·SKY HIGH·

RICHARD GARRETT
·SKY HIGH·

Heroic Pilots of the Second World War

Weidenfeld & Nicolson
LONDON

Contents

Illustration Acknowledgments

The photographs in this book are reproduced by kind permission of the following:

Central Press Photos 1 below; *Hulton-Deutsch Collection* 2, 3, 8; *Robert Hunt Library* 4 below; *Imperial War Museum* 1 above, 4 above, 6, 7 above.

Introduction

People are apt to ask an author all sorts of odd questions about his books. Why, they wish to know, did he write Title A? (If they read it, they might find out.) How long did it take to write Title B? (Too silly to be worth a reply.) How did he select the subjects for Title C?

This is rather more to the point in the present case. To take one example, twenty-two members of Bomber Command were awarded Victoria Crosses during the Second World War – thirteen of them posthumously. Each, surely, was a hero. Kenneth G.Wynn's *Men of the Battle of Britain* is described as a 'Who was Who' of the pilots and aircrew who flew with RAF Fighter Command from 10 July until 31 October 1940. The volume contains more than 2,000 entries. Heroes or not, they were by no means lacking in valour.

Why, you may ask, do I include Guy Gibson and Douglas Bader – men who have already received more than sufficient publicity? Are we not treading soil that has already been well trod? Perhaps. The truth is that this is to some extent a self-indulgent book. Having read a great deal about the subject, I chose the pilots that I found particularly interesting. I also wished to cover as many types of operation as possible. The bomber crews endured hours of cold, turbulence, and hazard, flying in unpressurized aeroplanes to targets deep in the hinterland of Germany.

The rightness of their missions, which resulted in the devil knows how much death and destruction, has since been questioned. But this is to misunderstand the mood of the day. As one of them has said, 'We did what we thought was right at the time.' Hatred was not their motivation. They did not gloat over the suffering they caused. They were trying to win a war – or helping to win it.

Fighter pilots were accorded the glory – though fewer VCs. When one considers the number of aircraft involved in their operations, the bursts of fire that had to be measured in seconds, and the shortness of the range that was essential for a kill, one concludes that these were indeed remarkable young men.

Technology has made sure that the conditions governing the actions of these bomber and fighter pilots will never occur again. The aviators of the Second World War are a vanished breed. This is not to say that, in similar circumstances, there are no longer young men who would perform equally well. We shall never know, for those circumstances will never be repeated.

The people singled out in this book, then, may serve to represent all the others who flew into hell without any great regard for survival. In many cases, they did not regard it as hell. They were addicted to flying and they flew regardless of the possible consequences. They were the knights of the sky, and my goodness how I admire them. What we have here, or what I hope we have here, is a tribute to a very special kind of person. It is right that the legends these people created should endure.

Richard Garrett
Tunbridge Wells

HEROES OR ACES?

Finding a sub-title for this book has not been without its problems. The word 'hero' is, perhaps, an example of male chauvinisn, for Hero was a woman. The hard work was done by a youth named Leander. Every night, he used to swim across the Hellespont, make love to Hero, and then swim home again. On one of these excursions, he misjudged the weather. The Hellespont became extremely rough, and Leander drowned. Far from bearing her loss with fortitude, Hero flung herself from a tower overlooking the water. Was Hero then, really a heroine?

My dictionary defines the word, among other things, as 'illustrious warrior' – something that, whatever her virtues, could not be said of the unfortunate Hero. In any case, so far as aviators are concerned, one tends to think of them as 'aces'. The trouble about aces, however, is that they are more precisely described. The concept was a French one. To join this exclusive community, you required qualifications. The Germans, who liked the idea, called them *experte* and insisted on ten kills for admission to the select ranks. The British and French were less demanding. Five were sufficient. But what was the form in cases where a fighter aircraft had a crew of more than one? Messrs Christopher Shore and Clive Williams solve the problem neatly in *Aces High*. Where a navigator/radar operator is involved, he receives a passing mention and only the pilot advances to 'ace'. But when the number two is a gunner (as in the instance of the Boulton Paul P82 Defiant – a night-fighter in which pilot and gunner sat, so to speak, back-to-back) he and the pilot share the glory.

But how do you define a victory? If you belonged to the RAF, you could destroy an enemy aircraft, or else cause it to become out of control. The French, when they first thought about it, were more fastidious. In the latter instance, the victim counted only as a 'probable' and did nothing for the score. However, they later relented and probables counted after all. The Germans had no truck with anything that suggested uncertainty: only a straightforward shooting down was acceptable. Nevertheless they often fudged the score.

As for the Americans, they tended to accept aeroplanes destroyed on the ground as well. But this was not quite the same thing, and so they introduced a new category, 'strafing ace', to cope with such situations.

In the First and Second World Wars, the attitude to the creation of aces (which was, after all, no more than an admission to an elite) varied. The French and the Germans saw the value of setting examples, and made much of their star performers. The British were less enthusiastic. Combat flying depended upon teamwork, and it seemed wrong to single out individuals for publicity purposes. This was the official view, which overlooked the fact that the public wanted heroes (or, in this instance, aces). The 1939–45 War was not very old before a young New Zealander began to make regular appearances in the newspapers. His name was Edgar James Kain, more commonly known as 'Cobber'.

'Cobber' Kain was born in Christchurch and, when he was old enough, he became a member of the Wellington Aero Club. In 1936, he sailed for England, where he joined the RAF. The autumn of 1939 found him flying Hurricanes in France. He scored his first victory on 8 November, when he shot down a Dornier Do 17 bomber. The action took place at 27,000 feet, which sent the record collectors rushing for their notebooks. No clash of arms in the sky had ever taken place at such an altitude before.

True to their policy of keeping aces out of the pack, the authorities kept quiet about his name. As his score mounted, they allowed mention of 'a 21-year-old New Zealand pilot'. They even let it be known that his nickname was 'Cobber'. Otherwise Edgar James Kain had to remain anonymous – at any rate for the time being. But this did not jeopardize his award of the Distinguished Flying Cross. Once this had taken place, his identity had to be revealed.

By the time he had done, 'Cobber' Kain had accounted for

seventeen German aircraft. Had he survived, the number would have been far greater. The trouble was that in June 1940 he was sent to England for a spell of leave.

He had, perhaps, become fond of his airfield and of his comrades. He no doubt wished to bid them farewell in the grand manner. Once he had got off the ground, he performed a roll at a dangerously low altitude. Then he did another and then, to make it a trio, he attempted a third. But by now he was too close to the deck. One of his wingtips smashed into Mother Earth. He was killed instantly. It was a shocking waste of a life and, come to that, of a perfectly good aircraft.

It is, indeed, surprising how many top-scorers survived aerial combat and lost their lives in situations that should have posed few dangers. There was the case of 'Chris' Le Roux, a young South African who, during 1940 and 1941, was shot down a dozen times. On every occasion, he bailed out without any trouble. He was duly awarded the DFC and then a Bar to it. By September 1944, he had dispatched twenty-three enemy aircraft. But then, on the 19th of that month, his life came to an end in a flying accident that should never have happened.

Richard Hillary, the Oxford rowing blue turned pilot and author (his *The Last Enemy* is essential reading), did much to justify his wings. On 3 September 1940, he dispatched a Messerschmitt Bf–109, bringing his score to five. But, shortly after the kill, his aircraft was hit and burst into flames. Getting the cockpit hood open posed considerable difficulties, but, despite fearful burns, he managed it and bailed out. That great plastic surgeon Sir Archibald McIndoe did a magnificent job of rebuilding him and, after a long period in hospital, he was judged fit to fly once more. He was posted to Charter Hall in Scotland to train as a night-fighter pilot.

There was nothing remarkable about the night of 8 January 1943. The sky was cloudy, the weather cold and there was the occasional shower of sleet. But such conditions were to be expected in January. At the controls of a Blenheim, Hillary made one flight without incident before midnight. Round about 1.00 am, he and his radio observer, Sergeant Kenneth Fison, went up again. Over the radio telephone, he was told to circle a flashing beacon. This amounted to making a series of circuits of the aerodrome. At some point the ground controller asked him whether he was happy, and he replied, 'Moderately. I am continuing to orbit.' When the controller called up again, there was no reply. An officer in the control tower noticed Hillary's navigation lights and remarked that he seemed to be losing height. The Blenheim crashed about three miles from the aerodrome. Hillary and Fison were killed instantly.

An official inquiry produced no satisfactory explanation, but there are suggestions that Hillary was not in the best of health. A Polish pilot stationed at Charter Hall thought that he had looked 'tired, strained, and very red about the eye.' After an examination by McIndoe in early December, the surgeon had been doubtful about his fitness to fly. As he wrote after the fatal crash, 'Richard was suffering from the common complaint where his body could not tolerate what his mind could contemplate. His nervous system had not brought his physical responses under control.' More work had needed to be done on his face and, in particular, his left eye seemed to be giving trouble.

McIndoe had written to the Station Medical Officer at Charter Hall, suggesting that Hillary should be grounded. The SMO agreed that McIndoe was right in principle, but '. . . I am also sure that Hillary's self-respect is an enormous obstacle.' The Station Commander does not appear to have been informed about the situation, but this can, perhaps, be explained by the fact that he was away from the station on leave when McIndoe's letter arrived.

All this may offer some clue as to what happened in the Blenheim on the night of 8 January, but it does not afford an explanation. Nor does it give so much as a hint of why, having survived one ordeal that so nearly claimed his life, he should have been killed on a flight he need not have made in circumstances that were by no means dangerous. But no man living can answer that.

Hillary became a kind of cult figure – largely due to his book, which was published in 1942 and is still in print. But what about Fison? How many people have heard of him? Hillary had been suffering from severe headaches during the previous month. When he had quite recently been examined by McIndoe, the surgeon must have expressed to Hillary his doubts about his fitness to fly. He was obviously aware of the condition of his left eye, but still he was determined to be treated as if he were 100 per cent fit: to respond to the challenge of going back into combat.

That was all very well so long as the matter concerned Hillary alone. Whose life was it, anyway? In fact, it was two people's lives: his and Fison's. He and the Sergeant Pilot had struck up a friendship. The latter was doggedly loyal to a pilot whose frailties he must have suspected. If Hillary said, 'We fly,' they flew. This devotion cost him his life; devotion and, of course, the fact that he had to obey an officer. But wasn't Hillary guilty of self-absorption – even of selfishness? To ask such a question smacks of heresy; but, on Fison's account, it ought to be asked. Men such as he shared the risks of the pilots whom they accompanied. Surely, when talking about 'aces', they deserved some of the glory, too.

Sergeant C. F. Rawnsley, who partnered John Cunningham, fared better. Cunningham had been employed as a test pilot by the de Havilland Aircraft Company before the war. In the late spring of 1940, flying a Blenheim, he had attacked troop-carrying Junkers Ju 52s that were parked on the Dutch coast. But he achieved fame later in the year when, now flying a Beaufighter, he was assigned to night-fighter operations. His and Rawnsley's score was impressive. By 22 August 1941, they had destroyed fifteen enemy aircraft. Cunningham became known as 'Cat's Eyes' by the press. His apparently exceptional night sight was attributed to a diet of carrots, and people were encouraged to eat more of them. The idea was to distract German curiosity about the reason for his successes. It may also have been that carrots were more readily available than some other kinds of vegetables. In fact, his victories had nothing to do with his diet. They owed a great deal to a new system involving radar. Controllers on the ground directed the pilot to within 1,000 yards of the target. Thereafter, a set in the aircraft brought about a more intimate relationship. Whether the carrot story fooled the *Luftwaffe* seems doubtful. But it turned Cunningham into a legend. He was rewarded with a DSO and two Bars, a DFC and one Bar, and eventual promotion to Group Captain. But Rawnsley was not overlooked. He was awarded the DFM and Bar and, after he had been made an officer, a DSO and DFC. But he was a gunner – unlike the unfortunate Fison.

Cunningham survived the war and returned to de Havilland, where he became chief test pilot. Among the aeroplanes with which he was involved was the Comet airliner. But even his skill was unable to detect the original design flaw that had such tragic consequences.[*]

Pilot Sergeant Derek ('Dick') Lord was less fortunate. By his twentieth birthday, he had taken part in more than a dozen

[*]For an account of this, see author's *Flight Into Mystery* (Weidenfeld and Nicolson, 1986).

bombing raids. When he celebrated his twenty-second, the number had reached thirty, or thereabouts. He came unscathed through all these operations. But then, when he was 'resting' (or, to put it another way, working as an instructor), he was killed in a flying accident.

In Germany, Werner Mölders wiped out twenty-five Allied aircraft during the fighting in France in the spring of 1940. In the Battle of Britain, he increased his tally by another twenty. There was no doubt about it: Mölders was the man to beat. In fact, a French pilot did shoot him down on one occasion. Mölders was confined to a POW cage, but not for long. The Panzers were advancing at such a rate that within fifteen days he was released. Soon afterwards he was back in business again.

Mölders was more than a good pilot, he was a brilliant tactician. One of his formations, known as the 'finger four' was so successful that the Allies adopted it.

After Germany invaded Russia in June 1941, he was posted to the eastern front, where he was given credit for the destruction of 101 Allied aircraft, and he was awarded every version of the *Ritterkreuz* that was ever conceived. But Goering had the idea – rightly, no doubt – that such skills should not be the exclusive property of one man. They should be spread as widely as possible. Still only twenty-eight years old, Mölders was removed from flying duties, promoted to *Oberst* (Colonel), and appointed Inspector of Fighter Aircraft at *Luftwaffe* headquarters.

In November 1941, he was paying a visit to units in the Crimea when Ernst Udet, the officer responsible for aircraft procurement, died. Udet had been a First World War ace – he was credited with fifty-two victories, had wit, charm, and courage. During the between-war years, he worked as a test pilot and as a stunt pilot – an occupation that suited him admirably. Unfortunately, as the clandestine *Luftwaffe* began to develop in 1935, Goering persuaded him to join its ranks in a staff job – a role for which he was manifestly unsuited. Nor was his task made easier by the Reichmarshal's refusal to accept his advice – or even to consider his opinions. When Udet urged the need for a night-fighter force, he was told that the need for such an organization would never occur. When he warned his superior about America's increasing capacity to build aircraft, his counsel was dismissed with the reply that the Americans could manufacture cars and refrigerators, but not aeroplanes. Udet knew that this was rubbish: he had, after all, been to the USA on several occasions. Goering had not.

Frustrated beyond endurance, Udet took his own life. The matter was hushed up and he was accorded a state funeral. Goering insisted that Mölders should attend it. He cut short his tour of the Crimea, and, on 22 November, boarded an He–111 that was to take him back to Germany. The weather was bad and, as it came in to land at Breslau, the aircraft crashed. Mölders was killed.

The Battle of Britain may not have won the war, but, beyond any reasonable doubt, it prevented Britain from losing it. Hitler's plan for an invasion depended upon command of the air. The exploits of the RAF made it plain that he would not have it. The plan was dropped.

In view of its immense importance, it may seem strange that only one Victoria Cross was awarded during those vital months. The recipient was a 23-year-old Flying Officer named James Nicolson. On 16 August 1940, Nicolson was patrolling the sky above Southampton when a formation of Ju 88 bombers accompanied by an escort of Messerschmitt Bf–109s made a surprise attack. In the skirmish his left foot was damaged and a splinter of perspex pierced his left eyelid. To add to his problems, his Hurricane caught fire. The logical thing was to bail out without further ado. He was about to do this, when he saw a Bf–109 dead ahead. He resumed his seat, fired a sufficient amount of ammunition to get rid of the enemy aircraft, and then took to his parachute. He was now suffering from severe burns in addition to his other injuries and his ordeal was not yet over. On landing, a member of the LDV (Local Defence Volunteers – the origin of the Home Guard) mistook him for a German. Without bothering to make sure, he discharged his shotgun into the unfortunate Nicolson's backside.

By February 1942, he was considered well enough to fly once more. He made a steady ascent up the ladder of promotion, picking up a DFC on the way. In April 1945, we find him as a Wing Commander on the staff of RAF Burma. Such a job should have ensured his survival, but, in May of that year, he decided to take a look around from the sky. He joined a Liberator belonging to 355 Squadron as an observer. Somewhere about 130 miles south of Calcutta, one of the engines caught fire. The aircraft plunged into the sea. Two NCOs survived. Nicolson did not.

We seem to have strayed rather a long way from the aces heroes question posed at the beginning of this chapter. The truth is that aces were men who flew fighters. They were the more glamorous members of air forces: the individuals who provided protection against the slings and arrows of outrageous enemies. In Britain, they were chaps who wore polka-dot scarves, who usually wore the top button of their tunics undone, and who owned sporty MG cars. That, at any rate, was the popular image. Bomber crews were different. They slogged it out for long hours, suffering all the shot and shell the enemy could throw at them. Whether the saturation bombing of Germany was right is something that had been questioned by hindsight. It is, perhaps, significant that whilst the heads of RAF Fighter Command received peerages from a grateful country, Arthur Harris, the C-in-C of Bomber Command, had to be content with a knighthood.

There were few, if any, who drew the line at the destruction flung at such cities as Hamburg, Munich, Berlin and Dresden – destruction that caused enormous civilian casualties. After all, Jerry had started this kind of thing when he attacked British cities. Now he was getting some of his own medicine. It should also be remembered that the supply of information was limited. There were no TV crews to report the scale of operations. In any case, the public had other preoccupations. There were problems enough without worrying about the fate of German citizens. Even the dropping of atom bombs over Hiroshima and Nagasaki produced little more than a feeling of relief. The Japs were compelled to surrender: the war, thank God, was over.

On the other hand, the achievements of bomber crews could not be measured on what we might call the 'ace scale'. Their gunfire was a matter of self-defence and not their primary purpose. It was, as they say nowadays, a different ballgame.

Thus, if we were to use the word 'aces' in the title, it would either be misleading, or else it would narrow the field too much. We should receive no opportunity to mention men such as Eugene Esmonde, VC. Esmonde was an Irishman who, after a short service commission in the RAF, had joined the Fleet Air Arm in 1939. His first posting was to HMS *Courageous*, the aircraft carrier that, when she was torpedoed by a U-Boat on 17 September 1939, became the Navy's first major loss.

Esmonde survived the sinking, and put in a spell training other pilots. Presently he was sent to HMS *Victorious*, a more recent addition to the fleet (*Courageous* originated as a battle-cruiser completed in 1916, and was converted into an aircraft carrier in 1924). In May 1941, *Victorious* was summoned from her anchorage in the Clyde to assist Admiral Tovey in his hunt for the *Bismarck*. At 8.00 pm on 24 May, the carrier was 120 miles from the prey. With the wind blowing at near gale force, Esmonde took off in his Swordfish torpedo bomber, accompanied by eight others. They sighted the German battleship, flew into an intense barrage of flak, and released their torpedoes. One hit was scored, which failed to cripple the giant warship (the one that did the damage to her steering was delivered by a Swordfish from HMS *Ark Royal*). Nevertheless, Esmonde was awarded the DSO for his leadership.

Afterwards, he was posted to *Ark Royal*, but she shared the fate of *Courageous*. On 13 November 1941, thirty miles to the east of Gibraltar, she was hit by a torpedo from the U–81. She sank on the following day. The general opinion is that she could have been saved if the damage control had been more efficient, but there you are. Esmonde had again got his feet wet.

January 1942 found Esmonde at Manston aerodrome in Kent in charge of a squadron of Swordfish. He had already volunteered to make a night attack on the German battlecruisers *Scharnhorst* and *Gneisenau* and their cruiser consort *Prinz Eugen*, should they attempt to come up the Channel from Brest, where they had lingered for some while, and make for their home ports in Germany. On the morning of the 12th, he was watching men clear the snow off the runway, when he learned that what he had foreseen had occurred. Indeed, the German warships had made such good progress that there could be no question of waiting for darkness. If he and his only partially trained squadron were not in the air by 12.30 pm, it would be too late.

To attack such a mighty naval formation without cover would be virtually suicidal. Three fighter squadrons had been assigned this role. The trouble was that they never turned up. One found the German ships, but missed the Swordfish. Another arrived fifteen minutes too late. The third was wrongly briefed. Its leader was told that the battle was a small affair involving German E-boats and their British equivalent, motor torpedo boats.

Esmonde was in a hurry, and if there was to be no fighter cover, it was just too bad. At 12.25 he and the rest of his squadron took off. Somewhere on his journey he glimpsed some fighters and their pilots glimpsed the Swordfish. But that was as far as it went. Unprotected, the fragile biplanes (they were known as 'String-bags') went into the attack. All their torpedoes sped wide of the mark. Only two of the Swordfish three-men crews survived. Esmonde was not among them. For his part in the action, he was awarded a posthumous Victoria Cross.

The targets of Esmonde and other likeminded individuals were strictly military. After all, torpedoes and not bombs were their weapons. Charles Pickard falls into a different category, though his is a comparatively rare case. In the early days of the war, the Crown Film Unit made a motion picture entitled *Target for Tonight*. It was more of a documentary, though it was by no means lacking in thrills. Intended to show British audiences that the German bombing of their country was incurring at least some punishment: that Britain was fighting back, it featured the experiences of an RAF aircrew during a night raid over Germany in a Wellington. After the war, bomber pilots were played, often very convincingly, by actors (Richard Todd, who was excellent as Guy Gibson in *The Dam Busters*, springs to mind). In this case, RAF personnel were used, with Charles Pickard starring (if one can use the word) as the bomber's captain.

During the early winter of 1941, it was noticed that the performances of German flak gunners and, particularly, night-fighter pilots, were showing a marked improvement. Was this due to greater skills, or had there been some advance in technology? On 4 December, a Squadron Leader named Tony Hill, who carried out photographic reconnaissance missions, flew over Cap d'Antifer (between Le Havre and Dieppe) and took pictures of what was obviously a new type of radar installation. Its aerial resembled a very large electric bowl fire – or, to put it in more up-to-date terms, a much bigger version of those dishes displayed on the outside of houses whose inhabitants can receive the alternative television. It was clearly something that should be investigated. The ideal way would be to drop a company of parachutists. They would help themselves to vital components, and then be taken off the beach by Commandos. The project was code-named BITING.

Major John Frost, who was later to distinguish himself at Arnhem, was put in charge of the parachutists, to whose ranks a section of airborne Royal Engineers and two RAF technicians had been added. Wing Commander Charles Pickard was assigned to get them over the target using Whitley bombers (the Whitley went on to serve as a training aircraft for paratroops and as a glider tug). He was a large, good humoured, pipe-smoking individual who generated confidence. Pickard and his squadron were stationed at Thruxton on Salisbury Plain.

The raid had originally been planned to take place on Monday 23 February 1942. At 5.00 pm, the actors in the forthcoming drama sat down to tea. But then it was announced that the weather had turned bad, and everything would have to be delayed for twenty-four hours. As things transpired, it was to be longer than that, and it was not until Friday the 27th that the day dawned clear and crisp and flying conditions were good. Frost had worked out that the delay had fouled up the time-table on the beach: the landing craft that were to evacuate them would depend on an ebb tide. But the Admiralty envisaged no trouble in this respect. The thirty-two men of 12 Commando who were to cover the withdrawal, put to sea – the five motor gunboats and the two destroyers (HMA *Blencathra* and HMS *Fernie*) assigned to protect them were brought to a state of readiness.

Despite his jovial, optimistic outlook, Pickard seems to have been less than confident. As the troops boarded the aircraft, somebody overheard him say, 'I feel like a bloody murderer.' He need not have done. The operation went off perfectly. At a cost of two killed, two wounded, and six taken prisoner, the raiders brought home the components and one German captive.

Pickard had established a reputation for himself as a low-level flier and as a pilot with a talent for spotting weaknesses in the enemy anti-aircraft defences. Consequently, he tended to be singled out for missions that required uncommon precision. He was, perhaps, a disciple of Air Vice Marshal Basil Embry – or was Embry, despite his higher rank, a disciple of Pickard?

The jail at Amiens was a cruciform building surrounded by walls twenty feet high and three feet thick. According to reports received from the French underground in early February 1944, it housed 700 prisoners, who were kept in their place of detention by special troops (the SS no doubt). Among them were common criminals, who had no business to be anywhere else. But there was also a considerable number of resistance workers, including a gentleman named Vivant. M.Vivant was in charge of operations in the Abbeville area.

Nearly all the men in the latter category had been sentenced to death. Word leaked out that, with a fine sense of Teutonic economy, the executions were to be carried out along the lines of mass production (mass destruction might be more appropriate) on 19 February. Could this be prevented? Breaking into such a well-fortified building was beyond the ability of even the most experienced and best-equipped underground fighters, and Amiens was too far inland for a Commando-style raid. The use of bombers was another matter. The Mosquito Mk VI was now available: a very frisky fighter/bomber, ideal for low-level attacks and with the speed and manoeuvrability to get itself out of trouble. Also available was Charles Pickard with his gift for dropping things in the right places.

A model of the prison was manufactured by workers who, in civilian life, specialized in the kind of decorations one finds on wedding cakes (they were very good at this sort of thing). Nineteen pilots and navigators were detailed for the task: six from 487 Squadron of the Royal New Zealand Air Force, six from the Royal Australian Air Force's 464 Squadron, and six from 21 Squadron RAF. They would be accompanied by a photographic reconnaissance aircraft.

The tenth of February was the date originally scheduled for the operation, but the weather was abominable and it had to be delayed. The weather was still bad on the 18th and again there was talk of cancellation. But the pilots, aware of what was planned to take place the next day, protested. Come snow, storm, and tempest, they would have a go.

Flying low across the Channel was by no means the easiest of tasks: the aircraft were beset by snow storms. But they reached Amiens in good order and the jail was perfectly visible. Pickard's idea had been to attack in three waves. Once the first two had gone in, however, their bombs were seen to be so well placed that there was no need for any more. Pickard signalled wave number three that it could go home.

Casualties among the prison inmates as well as their guards were inevitable. One hundred and two of the former were killed, but 258 – including Vivant – escaped. Many of them were recaptured, but Pickard and his aircrews had done all that anyone could have expected of them. It was a masterpiece of precision bombing.

It was, alas, also an operation that ended in tragedy. Pickard and his navigator, Flight Lieutenant J. A. Broadly, circled the target a mite too long. A couple of Fw–190s jumped them and their Mosquito crashed a few miles from the jail. Both men were killed.

However, it was now established that you could attack individual buildings. Gestapo headquarters in The Hague occupied what had once been the Kleizkemp Art Galleries, a five-storey edifice that contained a register of Holland's population – with appropriate comments against a number of names. If these records could be destroyed, a good many lives might be saved and the Gestapo would be put to no end of trouble.

Wing Commander R. N. Bateson and 613 Squadron were given the assignment. Flying at fifty feet, they followed a complicated route to conceal their intentions. The operation went without a hitch. Two bombs landed inside the front door, and two through windows on either side. A German sentry was seen to drop his rifle and run. Other bombs fell on a German barracks behind the art gallery, and razed it to the ground. The Dutch were quick to see the value of the raid. It would take the Gestapo some while to reassemble its shattered collection of records. They used the opportunity to replace genuine cards with fakes, which added to the confusion and doubtless saved a number of lives.

But let us return to Air Vice Marshal Basil Embry. Embry, who was born in 1902, had been shot down over France and taken prisoner in May 1940, but he managed to escape. He eventually arrived in Plymouth via Spain and Gibraltar on 2 August. This exploit earned him a second Bar to his DSO. He was doubtless pleased to learn that the Germans had been so impressed by his adventurous attitude that they placed a price tag of 70,000 Reichmarks on his head.

Embry was an officer who believed in leading from the front. Sending men on operations was all very well, but, when it was possible, he liked to go along too. Once, when in command of a squadron, he told its members that since they had to have a war they 'could damn well enjoy it'. His enjoyment was plain to see, but he was cautious after his fashion. Although by 1945 he was an Air Vice Marshal in charge of No. 2 Group, Bomber Command, he always used the pseudonym 'Flying Officer Smith' on his exploits. If he were shot down and survived, it might make those 70,000 Reichmarks more difficult to earn.

Among the raids in which he took part in 1944–5 were three attacks on Gestapo headquarters in Denmark. The most spectacular was against a building that, before its occupation by the secret police, had been the headquarters of the Shell oil company in Copenhagen.

In early March 1945, a Danish resistance worker had been airlifted out of his country and flown to London. He had a sorry tale to tell. Shell House contained so many vital documents and so many important prisoners that unless something were done about it the whole underground network would fall to pieces. As a result of these discussions, Operation CARTHAGE was mounted. Eighteen Mosquito bombers accompanied by twenty-eight fighters would be employed. The Mosquitos would be armed with high explosive bombs to bring down the walls, and incendiaries to send the embarrassing papers up in smoke. As at Amiens, the attack would be made at a very low level. The trouble was that the Mosquitos would be flying a distance pretty close to their limits. But Embry was not too worried about this. He was ever an optimist.

The wedding cake artists prepared a model of the building and of the area contained within one square kilometer around it. This was used to brief the pilots when they assembled at a base in Norfolk on 21 March. Normally they would have flown to their target at 335 mph, but, to lessen fuel consumption, Embry decided to reduce this to 250 mph over the sea and 275 mph over land.

Embry and his formation reached the sky about Shell House without any incident. The raid took four minutes: the documents burned brightly. Many Gestapo officers died (but not their commanding officer, one Karl Heinz Hoffmann, who happened to be attending a funeral at the time). The prisoners were quartered on the sixth floor and a surprisingly large number survived and escaped. One man, playing patience in his cell, suddenly discovered that he had descended to the fifth floor. Above him was a patch of blue across which a Mosquito could be seen streaking away. Others descended to the safety of the street by joining together the belts of dead Gestapo men.

Contrary to the pessimistic view, the Mosquitos returned to their base with petrol to spare. But there were prices to be paid. Most of the 200 casualties within Shell House were members of the Gestapo, or else Danish collaborators who were helping them with the clerical work. Nobody was going to mourn them. Four Mosquitos and two fighters were lost – they either crashed, or else were shot down, on the return journey. But the real tragedy occurred near to Shell House, where a convent school for girls, the Jeanne d'Arc School, was situated. Despite the model and the careful briefing, one of the pilots mistook this for the target. Eighty-six children and seventeen adults were killed. It was an awful business – not least because six weeks later Denmark was freed from the Nazis without the need to fire a shot.

Were people such as Pickard and Embry heroes? Or were they professionals doing the job they had been trained to do, and doing it very well? Pickard perished, Embry survived and had been admitted four times to the Distinguished Service Order. Pilot Officer Gibson (not Guy Gibson), who served under the latter in No. 2 Group, was an uncommonly valiant man. In November 1943, his unit (flying Bostons) was briefed to raid the village of Audinghen on the French coast between Calais and Boulogne. Normally it is a place of very little importance, but in those days it was suspected of being a headquarters of the Todt Organization – a body with wide ranging responsibilities which included the building of German defences against an Allied invasion. In this respect, as in several others, it made considerable use of slave labour.

The village was virtually destroyed. As the aircraft turned for home, a Boston of 99 Squadron, with Gibson at the controls, was hit by flak. Gibson's collar bone was broken, his face was badly gashed, and, for a moment or two, he was stunned. When he regained consciousness, he found that, as if all this were not enough, he had lost the use of his arms. He also discovered that his aircraft had lost 2,000 feet of altitude. However, he was an enterprising pilot and it transpired that, with a good deal of agility, it was possible to maintain flight by grasping the control column with his knees. Once he had brought the Boston back on to a level course, he invited his crew to bail out. They hesitated and then declined the invitation. Eventually some feeling returned to Gibson's arms, but he was in very great pain. Nevertheless, he brought them all back safely to the squadron's base at Hawkinge in Kent.

Or take the case of Sergeant J. A. Ward on No. 75 (New Zealand) Squadron who, in 1941, was returning from a raid on Munster. The starboard wing of his aircraft caught fire. By all that was reasonable, this should have been the cue for him and his companions to bail out. But Ward was made of sterner stuff. At enormous risk, he climbed out on to the blazing wing and put out the flames. The aeroplane and its occupants returned safely to their base. Sergeant Ward was awarded the Victoria Cross for what was patently an act of heroism.

To my mind, all the people I have mentioned in this chapter were heroes; only some of them were aces. In any case, it is perhaps a mistake to become too much in the thrall of words – proper nouns, at all events. You may like to consider the case of an ace (heroic, too, but nevertheless an ace) named Marseille and another named Clostermann. Who was the German pilot, and who the French? The answer is provided by their forenames. Marseille's was Hans-Joachim – otherwise known as Jochen. Clostermann's was Pierre.

Clostermann was, in fact, living in the Congo at the outbreak of war. He came to Britain and joined the RAF. Within a year, after a slowish start, he had destroyed ten enemy aircraft and been awarded the DFC. By VE-Day, he had accounted for thirty-three German aeroplanes in the sky and a further twenty-four that never got off the ground. He had also been awarded a Bar to his DFC. Ironically, although he had twice survived crash-landings, he bailed out on only one occasion. That was on a victory fly-past over Bremerhaven, when he collided with another 'plane. After leaving the RAF in August 1945, he became a member of the French House of Representatives. During this period, he wrote two books about his experiences. In the Algerian crises of the late fifties and early sixties, his services were required by *l'Armée de l'Air*, and he afterwards wrote a book about these operations. He is now living in comfortable retirement in France.

Marseille's life was painfully short. He was only twenty-one when he was killed in the Western Desert; but, by then, he had been credited with 158 victories – seventeen of them, it was said, on a single day. In *Wings of War*, Laddie Lucas recalls that after the thanksgiving service for Sir Douglas Bader he asked General Adolf Galland for his opinion of Marseille's ability. Without hesitation, the great German airman said, 'He was the best.'

Although his name betrayed his Huguenot ancestry, Jochen Marseille was a Berliner. After completing his education, he joined the *Luftwaffe*. His sense of discipline left a good deal to be desired. He was flamboyant: his hair was too long, his attire was scruffy. Had he joined the infantry, he would have been given very short shrift indeed. But, as a pilot, he possessed two qualities that were essential: indeed, he had them to an extent that he can safely be rated as exceptional. The speed of his reactions have been favourably compared to those of a present-day computer and his eyesight was remarkable. In short, and in his own line, he was a genius.

In the Battle of Britain, he claimed seven victories – which was not particularly impressive since four of them were not confirmed. Furthermore, he was shot down four times – on one of them, he ended up in the Channel. Thereafter, he took a dislike to parachutes and preferred to crash-land whenever he could.

But it was in North Africa that Marseilles made his name. He was high spirited, threw parties on the smallest pretext, and enjoyed practical jokes. The Germans heaped decorations upon him and so did the Italians. When Mussolini presented him with Italy's highest award, he had to undergo the ritual ordeal of being kissed. Afterwards, he remarked to a fellow pilot, 'It was terrible. The Duce was unshaven.' But he should not really have complained. The decoration was the Italian Gold Medal for Bravery. Rommel received it, too, but his was only the silver version.

There was, of course, a more serious side to his nature, and he liked nothing better than to discuss tactics with his companions. In June 1942 he was sent home for a period of rest (rare among *Luftwaffe* pilots: rest received a very low priority). On 23 August he was back in action and piling up more victories. The trouble began on 5 September, when his best friend – a pilot named 'Fifi' Stahlschmidt, whose score stood at fifty-nine – was killed. Marseille took the news badly. The good-looking playboy was replaced by a very much more withdrawn individual. On 30 September he took off with two other aircraft to carry out a sweep in the direction of Cairo. The patrol was uneventful; but, on the way back, a fuel line in his Me–109 broke and caused a fire. The cockpit became filled with smoke. His fellow pilots more or less beseeched him to bail out, but Marseille would have none of it. They were only three minutes away from the German lines: he did not want to become a prisoner of war. He also mistrusted parachutes.

A moment or two after they had crossed the line between the opposing armies, he accepted the inevitable. He would have to jump for it. But the aircraft was now in a nose-down attitude: centrifugal force pushed him back, helpless, into the cockpit. At last, he managed to break free, but again the wretched aeroplane acted against him. As he fell, he hit the fin and became unconscious. He did not recover in time to unleash his parachute. The brief life of Jochen Marseille was over.

Hero or ace, it doesn't matter. Whatever the word, these men made us proud to belong to the human race. And those who died were not expendable. The pity of it is that more of them did not survive. We could do with people like these in the avaricious, consuming, self-absorbed, money-grubbing world of today.

2

Guy Gibson
THE MASTER BOMBER

On the night of 16 May 1943, sixteen Lancaster bombers belonging to the RAF offloaded their freight on to a trio of dams adjacent to the industrial heartland of the Ruhr. At the cost of half the aircraft and fifty-six men, they accounted for 125 factories, 25 bridges, and at least 1,294 lives. When Albert Speer – Germany's minister for armaments and munitions, inspector of roads, water, and power, etc. – reported the raid to Hitler, the Führer was deeply impressed. About the only German to derive any satisfaction from the operation was *Oberburgermeister* Dillgardt, but his must have been a hollow victory. For some while, he had been insisting that the walls, which helped to enclose nearly half-a-million gallons of water, were vulnerable. Surely their defences should be strengthened? People listened politely and did nothing. It was, they said, unnecessary.

Thus the legend of the 'Dam Busters' was created. The surviving aircrews were rewarded with a week's leave, one Victoria Cross, five DSOs, four Bars to DFCs, ten DFCs, and twelve DFMs. The ground crews received three days' leave. The Victoria Cross was for Wing Commander Guy Gibson, leader of the squadron – a 25-year-old veteran of 173 missions, who, when he heard about his award, rang up Flight Sergeant Powell, the squadron's disciplinary NCO. 'Chiefy,' he said, 'if I ever change, tell me.'

When, in 1936, Guy Gibson left St Edward's School, Oxford, he had no doubt about what he wished to do. He was determined to become a test pilot. It was, he had decided, 'a good job with plenty of money in it.' Among those to whom he turned for advice was Captain 'Mutt' Summers, who was employed by Vickers.

Summers pointed out that, as a first step, one should learn to fly. The best way in which to do it would be to take a short service commission in the Royal Air Force. Gibson agreed.

Guy Gibson was built on the short side, with a pleasantly open, rather good-looking face. He played rugby football, was fond of dogs, and very gregarious. He was seldom happier than when he had a can of beer in his hand. The very word 'party' brought a gleam of expectancy to his eyes. When on holiday, he enjoyed sailing.

His house master at school described him as 'strong minded without obstinacy, disarmingly frank and of great charm.' Few people would have disagreed with this verdict. They say that the world is divided into those who do and those who think. Gibson, it seems fair to say, was proficient at both. In his book, *Enemy Coast Ahead*, we find a relish for action; but, now and then, a more contemplative spirit emerges – a man who thought beyond the war and was concerned about the recurrence of any similar disaster. Nor was he unmindful of his victims. 'Nobody likes mass slaughter,' he wrote, 'and we did not like being the authors of it. Besides, it brought us in line with Himmler and his boys.'

It is significant that after the raid on the German dams he delayed setting off on leave for two days. The mothers of all those fifty-six casualties had to receive letters. The task could have been accomplished in a very much shorter time. Typists were available to help him and, anyway, there was a more or less standard form for such correspondence. But Gibson insisted that whatever was written should be in his own hand, and that each letter must be composed individually.

During the late summer of 1939, Guy Gibson was enjoying a sailing holiday off the south coast of Wales. One afternoon he was surprised to see a boy swimming toward his boat from the beach. In his mouth, he carried what seemed to be a telegram. He came alongside and delivered what was now a somewhat damp message. Seeing that it was marked 'Urgent', Gibson opened it immediately. Its contents were brief and uncompromising. 'Return to Unit immediately,' it instructed.

A few minutes earlier, all thoughts of war had been pushed aside: in the calm of a sun-drenched day and with a glamorous companion, the probability 'just did not exist'. But now it seemed to be at least that and, more likely a certainty. Within two hours of receiving the message, he had packed and was on his way. A friend drove him to Oxford where they stopped at a pub near the station. Inside were a number of convivial spirits, each bound for some similar destination. The beer flowed, the conversation flourished, and it was all very pleasant. Nevertheless, at the back of his mind, there was an awareness of how wretchedly ill-equipped Britain was for whatever lay ahead. Neither the British nor the French air forces were at anything like the strength they should have been. In a moment of more or less sober reflection, he rather doubted his chances of survival.

The train journey was slow and uncomfortable, and it was not until 4.00 am that, tired and with a sizeable hangover, he arrived at Lincoln. With some difficulty, he managed to obtain transport to the aerodrome at Scampton – a relic of the First World War where his squadron of Hampden bombers was based. Normally at such early hours, the officers' mess was deserted, but everyone had been standing by since dawn. When, at 6.00, he applied himself to breakfast, the place was crowded and with good reason. Not long afterwards, they learned that the Nazis had invaded Poland. There was clearly a great deal to be done, and Guy Gibson, with his unerring grasp of essentials, saw how best to equip himself for these duties. He went to bed. At least it would overcome the fatigue. It might even cure the hangover.

A South African, Group Captain Emmett, was the station commander at Scampton; the aircraft with which the pilots were intended to bring havoc to the Third Reich were Hampdens – a Handley Page product that had come into production during the previous year. Manned by a crew of four, the more lethal aspects of the bomber were concentrated up front. Thereafter an almost pencil-slim fuselage connected the compartment with the tail unit. With a top speed of 245 mph, it has been described as 'a truly outstanding aircraft,' and, less respectfully, as the 'Flying Suitcase'. The trouble in these early days of its life was that nobody seemed to be sure how it would react to the imposition of a tolerably heavy load of bombs. There were even doubts in some people's minds about whether, with 2,000lbs of them on board, it would deign to become airborne.

One says 'bring havoc to the Third Reich'. This is only partially true. The idea that, in the event of another Great War, Britain would be immediately reduced to rubble was conceived by H. G. Wells in a work of fiction. As time went by, it seemed possible that, if the word 'immediately' were deleted, this might happen.

In September 1939, however, the British had rules. To bomb a warship was all right, providing it was at sea or riding at anchor. If, however, it was in dock or berthed alongside a quay, it was no longer fair game. In such instances, the bombs might fall wide of their targets and hit civilian houses. That was not acceptable. Similarly, and for example, there were several ammunition dumps at a place called Marienhafe between the Jade and the Ems. They were legitimate prey – on the strict understanding that the citizens of Marienhafe should not be unnecessarily inconvenienced (nobody seems to have considered the possibility that, in such circumstances, there would probably be a much larger secondary explosion that would erase the village from the map). Whether the German intentions were equally scrupulous is uncertain. A number of their pilots had been involved in the raid on Guernica in the Spanish Civil War, and they were showing no compunction about hitting civilian targets in Poland. However, an early *Luftwaffe* attack against Scapa Flow is said to have produced only one casualty – a rabbit*.

Gibson had been allocated a Hampden designated C 'Charlie'. 'It was,' he wrote, 'my own aeroplane, and a lousy one at that.' Among its foibles were a tendency to swing round to the right on take-off, to fly with the left wing in the descendant, and for either engine, as if upon a whim, to cut out. But 'Charlie' was his and he loved her – just, one supposes, as an affectionate spouse may tolerate the shortcomings of a far from perfect partner.

C 'Charlie', Gibson, and his crewmen were to have their first taste of action within two or three weeks of war breaking out. At this time, 'Charlie's' complement was one man short: there were just Gibson, the second pilot, and a radio operator. The squadron had been ordered to contribute six aircraft for a raid against naval shipping in the Schillig Roads at the entrance to the Kiel Canal. The briefing contained all the usual stuff about not bombing civilians, and offered Marienhafe as an alternative target if there were no pocket battleships in the roads. The intelligence officer quite wrongly insisted that these vessels' only defence against aircraft was machine guns. He suggested that the best height from which to attack was 3,000 feet. This would be beyond the range of

*According to Bud Flanagan, this inspired the song 'Run Rabbit Run', which he and his partner, Chesney Allen, sang with such success in the 1940 London Palladium show *The Little Dog Laughed*.

the presumed machine guns and below that of heavier flak. The weather promised to be bad, which produced all sorts of complications as weather so often does. Not the least of them was that they would not be able to see the barrage balloons that cluttered the sky. If the conditions were too awful, they should abandon the mission. The reason seems not to have been concern for the safety of the fliers, so much as fear that they might accidentally bomb German soil and thereby present the enemy with a nice propaganda opportunity.

Before setting off, Gibson was understandably nervous – as, indeed, were all the others. It was, then, reassuring when, as he settled into the pilot's seat, a rigger named Taffy wished him good fortune. 'Now don't you worry,' Taffy said, 'You will be OK. You will always come back.' He spoke with such assurance that it was hard to doubt him. To some extent he was correct. Guy Gibson perished in the end, but he outlived the others who took part in the raid.

The take-off was twice delayed, though no reasons were given. When at last the squadron was sent on its way, the aircraft took off in formation, with C 'Charlie' heaving itself arthritically into the sky. True to forecast, the weather was pretty awful and 'Charlie' took time to pick up speed. The moody bomber felt heavy – as if protesting against her load of four 500-lb bombs. Crossing the North Sea at a height of 1,000 feet, they spotted a German Dornier 18 flying boat ambling along at about 500 feet below. The D18's pilot very sensibly disregarded them, and the Hampdens disregarded him. When they were forty miles from Wilhelmshaven, the cloud descended to 300 feet. They came down beneath it. It was raining heavily, and from what they could see, the sea appeared very rough.

Optimistically they plodded on until they were ten miles from the target. The cloud was now down to 100 feet. Ahead of them there were discouraging crumps of anti-aircraft fire. From being an adversary, the too plentiful cloud now became an ally – at least it provided a hiding place from the flak.

However, what with one thing and another, the squadron commander (a former contestant in the Schneider Trophy race named Leonard Snaith) decided to abort the mission. The aircraft turned for home. They jettisoned their bombs into the North Sea; saw the same flying boat pounding, so to speak, its beat; and eventually crossed the English coast at Boston. From there it should have been a simple matter to navigate back to Scampton, but the beacons had all been moved from their customary positions. For the next two hours, the aircraft wandered about the sky, searching for some indication of where they might be. It was not until the moon came up that one of the crew was able to notice a canal leading to Lincoln. With this priceless piece of information, it was not too difficult to find the airfield.

On entering the mess, Gibson was told that he should have been dead. A wireless operator in another aircraft asserted that he had seen him dive vertically into the sea. The only individual to benefit from the raid was a Squadron Leader named Doran from another unit, who managed to land a bomb on the pocket battleship *Admiral von Scheer* (destroying the ship's aircraft and catapult gear). Doran, who later became a POW in Germany, was awarded the DFC. Forgetting the rules, the Nazi propaganda machine claimed (quite wrongly) that civilians had been attacked. Substantial reprisals were threatened – not least the dispatch of 100 bombers to London. Goering, it seems, was keen on the idea, but Hitler was less enthusiastic.

Looking back on those early days of the war, the bombing offensive (if such it could be called) seems to have been a very rudimentary affair. Targets were set, but pilots were often permitted to take off when they chose and to follow whatever route seemed best. Radio was so inefficient that one wonders why it was deemed necessary for each bomber to carry a wireless operator. Navigational aids were virtually non-existent, and most people had to depend upon that least accurate means of getting from A to B, dead reckoning. The Germans, admittedly, had a device named *Knickebein*, which was really quite clever. The pilots simply had to follow a radio beam. When they were over the target, another beam converged on it. The sound in the earphones changed, and this was the moment to drop the bombs. It was reckoned to be accurate to within about one square mile. Curiously, it was defeated by a device based on the medical treatment provided by diathermy (the application of high frequency currents to product heat in the deeper tissues of the body). This had the effect of blocking out the sound.

Not long after the excursion to the Schillig Roads, Gibson was injured. The villain was neither flak nor any other enemy war machine. It was, of all things, the station commander's dog

Zimba. Zimba was in the habit of biting people, and he saw no reason to make an exception of young Guy Gibson's legs. Indeed the inroads of the creature's fangs were so severe, that the medical officer insisted he should take thirty-six hours' sick leave. It suited him very well, for it enabled him to attend his brother's marriage at Rugby.

By the time his sick leave had expired and his ailing limb had recovered from the ravages of Zimba's teeth, Poland had fallen. It now seemed possible – probable, indeed – that the expected wrath of the German air force might be unleashed over Britain. RAF bases, the assumption went, would be among the prime targets. Scampton, being on the eastern side of the country, seemed a likely candidate. To save the bombers from extinction on the ground, the aircraft were removed to Ringway near Manchester, and it was to here that Gibson (known to his friends as 'Gibbo') reported.

The torrents of death were not poured from the sky: the so-called Phoney War was still phoney. The more thirsty air crew personnel discovered an admirable pub about midway between Ringway and Manchester, and there were parties galore. Gibson fell in love with a girl named Barbara, remarking that 'It struck me as funny that it should take a war to make a chap even think of falling in love.' But Barbara's heart was pledged to a member of the Fleet Air Arm. As for Gibson's, it was a robust organ, and there was no damage that time, work and beer could not heal.

In fact, there was not a great deal of work to do. Some squadrons made flights over Germany, dropping leaflets designed to convince the population that, as causes went, this was a lost one. Down on the ground in France, the troops of both sides largely contented themselves with taunts amplified by loud speakers. There was one example of black humour that Gibson rather enjoyed and doubtless went the rounds of countless messes. It seemed that a Messerschmitt 110 had made a forced landing between the Maginot and Siegfried Lines. This might indeed be treasure trove, and the French troops planned to capture it. Fumbling in the dark, working very quietly, they made preparations to haul it Maginotwards. The soldiers had succeeded in attaching a rope, when the scene was suddenly illuminated by German searchlights. From the enemy lines, a greatly enlarged voice called, 'If you want a light, why the hell didn't you say so?' It was a good joke spoiled by the bursts of machine guns that followed and which wrote off the working party. The French replied with an artillery barrage and then the hostilities went back to sleep.

Life at Ringway was too good. There was the tale of a dozen bombers that had set out to sink three German destroyers going about their business off Heligoland. It put an end to the myth of machine guns being used for anti-aircraft purposes. Instead, the vessels were armed with extremely efficient light ack-ack weapons. They, themselves, turned out to be very manoeuvrable. Of the twelve aeroplanes, only six survived the low-level attack.

But at Ringway there were no such sorties, and the half-way house of a pub did an excellent trade. Back at Scampton, accounts of young aviators enjoying a somewhat libertine existence were viewed with disfavour. A more senior officer was dispatched to lead them to the path of righteousness. The convivial pub was put out of bounds and a temperance hotel stipulated as a social rendezvous. By the time its clientele had done with it, it was somewhat less than temperate, but this didn't much matter. The *Luftwaffe* was clearly not about to remove Scampton from the map and, shortly before Christmas, they all went back there.

They made two attempts to find the pocket battleship *Deutschland* and failed on each occasion. On 1 December, having a few days leave, Gibson drove to Coventry to stay with his brother. He played a game of rugger, kept his beer level adequately topped-up and, more to the point, met a girl named Eve. Her father was something to do with shipping at Cardiff; she was currently employed as an actress. She was very attractive and a stimulating conversationalist. Barbara could have her Fleet Air Arm pilot: this was different. If lives really do have turning points, this was just such an occasion in Gibson's. He returned to Scampton with a hangover (predictable) and a new understanding of love (not predictable).

On Christmas Day, Eve rang him up to wish him happiness, and he made every effort to do her bidding. Alas, the day had a less than happy conclusion. On his way to bed, he tripped over a fire extinguisher. Not realizing that there was no fire to be extinguished, the wretched thing spewed out its content of liquid foam with abandon. Ever a man of action, Gibson decided that the only answer to such inane exuberance was to hurl it outside. The way to the outside world lay through an ornamental glass door. This was no occasion to consider the niceties of decoration. The glass was shattered; the extinguisher no doubt expended itself; and Gibson went unsteadily to bed.

Next day, he was summoned to see the mess secretary. Such conduct, he was informed, was unbecoming and, as a penance, he was not to touch one drop of alcohol for a month. It seemed unfair, but what could he do? He appealed to his squadron commander, who made clear his inability to quash the sentence, but at least he put the matter in a better perspective. He invited him to reflect on how much money he would save; money, that is to say, that could be spent on Eve.

It snowed heavily that winter – to such an extent that Scampton had to receive an airlift of beer from some other station. Nevertheless, by the spring the pilots had become more proficient at navigation; they were able to bomb more accurately; and they had mastered the art of night flying (on the other hand, the ban against harming civilians in Germany remained until April). The war may have been phoney, but it at least afforded a much needed training period. As Gibson had remarked earlier, 'We did not know a thing about aerial warfare and it was up to us to learn.' He also observed that 'to be successful, bomber pilots have to have a large amount of skill and dash.' By conviction, he was now a low-level enthusiast and he never saw any good reason to doubt the wisdom of this. At its most simple, the object was to hit the target with bombs. Everything else was secondary to this – including survival. In his book, he frequently expresses doubts about his ability to live through his experiences; and, as time went by, there was plenty of evidence to support them. Few of his contemporaries managed to come through alive. It may be rubbish, but his accounts of many of his missions include a happy expectation of bacon and eggs and coffee in the mess afterwards. Does this really suggest that these excursions into the dangers of the night produced a healthy appetite? Does it indicate a liking for the traditional English breakfast? Or could it be symbolic? On such occasions, do bacon and eggs, in the subconscious at any rate, represent survival? Does the ability to consume them indicate that one has come home in one piece and will live to bomb another night?

On one occasion, his squadron took part in a raid against Hamburg. The objective was the city's oil tanks and it was by no means an indication of the awful excesses to come – when that hapless place was to be demolished by fire and high explosive. There was no sign of any night-fighters, which was as well. On the other hand, there was plenty of flak, searchlights pierced the darkness and served also to illuminate an ominous number of barrage balloons. On C for 'Charlie's' first attempt, the bombs remained obstinately on board the aircraft. Gibson climbed to 5,000 feet; put the aircraft into a dive in which the speed reached a fantastic 320 mph. As he pulled out of it, they all blacked out for a few brief moments, but the bombs obediently fell from their nest and they were rewarded by the sight of something on the ground going up in a blaze of fire. But now they were in the very thick of the action: blinded by the searchlights, flak exploding on every side, and the way to safety encumbered by the innumerable strands of balloon cables. A wing snagged one of them and an enthusiastic ack-ack shell damaged the rudder. But 'Charlie' was still in business and, making allowances for the aircraft's infirmities, Gibson was able to nurse it out of hell and back to Scampton.

They returned to Hamburg on another occasion, when the target was again oil tanks. In this instance, it was a small refinery owned by Hermann Goering. The income accrued from it was said to finance the Reichmarshal's expenditure on uniforms, but that was probably a joke. When the raid was over, the damage was such that its owner moved the whole installation many miles to the east. After all, a man must look after his investments.

Working it out with billiard balls, somebody conceived the notion that, if you got it absolutely right, you could send a bomb *inside* a railway tunnel, fly to the far side and repeat the performance – thus blocking the line for a fairish time. Gibson accomplished this demanding manoeuvre, but one of his friends did even better. He pulled it off when there was a train inside.

After Dunkirk, Hitler got busy on what was to be the invasion of Britain. Everything depended on air superiority, and the Battle of Britain settled that. Nevertheless, there was a sizeable assembly of sea-going barges in ports from Antwerp to Dieppe and these had to be demolished. Each squadron was given a specific port – in Gibson's case, the basin at Antwerp. The defences were substantial and, with the emphasis on low flying, the demands on the pilots' skills exacting. Somebody reckoned that they must have sunk about 100 of these vessels, but at a cost. Many did not return, and several only just managed it. One member of the squadron, his name was Hannah, received the Victoria Cross for attempting to put out a fire on board his aircraft, using his bare hands. Gibson was in trouble when a missile pierced the underside of his Hampden, missing one of his feet by half-an-inch. However, it demolished part of the rudder bar and, consequently, put the steering out of action. In a single-engined aeroplane, this would have been fatal. But, with two, and by adjusting the speed produced by one or the other, it was possible to bring 'Charlie' home.

And then there was the raid on Berlin. Two hundred bombers were involved, which made it the largest so far. Military targets were still only deemed legitimate by the RAF, which made it difficult. Enemy air defences were not the only hazard attending the aircrews. There was the weather. On this night, it was a great deal less than co-operative. Cloud covered much of Germany and, on the return trip, the aircraft had to punch a gale-force headwind. Flak, predictably, was abundant. With some ingenuity, the Germans had managed to jam the somewhat rudimentary navigational systems – with the result that they had to fly entirely by dead reckoning. Unable to see Berlin, they dropped their bombs where they thought it might be. A lot of them fell where it wasn't. The American journalist William Shirer (the USA had not yet entered the war) was down below, and he observed that few had landed on the city and had done little damage. It was all rather disappointing.

Gibson experienced one of his rare moments of depression. Lying in bed afterwards, he worked out that he was the only surviving member of the squadron who had been on its strength since the outbreak of war. 'I did not see any point in living,' he wrote. 'For the moment I didn't even care about Eve. All my friends had gone now – there were new people – different – with different views on life – different jokes and different ways of living. I was the last one left.'

But there were changes in store for him. Some weeks (and some more missions) later, he was posted to Fighter Command. To be more precise, his destination was some miles to the south of Lincoln – an aerodrome at Digby, where he was to fly Beaufighters. These twin-engined aircraft should have been the terror of any German aircrew that dared intrude over Britain by night. In Gibson's estimation, they were often a lot less than perfect. Nor was his welcome to the mess at Digby enthusiastic.

The fighter lads regarded bomber pilots as 'bus drivers' (a state of mind that prevailed until Hurricanes and Spitfires escorted heavy bombers and the two arms of the service worked together). To make matters worse, he had been given command of 'A' Flight, replacing a very popular officer who was compelled to drop his acting rank.

In theory, night-fighter operations were a less hit or miss affair. Ground Controlled Interception (GCI) directed the aircraft to within about 1,000 yards of the enemy, after which Air Interception (AI – radar on board the aeroplane) brought the intruder into view. But it was still a matter of being in the right place at the right time. As Gibson observed, 'The night sky is very, very big.'

His personal life experienced two improvements. On 22 November 1940 he flew to Cardiff, where Eve and he were married. After a short honeymoon, they established themselves in a small hotel in Digby. Later, he acquired a Labrador pup named Nigger. Nigger, like his master, enjoyed beer and, again like his master, was by no means reluctant to go up in an aeroplane. When the squadron was moved to West Malling in Kent (to assist in the defence of London), he found the countryside very agreeable; and he, Eve, and Nigger were able to move into a cottage near the base.

'In many ways,' he reflected, 'these were the happiest days I ever had.' By bombing standards, the duties were not too arduous, nor too dangerous. During one year, he flew seventy night sorties and thirty day patrols, and yet saw only about twenty Germans. Others will probably dispute this, but he regarded it as 'the safest game of all'. The main problem was the weather which, as always in Britain, was unpredictable and often ghastly.

In periods of self-examination, however, he decided that he was not a very good shot and that 'bombing was still in my blood.' The climax came when he was suddenly posted to an Operations Training Unit. When he asked the reason, he was told that it was for a rest. The argument was not accepted. In a fit, one must assume, of pique, he borrowed an aircraft and flew to Scampton. It had to be regarded as a social visit, but he learned a great deal.

The flak situation over Germany was much as it had been. There was a huge belt of searchlights, about twenty miles wide, extending from the Dutch coast to Paris. The authorities were less fussy about the bombing of civilians, but aircraft were now being fitted with cameras. A flash bomb was released at the same time as the more lethal missiles. It exploded at about 3,000 feet and the camera shutter opened. The results were sometimes sobering. The pictures, it was estimated, were accurate to within ten miles. If you were over the target, they registered success. Quite often, however, they showed that, contrary to a pilot's belief, he had been nowhere near his objective. The only reward for a dangerous night's outing was a field pitted with a few craters.

The enemy, of course, did all that could be done to deceive. In this respect, they were following the example of a retired army officer in England. Colonel John Turner had become Director of Works and Buildings at the Air Ministry. Not long after the outbreak of war, he conceived the idea that it might be no bad thing to lead the *Luftwaffe* astray. What became known as 'Colonel Turner's Department' was set up. It built seventy dummy airfields, most of them equipped with flare paths and which, in June 1940, attracted thirty-six attacks. As well as this, he lit decoy fires that were known as 'Starfish'. During a raid on Portsmouth, or so it was said, one of them received 170 high-explosive bombs, thirty-two parachute mines, and the flames burned brighter from the downpour of 5,000 incendiaries (unfortunately other German pilots were not misled, and Portsmouth burned brightly, too).

After a lot of service, the Hampdens were beginning to wear out, but there was promise of new and better aircraft. By the time he returned to the OTU, Gibson's mind was made up. He must, at all costs, return to Bomber Command. The path was by no means easy, but he pulled just about every string there was – including an interview with Air Marshal Arthur Harris, C-in-C of Bomber Command. Eventually, on 14 March 1942, he was promoted to Wing Commander and given command of 106 Squadron, which was based in the North of England. The instruction came two days after his meeting with Harris, which seems to show the sense of going right to the top.

When Wing Commander Guy Gibson presented himself and Nigger, he found that the station commander was an amiable gentleman with a passion for dahlias. He was an easy-going officer, and 106 had a good record for its work in Hampdens. These had been replaced by Manchesters, which were not very satisfactory, but any day now they were due to be re-equipped with Lancasters. The Lancaster was an almost instant legend: a turning point in the evolution of British bombers. Unlike the

Hampden, with its crew of four, it was manned by seven men. On the ground, it was heavily guarded, for it was fitted with new and highly secret instruments. In many instances, runways had to be lengthened to accept it.

The Lancasters arrived in batches of five. Since there was no conversion unit on the station, the pilots had to train themselves to fly them – and, what was more, they had to be ready for a maximum effort against Germany in two weeks' time.

At night and in the daytime, they worked, and worked. Gibson: 'The most important thing of all is this cockpit drill, when flying modern aircraft. All it means is getting to know the position of every tap so that you can fly the aircraft without having to look down for the controls. All the movements have to be made automatically, as one does when driving a car. When flying a big bomber on a misty night, that split second when the pilot might turn his head away from the instruments might make all the difference between life and death.'

Just so. The raid due to take place in two weeks' time was meant to be against Hamburg. One thousand three hundred aircraft were to be assembled, some of them on loan from Coastal and Training Commands. But the weather was on that often less fortunate city's side. The raid was delayed for a night. With the cloud still bestowing its favours on Hamburg, the target was switched to Cologne. On the night of 27 May, 1,500 bombs were showered down within the space of 90 minutes. That, as they said, was showing them. The city's industrial area was supposed to be the victim; but, with bombing on such a scale, who knew where death and damage would occur. In any case, another purpose was to raise morale in the UK. Britain could take it; Britain could hand it out (as they also said).

Similar raids took place on Essen and Bremen, but these were less successful. Thereafter, the number of aircraft employed was reduced to between 400 and 600. But this was by no means the end of the problems. When you have half a thousand aeroplanes milling about in a smallish airspace, their crews concentrating on their targets and, at the same time, trying to avoid the flak, the possibilities of collision are considerable. There was also the chance (likelihood, indeed) that the formation might be split up – thus making the stray bomber an easy prey for the night fighter.

To Gibson's way of thinking, the worst part was before take-off: 'Your stomach feels as though it wants to hit your backbone. You can't stand still. You smoke far too many cigarettes, usually only half-way through, then throw them away. Sometimes you feel sick and want to go to the lavatory. The smallest incidents annoy you and you flare up on the slightest provocation . . . All this because you're frightened, scared stiff.'

All the while, the night sky's population of hostile fighters was increasing. This introduced another difficulty. To see the target, you needed a clear sky or, at least, high cloud level. But these very conditions also favoured the German interceptors. Given a full moon, they could see their potential victims and make the most of the opportunities. On occasion, the men of Bomber Command, who travelled by night, envied their American friends, who toured the skies of the Third Reich by day. A Boeing B–17 Fortress was armed with thirteen 0.5 Brownings, whilst a Lancaster had only eight.

As squadron commander, Gibson was unable to take part in every mission. There was paper-work that required attention, letters to be written to the relatives of casualties, and all the other tasks of administration. By and large, he managed to fly in one in five operations, but this does not mean to say that he slept quietly at nights. When his crews were going about their business, he did not sleep at all. He was in the control tower, anxiously awaiting their return.

He had considerable sympathy for the wives of his men. A couple might spend the day together, and then, come night-time, the husband would go off to work. The wife would count the sounds of the aircraft taking off, and count them again when they returned. Inevitably, the latter tally would be less than the former. What of those that did not come back? Was her husband among them? The suspense was dreadful. Eventually a rule was made that, except in exceptional circumstances, a wife could not live within forty miles of the aerodrome. The Gibsons were less plagued by this anxiety. Eve, who had given up the stage, was now doing war work in a factory near London.

It is impossible to give details of all Gibson's operations here. He had earned himself the DSO and Bar and the DFC and Bar. He had carried out an inordinate number of operations. But to find out more about them, you had best read his book *Enemy Coast Ahead*. The narrative moves along at a spanking pace; there is comedy as well as seriousness in it; and, when one considers that it was written in wartime, it is amazingly frank (it may be significant that it was not published until 1946).

In the middle of March 1943, he took part in a raid against Stuttgart. It seemed an age since he had enjoyed any rest, but his tour of duty was coming to an end. Afterwards, he and Eve were due to go on holiday to St Ives in Cornwall. Accompanied by lively and devoted Nigger, they planned to do some sailing, go for walks, and generally enjoy the relaxation that had been missing for so long.

Not long after the Lancaster took off, the port outboard engine developed a fault and cut out. The aircraft began to lose height. The question was whether to turn back. It was common knowledge that you could fly a Lancaster with the assistance of only one engine. Knowing this, Gibson decided to press one albeit at less than the stipulated altitude. The point was that to qualify for a rest one had to accumulate a sufficient number of operations. If they opted out of the visit to Stuttgart, there would have to be another sortie. It might be the next night, but then the weather might be bad and it would have to be the night after that. Goodness knows when it would be. It did not do to take chances with such a pleasant prospect in sight.

It was a curious experience to be flying beneath the rest of the bomber force: to see high explosives and incendiaries hurtling downwards not many yards away. On the other hand, the German air defences paid no attention to this solitary aeroplane. They may even have mistaken it for one of their night fighters. Gibson dumped his load and flew home. He went immediately to his room, packed some clothes and went to bed. He did not wake up until several hours later.

When he was pushing aside the mists of sleep, the station adjutant came into the room. There was a mournful look on his face; the expression people adopt when they have bad news to impart. Gibson, he informed him, was to be posted to 5 Group at Grantham. This seemed to be questionable: not only was he about to go on leave, he was due to be rested afterwards. He picked up the 'phone by his bedside. Yes, the officer at Group said, it was true. His squadron was to be handed over to somebody else. The reason, he gathered, was that the Air Officer Commanding wanted him to write a book – something that would help aspiring bomber pilots. He should postpone his leave, come to Grantham, and report at the headquarters unit on the following afternoon.

Eve was sent a telegram cancelling the holiday arrangements; there was the inevitable party that night, and, next day, Gibson drove to Grantham. He spent one or two days trying to think himself into the role of author. Then the AOC, Air Vice-Marshal the Honourable Ralph Cochrane, sent for him. He congratulated him on his latest DSO, more or less indicated that the business about a book was just a blind, and asked him whether he would care to make one more trip. It was, he insisted, something of great importance though he could tell him nothing about it. Gibson replied that he thought it would be all right. He was given two more days to consider it.

He thought about it and, such was his nature, he decided to fall in with Cochrane's wishes – whatever they might be. He assumed, wrongly, that it would be another attack on the German super-battleship *Tirpitz*, which was lurking in a Norwegian fjord and greatly perturbing Russian-bound convoys (in fact *Tirpitz* was beyond the range of British based aircraft. She was eventually destroyed by Lancasters that took off from Lossiemouth for an aerodrome near Archangel, refuelled, and then flew on to the target). The Air Vice-Marshal divulged no more than to reiterate that the unspecified mission was of extreme importance, and that a special squadron of carefully chosen men was to be formed to execute it. It could not be carried out for two months, but this was little enough time in which to assemble the air crews and the aircraft, and to carry out the extremely exacting training that would be needed. Scampton would be used as the base.

The task of assembling the squadron began. Twenty-one crews equalling 147 men were required. Such is human nature that there was always the danger that other units might see it as an opportunity to dump personnel they regarded as less than satisfactory. Consequently the list had to be carefully scrutinized. Eventually Gibson considered that he really did have a pack of aces. Among them were several Australians, all of them with DFCs, several British aviators who had won this award, a DSO (in addition to Gibson), Canadians and one American – all of them with good medal-winning potentials.* The mission would involve very low-level flying indeed. It would take place at night with, hopefully, assistance from a full moon. Water was involved in some way or another.

*The score added up to 2 DSOs, 13 DFCs, and 5 DFMs.

It would obviously be best if the daytime as well as night-time could be used for training. But how do you simulate darkness? The solution came from one member of the squadron, who had read somewhere that it could be done by wearing blue-tinted goggles and colouring the aircraft's windows yellow. This was done, and it worked.

The squadron was organized into two flights. Ten routes over Great Britain were mapped out. Since it was necessary to fly at a specified low altitude these were rigorously maintained. Apart from such potential problems as hitting trees and houses, it was as well to avoid throwing the Observer Corps into too much confusion. A reservoir in the Pennines near Sheffield, which was hemmed in by hills, provided the water element; a bombing range at Wainfleet in Lincolnshire received considerable attention. In all, 1,500 practice bombs were dropped there.

Initially, for want of any better idea, the new unit was called 'Squadron X'. After a week or so, the Air Ministry came up with a less flamboyant designation and it became known as 617 Squadron.

The time was approaching when Gibson would have to know rather more about the nature of his assignment. He travelled to London, where he caught a train to Weybridge. Much to his surprise, he was met at the station by his old acquaintance and mentor, 'Mutt' Summers. Summers drove him to a large country house at Burhill where security was obviously taken very seriously. After a series of checks, he was shown into a pleasant room overlooking a golf course. A rather tired-looking gentleman rose to meet him.

In his book, Gibson refers to him only as 'Jeff', just as 'Mutt' Summers is mentioned only as 'Mutt'. In fact, his host was the celebrated inventor, Barnes Wallis. It was he who had designed the airship R100 which, in contrast to its ill-fated rival R101, performed perfectly. It was he, too, who had devised the ingenious system of construction that made the Wellington bomber so successful. At present, he was engaged in the conception of specialist missiles with which to confuse and confound the King's enemies. Among them was the massive Tallboy bomb that was eventually to deliver the *coup de grace* to *Tirpitz* (appropriately, it was dropped by 617 Squadron). He was quiet, gentle, an apparently diffident man who, when pressed, could argue his point with urgent conviction.

The meeting might have got off to a poor start. Wallis said that he presumed Gibson knew the purpose of the operation. Gibson replied that he had no idea. Wallis shook his head sadly, looked at a list of names in front of him, and noticed that Gibson's was not on it. For want of this authority, he was unable to tell him anything about the intended target. He did, however, explain that there were certain objectives in enemy territory that were impervious to conventional bombing. Wallis, however, considered that he had the answer to this. He had, indeed, conceived it some while ago, but there had been no bomber capable of carrying a mine of above-average size and flying at the speed required to launch it. The coming of the Lancaster had solved this part of the problem.

He confirmed that whatever had to be done must be performed over water, and he showed Gibson a film of an aircraft dropping a cylindrical object into an estuary. Such was the altitude of the aeroplane, that it should have been blown to bits by the explosion. But it wasn't. What the weapon was doing was to produce shock waves: simulating, that is to say, an earthquake. If you dropped more than one, the effect would be cumulative – rather as, in a game of shove ha'penny, a coin hitting the one next to it will cause the one beyond that to move.

The important thing, Barnes Wallis insisted, was that the aircraft must fly at about 240 mph at 150 feet above smooth water (later it was amended to sixty feet. At altitudes above this, the impact of landing fractured the mine's casing). The code name of the operation, he said, would be DOWNWOOD.*

Gibson returned to Scampton and took Nigger for a walk. The dog was happy, for there were plenty of rabbits about. Gibson was in a less congenial mood. There was so much to worry about. Wallis had put up a convincing case, but the stipulated height and speed were alarmingly exacting.

By the time they next met, it seemed that Guy Gibson's name had been added to the list and Barnes Wallis was able to explain the purpose. Because of its coal and steel industries, the Ruhr Valley was the most industrialized area in Germany. The river was not large enough to supply it with all the water it required, and the Rhine was too far away. Consequently, it depended considerably upon three reservoirs that had been built a good

*A search of the Public Record Office list of code names makes no mention of DOWNWOOD.

many years ago. The Mohne (constructed in 1911) regulated the Ruhr's level, supplied water to homes and factories, assisted the hydro-electric system, and improved the navigability of the lower Ruhr. The dam that contained it was a fine Gothic structure, 850 yards long and 140 feet thick. No less than 140 million tons of water were contained within it.

Nearby, there was the Sorpe: smaller though nonetheless important. Between them, the Mohne and the Sorpe provided 76 per cent of all the water available in the Ruhr valley.

Finally, there was the Eder, built in 1914. This was mainly to prevent winter flooding, but it also helped to improve navigation on the lower Weser River and the Mittelland Canal, which linked the Ruhr with Berlin. Unlike the Mohne and the Sorpe, it supplied no water – though it had much to do with the generation of electricity.

If these three dams could be breached by high explosives, the productivity of the Ruhr would be greatly diminished and the resulting floods would wreak a lot more havoc. Models had been made of them, and were now at group headquarters. However, the dams could be attacked only when the reservoirs were full of water. Calculations suggested that this would be between 13 and 19 May – in other words, in six weeks' time. By a happy coincidence, the moon would also be suitable during this period – hence the tight deadline.

There was so much to do. Barnes Wallis's 'bouncing bomb' (as it came to be known) was by no means yet ready for its task. On one occasion, when testing off the Chesil Bank in Dorset, it fell slowly into the sea from a Lancaster and smashed into six pieces. On another, it simply sank. As for Gibson and his air crews, there was a great deal more training to be done. The River Trent was used to simulate the Rhine; the Cotswolds became the Ruhr hills; Uppingham reservoir became the Mohne; and Colchester's lake the Eder. Sometimes the aircraft returned with fragments of trees attached to them – evidence, surely, of their low-flying capability. Once, they were attacked over the sea by ships of the Royal Navy that mistook their identity and viewed their antics with some alarm.

Meanwhile, Avro's (A. V. Roe and Co.) had to adapt twenty-five Lancasters to carry what was obviously going to be a somewhat unusual bomb load. Barnes Wallis had at last got it right. On 29 April a Vickers test pilot named Shorty Longbottom flew low over the Thames estuary, and dropped what might be regarded as the prototype. It performed faultlessly. But they still had to be manufactured in sufficient quantity. Eventually, the mines arrived at Scampton on eight-wheeled trucks, each one covered by a tarpaulin.

There was, of course, the question of getting to the targets through an area that was known to be crammed with anti-aircraft defences. To find the solution, Gibson consulted his friend, Charles Pickard (see previous chapter) who, in Gibson's opinion, knew more about light flak in the coastal areas of Holland and Belgium than 'any man living'. Pickard suggested a somewhat tortuous route that would avoid the worst of it.

What with planning the operation, carrying out the considerable task of administration, and putting in his own hours of training, Guy Gibson was severely stretched. He felt sick, irritable, and a large carbuncle appeared on his face. The MO suggested two weeks' leave, but there was no time for that. In the end, he dosed himself with a tonic that seems to have worked.

By 15 May they had carried out 2,000 hours of practice and made 2,500 practice drops. The weather was perfect. Sometime during the day, Cochrane came to Scampton; a while later, Barnes Wallis arrived in an aeroplane painted white. The raid, Cochrane said, would take place on the following night. Gibson busied himself with composing the operation order.

The formation, he decided, should be divided into three flights. One would attack the Mohne dam and then proceed to the Eder. A second would apply itself to the Sorpe and also act as a diversionary force to distract attention from the first. The third would serve as a reserve to fill any gaps left behind by numbers one and two. Two of the crews had fallen sick, which left nineteen to carry out the assignment.

On the night of the 15th, all the aircrews involved were issued with sleeping tablets to ensure that they got a good rest. Having put the finish on his orders, Gibson turned in at midnight. He had not been in bed long, when Charles Whitworth, the station commander, came to his room. Nigger had strayed beyond the camp boundaries and had been killed by a car. He had died instantly. Gibson was wretchedly depressed. Not only had Nigger been his friend, he had also been the squadron's mascot. It seemed a bad omen.

Security was everything. The adjutant, Flight Lieutenant H. R. Humphries, was told to draw up a 'night flying programme' in a no doubt fruitless attempt to mislead anyone who showed too much curiosity. At about noon on the 16th, a Mosquito landed. Its crew had been busy taking pictures of the dams. The water was at the correct level. The meteorological officer at Grantham promised good weather. By 9.00 that evening, the crews were ready and waiting in one of the hangars. One of the pilots, an Australian named 'Micky' Martin*, had a small koala bear mascot in his pocket. It had been given to him by his mother at the outbreak of war. Martin always took it with him. One of Gibson's last instructions on the ground was to 'Chiefy' Powell. He was to bury Nigger outside the squadron commander's office at midnight.

At 9.10 pm the first aircraft took off.

On the way, one pilot misjudged his altitude, hit the sea, bounced off it, and put paid to both outboard engines. What's more, its bomb was now in a far from lethal condition. He had to turn back. Over the Dutch coast another Lancaster was so badly shot up, that all its radio equipment was put out of action. That, too, had to go home. A little later, an aircraft flown by Bill Astell veered off the track, was hit either by flak or a night fighter, and was consumed by flames. The others flew doggedly on, weaving their way through the defences, and doing, all things considered, very well.

Eventually the Mohne dam came into view, brightly illuminated by the moon. Gibson called up the other aircraft and said, 'Well, boys, I suppose we'd better start the ball rolling.' He then informed them that he was going in to attack.

The Ruhr hills provided the perfect hiding place: a flak-free area in which the Lancasters could take cover before getting down to business. Gibson was the first to fly from the sanctuary. With faultless precision, he swooped down to sixty feet, saw the light beams converge, and released his mine. Down below, the anti-aircraft fire opened up with fearful intensity. Gibson recalled, 'We skimmed along the surface of the lake and as we went my gunner was firing into the defences and the defences were firing back with vigour, their shells whistling past us. For some reason, we were not being hit.' And later, '. . . we could see

*Later Air Marshal Sir Harold 'Mick' Martin.

that the explosion of the mine had caused a great disturbance upon the surface of the lake and the water had become broken and furious as though it were being lashed by a gale.'

Barnes Wallis, who was sweating it out in the control tower at Scampton, would have been proud. His invention had performed just as he had imagined it would. The snag was that success depended upon still water, and the surface of the Mohne was now anything but tranquil. They had to wait an agonizing ten minutes before things calmed down, and the next mine was dropped. Fighters were now gathering in the sky above, but, for the moment, they posed no threat. The Lancasters were flying too low to be intercepted.

'Hoppy' Hopgood made the next attack. A shell hit one of his petrol tanks and his aircraft was immediately ablaze. The bomb landed behind the power house and exploded with the glare of doomsday. But this was of no assistance to Hopgood and his crew. They all died in the burning Lancaster.

Micky Martin was more fortunate. His aeroplane was hit several times, but he and his bomb aimer got it right – though they had to abandon the rest of the mission and head for home. Two more of the intrepid band of brothers were equally successful and, unlike Martin, escaped damage. Meanwhile, Gibson and his crew were diverting the attention of the gunners down below; spraying their positions with machine gun fire and doing so with zest and anger. With seven men killed in Hopgood's Lancaster, there was a lust for revenge. But there was vengeance enough in the condition of the Mohne. Gibson: 'Now there was no doubt about it; there was a great breach one hundred yards across and the water, looking like stirred porridge in the moonlight, was gushing and rolling into the Ruhr Valley towards the industrial centres of Germany's Third Reich.'

Fog was now beginning to form in the valleys, which did nothing to assist the location of the other two dams. Sorpe was torn asunder after the aircraft had made a dozen dummy runs. But this was not a priority target: the reservoir contributed little to the Ruhr Valley catchment area, and this mission was entrusted to the second formation. The Eder, on the other hand, was important and it was now difficult to see. Gibson went in search of it, and promised to fire a red Verey light when he was over the dam wall. It took several attempts, and cost another aircraft and its crew, to get it right. But get it right the survivors did. 'We saw the tremendous earthquake which shook the base of the dam, and then, as if a gigantic hand had punched a hole through cardboard, the whole thing collapsed. A great mass of water began running down the valley . . .'

They could now go home. Owing to the full moon, there were no other raids over Germany that night: the brightness would have made things too easy for the fighters, and the firepower of a Lancaster was not comparable to that of a Flying Fortress. Consequently their exit did not go unchallenged. But Pickard's advice had been sound and they managed, you might say, to wriggle through the gaps and gain the comparative safety of the North Sea.

A lot of damage had been created, though the cost – eight aeroplanes, fifty-five men killed, and one taken prisoner – was high. The dams were repaired in a matter of weeks. Nobody involved in the operation would have been pleased to know that among 1,294 people drowned by the consequent flood there were 749 inmates of a Russian POW camp not far from the Eder. Nevertheless, somebody estimated, the result added up to the loss of production by 100,000 men for a substantial time. It was, in its way, a glorious victory. Scheer's verdict was, 'That night, employing just a few bombers, the British came close to a success that would have been greater than anything they had achieved hitherto with a commitment of thousands of bombers.'

Back at Scampton, the first suggestion of success was received when the one word 'NIGGER' was received over the radio. Used out of respect for Gibson's late dog, it signalled the destruction of the Mohne. The completion of the attack on all three dams was announced by 'DINGHY'. The mess staff could begin preparing breakfast.

There were honours galore. For Gibson, the Victoria Cross; for others, five DSOs, four Bars to DFCs, ten DFCs and twelve DFMs. The investiture was carried out *en masse* by the Queen. Afterwards Avro put on a huge party for everyone involved in the raid – and that, of course, included Barnes Wallis, who was now a kind of honorary member of 617 Squadron.

For Guy Gibson, a long period of rest should have followed. He had done enough. The squadron was taken over by George Holden, DSO, DFC, and given the motto *'Après nous le déluge'* (which somebody wrongly attributed to Marie Antoinette – in fact, it was said by Mme de Pompadour, but never mind. A deluge there had certainly been). To keep him away from the flight deck of a bomber, Gibson accompanied Churchill on a tour of the USA. At the beginning of July 1944, he was seated behind a desk, all too firmly fixed to the ground. He did not enjoy it and, briefly, he considered standing for Parliament. He might well have been elected, but his impression of the House of Commons was that its members were not of the same calibre as that of his Air Force friends. He abandoned the idea.

On 11 July Micky Martin visited him in a Mosquito. He took Gibson up for two circuits and then suggested that his friend might like to have a go. It was love at first sight. Gibson made such a nuisance of himself, pulled so many strings, that he was allowed one last trip as master bomber of 5 Group. The target was a factory at Rheydt on the edge of the Rhur.

Once the attack was over, Gibson told his flock, 'OK, chaps. That's fine. Now beat it for home.' Quite what happened after that is uncertain. His Mosquito was probably hit by flak. Whatever it was, he crashed into a hillside in Holland, sixty miles from Rheydt. He must have died instantly: his body was buried nearby. For the first time in his brief career Guy Gibson, VC, DSO, DFC, went without egg and bacon for breakfast. As for 617 Squadron, it continued to be used as a kind of elite unit – employed to attack such targets as battleships, bridges, and ballbearing factories: targets, that is to say, where the utmost precision was needed.

3

George Beurling
THE MELANCHOLY
SOLOIST

Guy Gibson has been referred to as 'Gibby', although, in *Enemy Coast Ahead*, he always quotes others as calling him 'Gibbo'. It's a matter of one letter, and perhaps not very important. Whatever his sins may have been, and there is no evidence that there were any, he was a conformist. He recognized the importance of teamwork, knew when to make a stand for his convictions, and was a natural leader. He was, I daresay, the very model of a high-spirited public schoolboy turned aviator. But, then, in a bomber crew there had to be teamwork. In, say, a Lancaster, each of the seven men depended upon the others for survival.

The Canadian outsider George Beurling was quite another matter. He has been dubbed 'The Falcon of Malta', 'The Knight of Malta', and 'Buzz'. But the more apposite nickname – and the one, possibly, that he preferred – was 'Screwball'. Beurling (pronounced 'Burling') was, to say the least, eccentric. According to Laddie Lucas, who was his commanding officer when he arrived on Malta, the name derived from a rather quaint habit of his. The RAF station at Takali was infested with flies. It was Beurling's habit to place some fragments of bully-beef on the ground. The flies would come in their masses to enjoy this apparently generous snack. When sufficient had assembled, one of Beurling's flying boots would come smashing down on them, crushing them into whatever afterlife these obnoxious insects experience (assuming, of course, that they experience any). It smacked of eccentricity – hence 'Screwball'. To the more discerning eye, it may also have given some indication of his attitude to combat. There was killing, but it had to be done efficiently and, ideally, with an element of surprise.

George Beurling was born in Verdun, Quebec, on 6 December 1921. His father was a signwriter: a deeply religious man whose faith was handled by an organization known as the Exclusive Brethren. In fact he displayed an amazing tolerance of his often errant son. But, then, the two had at least one thing in common: single-mindedness. Just as Beurling Snr pursued his quest for grace with a zeal not far short of fanaticism, so did Beurling Jnr dedicate himself after his own fashion to aviation.

In a passing encounter, you would never have considered George Beurling to value precision. He was a tall, gangling figure, chronically untidy, and with small respect for the niceties of military behaviour. But put him into the cockpit of an aeroplane, and everything had to be just so. This almost obsessive attention to detail was complemented by quite exceptional eyesight and, when he cared to use it, considerable intelligence.

Aircraft and George Beurling first became acquainted with each other when the latter was aged about seven. Not too far from his home there was an aerodrome. Like many youngsters he was a keen model-maker – devoting himself exclusively to aeroplanes. These were long before the days of plastic kits and a lad had to start his project from scratch. The first step was to acquire a reasonably good idea of what the end product should represent. To find out about this he made innumerable trips to the airfield. So frequent, indeed, were his visits, that he eventually came to the notice of the chief flying instructor, an amiable individual named Ted Hogan. One day, Hogan offered to take him up on a flight. It lasted for ten minutes, but those minutes were crucial to Beurling's life. Thereafter, he spent all his free time at the airfield, doing odd jobs – anything that might, conceivably, further his ambition to fly.

There is no knowing the cost, financially and emotionally, that this obsession inflicted on his father. That devout gentleman would have liked his son to have become an academic: occupying, perhaps, some post at a university. But school and the aspiring pilot were not compatible. He left at the age of sixteen without passing any of the required exams. He had, on the other hand, already prepared himself for that moment of moments, his first solo flight.

He was an unusually quiet youngster who made few friends. At school, his only interests had been geography and meteorology. It later transpired that there was a rich vein of mathematical ability waiting to be mined. But the teachers never discovered it and, for example, when years later he decided he needed to know about trigonometry, he taught himself.

Were there tensions within the Beurling ménage? Certainly, once his education was done, George left home and found a job assembling radio sets. On the other hand, at whatever price to himself and the rest of the family, father Beurling continued to finance his son's flying. No matter that he had failed the exams of the classroom: those to do with flying posed few problems. In February 1939 he was able to stow away on a freight train heading for Toronto and apply for the post of second pilot to an entrepreneur running a cargo service to the goldfields in northern Quebec. He was accepted. His duties were mostly confined to on- and off-loading equipment, but the journeys were beset by sudden blizzards and other meteorological nastiness. They served to improve his skill at navigation.

The object of life – his life, anyway – was to fly: to sit at the controls and drive the aircraft through the sky. Man-handling crates was certainly not this and, before long, he had tired of the experience. Reading that the Japanese had invaded China, he assumed that the Chinese authorities would be grateful for his services. The problem was how to get there.

An uncle contributed $500 to the cost, which was nothing like enough. Nevertheless he headed westwards towards San Francisco, the port of departure for China. His journey came to an end at Seattle, where he was arrested for entering the United States illegally. After two months in jail, he was returned to Montreal. It was, no doubt, just as well. By this time, the Second World War had broken out in Europe. It seemed improbable that a qualified pilot would have to travel all the way to China to find a job.

His first reaction was to suggest that the Royal Canadian Air Force should accept him as a fighter pilot. The RCAF was less enthusiastic. Beurling attributed this to some unkind remarks he had made at a flying display given by Air Force personnel. Somebody had overheard them and harboured a grudge. A more probable explanation is that his academic record was not sufficiently good, but this was Beurling all over. He was honest after his fashion, but he was capable of employing what the late James Agate used to call the 'higher truth'. In other words, and doubtless with a kind of sincerity, he sometimes saw things not as they were, but as he thought they ought to be.

If the RCAF wouldn't have him, the RAF might be more amenable. Employed as a deckhand on a Swedish ship, he travelled to Glasgow and checked in at the nearest recruiting office. Yes, he was told, he did seem to be the right stuff. Could they please see his birth certificate? Unfortunately, it was back in Montreal. Undismayed, he worked his way back across the ocean, picked up the document, and then worked his way back again. The authorities were satisfied. They signed him on as an aircraftsman second class. He was posted to a depot at Hendon on the north-western edge of London, where he spent several weeks on various duties – the greater part of which seems to have been peeling potatoes.

Come December (it was now 1940), however, and this particular phase of initiation was judged to have achieved whatever it was supposed to have done. He was moved on to an Initial Training Wing in Devonshire. The course was important if unexciting. The studies included mathematics, meteorology, and navigation. He seems to have absorbed the knowledge without any great difficulty and, when it was over, he passed all the tests. In the spring of 1941 he was moved on to an Elementary Flying School in the Midlands. At last the authorities were to be rewarded with a glimpse of what he regarded as the true Beurling. Had they realized it, they were also to be rewarded with a foretaste of the Beurling to come. As a wager, he made a series of dangerously low 'attacks' on the control tower. If he had expected to be rewarded with a round of applause, he was to be disappointed. On landing, he was brought before the chief flying instructor, who had some rather harsh things to say. He even threatened to ground him – no penalty could have been more terrible. It may have been that the instructor was a kindly individual with a tolerance for youthful exuberance, or it could have been a realization that here was an above-average flier. At all events, the threat was never carried out. Thereafter Beurling behaved himself, revelling in the aerobatics, the low-flying exercises, the sheer joy in doing what he, more than anyone else, knew that he could do well.

That summer, he progressed again – this time to No. 8 Service Flying School at Montrose in Scotland. The aircraft were Miles Masters which, in some respects, had similar characteristics to those of the Hurricane. The course was very much tougher. The Cairngorm Mountains and the North Sea were ample deterrents to pilots who might have got it wrong. The weather was unreliable and the schedule was severe. Some never got beyond this phase: they did get it wrong and their mistakes cost them their lives.

Beurling himself had a narrow miss when his engine cut out. His instructor grabbed the controls and made an unacceptably hard landing in a stone strewn field. The aircraft was a write-off. He and Beurling, attended by amazing good fortune, were unharmed. On the credit side, however, his very considerable shooting ability now became apparent. As a pilot, he was considered good but not exceptional. At the conclusion, he was rated as 'useful as a service pilot,' though it was remarked that he needed to cultivate a 'sense of responsibility'.

He now ranked as a sergeant pilot and was able to wear his wings. But he was still not ready for combat. A course at an Operational Training Unit had to be carried out, and that would occupy another three months. Nevertheless, it was the beginning of the only love affair in his life that endured – with the Spitfire. His upbringing may have helped: not only did he not drink, he actually disliked the stuff. For him, there were no rowdy evenings in the mess or in one or another of the neighbourhood's pubs. He worked like one possessed. People remarked on his apparent inability to relax, on his restlessness, and on his determination to fly whenever he could. His flight commander, 'Ginger' Lacey, had destroyed eighteen enemy aircraft during the Battle of Britain, damaged six more, and probably accounted for another six (he is thought to have shot down the Heinkel that bombed Buckingham Palace). Lacey was impressed and wanted to recommend him for a commission. Much to his surprise, Beurling turned the offer down. He did not, he said, feel like an officer. He had not, presumably, yet cultivated a sense of responsibility. But Beurling's world was a narrow world. He was not even greatly interested in the progress of the war. It was a God-given opportunity to fly and he asked for little else.

Thus this inclined-to-be-friendless individual – a man who actually tried to avoid close friendships, with a remarkable ability to concentrate on whatever interested him, and a deplorable inability to tolerate whatever bored him – became ready for combat. He was posted to 403 Squadron based at North Weald in Essex. On Christmas Day 1941 he flew on his first mission. It did not live up to his expectations: indeed, he described it as 'exciting as Toronto on Sunday.'

George Beurling had no liking for the Royal Canadian Air Force. The sense of its rejection had been strengthened by the RAFs willingness to enlist him. As he admitted later, '. . . I still had a chip on my shoulder.' By the spring of 1942, 403 Squadron had virtually been taken over by Canadians. This he found unacceptable – to such an extent that he arranged a transfer to 41 Squadron in Sussex. Another offer of a commission on the eve of his departure did nothing to deter him. He brusquely turned it down and left North Weald with no regrets. Poor Beurling: life seemed to be compounded of one disappointment on top of another. Despite the fact that he had been flying in combat for three months – unsensationally it's true, but flying nonetheless – the pilots at 41 treated him as little more than a novice. He was assigned to number four position in his section – a position commonly known as 'tail-end Charlie'. For the others, there was an aggressive role to play, a grappling with the enemy with the chance of glory at the end. 'Tail-end Charlies' were there to ride shotgun. Theirs was a protective role made none the better by the fact that it was also the most vulnerable. Newcomers usually got the task on the reasoning that, if a pilot had to be lost, it was better to lose somebody with less experience than the others.

It was not a task to be meekly accepted – at any rate in his case. On his third mission, he became separated from the formation when five Focke-Wulfs produced a good deal of excitement.

Beurling's Spitfire was dreadfully mauled. Fifty per cent of its armament was put out of action and this was by no means the full extent of the damage. Nevertheless, with his faultless aim, he caused one of the F-Ws to explode in mid-air. Then he nursed his stricken aircraft back to Sussex.

Not unreasonably, he felt that he had done well. The others were less enthusiastic. He had broken formation and left them to face heaven knows what perils on their own. His chances of achieving popularity were badly impaired. Nor was the situation improved two days later. Again he left his appointed position –this time to destroy a solitary F-W 190. On this occasion, his rake-hell individualism was reported to the commanding officer. There was nothing that could be done about it officially, but henceforth he was cold-shouldered by men who should have become his friends. Furthermore, his name was often absent from the lists of those detailed for sweeps over Europe.

In fact, he carried out three more missions – all of them lacking in incident – before an unexpected answer to his tribulations occurred. One of the pilots had received an overseas posting. Since his wife was expecting their first baby, he was somewhat less than pleased about the matter. Beurling overheard him grumbling about it and promptly sought an interview with the squadron commander. Could he take the future proud father's place? To resolve the business of a pilot's problem and that of a problem pilot at one swipe of a pen was uncommon good fortune. The squadron commander agreed. No tears were shed when the brooding Canadian departed from 41 Squadron for goodness knew where.

The trouble with Beurling was that he was his own man and nobody else's. The idea was surely to destroy German aeroplanes and to kill German aviators – no matter how. The fact that it might best be done by well-disciplined teamwork, that there might be an inter-dependence about the business, does not seem to have occurred to him. His was by no means a simple mind, but it was narrow. It was, perhaps, surprising that he had already been twice singled out as officer material. It is, again perhaps, a tribute to his self-knowledge that he had refused. Officers do, after all, have to think of others.

It was not until he reached Gibraltar that he was informed of his destination: Malta. The island was a considerable threat to Rommel's line of communication between Italy and North Africa. Attempts by Axis aircraft to put its airfields out of action had failed, but there was another solution. Its very survival depended on shipping: if convoy after convoy could be severely hit, it might be starved to the point of death.

Thus there were shortages of food, aircraft, spares, gasoline, ammunition – pretty well anything you can think of. Somehow, some ships managed to get through, but at enormous cost. The fact that its distance from Gibraltar exceeded the range of a fighter did not help. But then somebody had the idea that the aeroplanes might be taken part of the way by aircraft carriers. At this point, equipped with extra fuel tanks and decreased in armament and ammunition to extend their limits, they would take off. It was a perilous business, not least because of the considerable demands it made upon navigational skill. Malta is a mere dot in a large sea. Under such circumstances, mere dots are easily missed.

Beurling and forty-eight others were embarked in HMS *Eagle*. After two days at sea, they took off from the carrier's deck for a flight of about 660 miles. Some while later, Beurling landed at

RAF Takali. The scene was by no means promising. The buildings were sadly dilapidated; the airfield itself was cratered by the depredations of enemy bombers. But, by some miracle, it was still in business. Some people might have found it depressing, but Beurling was undismayed. It was all so different from the well-ordered appearance of an airfield in Britain. There was a kind of informality about it; an atmosphere of adventure that appealed to his adventure-seeking mind. Here, he felt, was a place in which he might, just possibly, be happy.

The impression of informality was reduced slightly when he came face to face with his squadron commander, a former Fleet Street journalist named P. B. ('Laddie') Lucas. Lucas was a leader who demanded results, and it was no act of chance that his was to become the island's top-scoring squadron. He had, however, a shrewd insight into human character and behaviour. Beurling's reputation as a difficult subordinate had followed him from England, but Lucas preferred to make his own judgement. In *Five Up: A Chronicle of Five Lives*, he summed up his impressions of the newcomer: 'He was something of a rebel, yes; but I suspected that his rebelliousness came from some mistaken feeling of inferiority. I judged that what Beurling most needed was not to be smacked down but to be encouraged. His ego mattered very much to him and, from what he told me of his treatment in England, a deliberate attempt had been made to assassinate it.' He would, he said, give the young Canadian his trust. But, if he abused it, he would be put on the next aircraft leaving for the Middle East. Beurling thought it a fair deal. He was even prepared to go along with Lucas's insistence that whilst there might be a place for loners in the world it was not in the RAF. He might be – indeed, he was – a singularly good shot, and his handling of an aircraft undoubtedly displayed an uncommon sensitivity: nevertheless, whatever his virtues, he would be just another pilot. Very well, Beurling decided, if that was the truth, the truth must be accepted.

There are, roughly speaking, three ways in which to attack an enemy aircraft. The first is head-on (risky: there might be a collision). The second is from the rear, and the third is at an angle. Of the three, the last is by far the most difficult. Since both aeroplanes are moving, you have to work out the angle and the speed of the opponent in relation to your own. You have to do this, and you have to do it very quickly.

Deflection, as it is called, became an obsession. The estimated effective limit to the range of a Spitfire's guns (in terms of accuracy) was 300 yards. Beurling preferred to reduce it to 250 whenever possible. He spent much of his spare time hunting lizards. The others dismissed it as one of his many eccentricities, but there was method in it. The hapless reptiles represented in miniature the sizes of the German Messerschmitt and the Italian Macci fighters. The distance at which he aimed his revolver was, he calculated, a scaled down approximation of 300 yards. Since the lizards were moving, he had to aim correctly. It was one way of learning to overcome the problem of deflection.

Another was to keep a record of all his encounters with enemy aircraft: to record statistics, to draw graphs, and to compose formulae. It was a scholarly business and revealed the mathematical ability that, all those years ago (or what seemed to be so), his high school teachers had missed. On one occasion, he tried to explain his ideas to one of the squadron commanders. Whilst agreeing that they made sense, that officer had to admit that he would find it impossible to memorize all the data. Beurling it seemed, had no such difficulty. He not only killed, but he killed cleanly. He could actually anticipate the exact point on an enemy aircraft where his bullets would strike.

The Spitfires flew in pairs, which meant that each pilot could keep an eye on the other's blind spot – thus reducing the danger of a surprise attack. During his first month on the island, Beurling achieved nothing worth talking about. But then, on 6 July, his fortunes took a decided turn for the better. In the morning, with seven other Spitfires, he was involved in a battle against three Italian bombers and thirty fighters. He damaged one of the bombers and shot down two fighters. A sortie in the afternoon yielded nothing, but in the evening he accounted for a Messerschmitt Bf–109F.

His score now began to mount. During the following week, he destroyed another eight, and by the end of the month he had been awarded the Distinguished Flying Medal. He was well on his way to becoming Malta's top-scoring pilot. He still turned down any offer of a drink: whilst, in the evenings, others consumed beer in the mess, he occupied himself with his self-imposed studies, bringing his records up-to-date and looking for lessons in them. Somebody once described the poet Dylan Thomas as looking like an unmade bed. Beurling made a rather similar impression. But, in Malta, nobody minded much. Instead, he was awarded a Bar to his DFM and another offer of a commission – which, naturally, he turned down.

In seven flying days during July 1942, he shot down no fewer than fifteen enemy aircraft and damaged five more. His own aeroplanes did not come through the experiences unscathed: more often than not, they were seen to be riddled with holes on landing. But he was unharmed. The real enemy, and one about which neither he nor medical science could do very much, was a particularly nasty form of dysentry that was rife on the island and which was known as 'Malta Dog'. Like more or less everyone else, he succumbed to it. What with this and the lean diet available on the besieged island, his weight fell from 175lbs to 140lbs. But he was happy. The only flaw in the pattern was yet another offer of a commission. On this occasion, he was sick with 'Malta Dog' and one must assume that his defences were very much reduced. At all events, he accepted. As Hugh Halliday remarks in *The Tumbling Sky*, 'For both the man and the service it was a tragic mistake.' Beurling had been right all the time: he was not the officer type.

Under the immediate circumstances, however, it didn't matter much. He had become accepted as a popular eccentric, and no matter whether you wore chevrons on your sleeves or stripes on your cuffs, there were still aircraft to be destroyed: still the thrill of the chase and those lightning calculations to be made that would slam home the bullets in the places he intended.

He was fastidious to the point of perfection about the preparation of his aircraft. He disliked using tracer, for he felt it spoiled his concentration. In flight, he was economic in his manoeuvres and sparing with his ammunition. With four Browning machine-guns and two 20mm cannons, they reckoned that you could discharge the full quota in 13 seconds. He rationed himself to seven bursts, each lasting two seconds. With such marksmanship, the idea served very well. It meant that you could attack more aircraft on a sortie, with correspondingly better results.

As an officer, he now lived in the more comfortable surroundings of the Xara Palace, the former home of a baroness, that overlooked the airfield. The food was not very much better and it seems doubtful whether he appreciated the relative luxury.

In July 1942, enemy air attacks on Malta had been more numerous than ever: the siege at its worst. But then, at the end of the first fortnight in August, a convoy got through. The losses were fearful. *Eagle*, the veteran left-over from the First World War, was sunk. *Indomitable* was put out of action. The cruiser *Manchester* had to be scuttled. Five out of the fourteen merchant ships that had set out in the convoy codenamed PEDESTAL reached their destination. The attacks by submarines, E-boats, and aircraft were unremitting. But those five ships did get through. The first arrivals reached Valetta on 13 August. On the 16th, the tanker *Ohio*, which had been hit three times, was towed into the port. Malta was now the richer by 32,000 tons of general cargo and 15,000 tons of oil. The island's ordeal was by no means over, but the breakthrough had taken place.

Beurling had been among those escorting the survivors on the last part of their voyage. When the *Ohio* berthed, he celebrated the occasion by flying upside down at zero altitude along the main street of Valetta. It may have seemed to be a somewhat flamboyant gesture by a flamboyant man. He certainly enjoyed flying upside down and would do so on the smallest excuse. Nevertheless, on the face of it, it does not seem to be entirely characteristic. But Beurling was such a mass of contradictions. Sometimes he seemed like a pilot playing the part of an actor playing the part of a pilot. You never quite knew where you were with him – unless you skimped the preparation of his aircraft, or offered him an alcoholic drink.

On 14 October, at 1.00 pm, fifty fighters and eight bombers were seen to be approaching the island. Two squadrons of Spitfires were scrambled, which set the odds at two to one. Beurling shot down a Ju 88 bomber and two Messerschmitt fighters. But then an enemy got on to his tail. The result was that his controls were shattered and the aircraft went into a dive from 16,000 feet. By the time the Spitfire had reached 2,000 feet, flames were enveloping the cockpit. With a good deal of difficulty, he climbed out on to the wing and, at 500 feet, bailed out. His left heel had been badly damaged by shrapnel, but this did not seem to be very important. He had been quite certain that he was going to die.

The crew of an air-sea rescue launch hauled him out of the water and he was taken to a hospital near Takali. As he lay in bed, he doubtless considered the state of his accounts. On the credit side were 27 victims over Malta, plus the two he had dispatched when he was based in England. He had been awarded two DFMs and, more recently, the Distinguished Flying Cross. On the debit was the fact that 'Laddie' Lucas had been posted elsewhere. Few of his original comrades had survived. His health had suffered from the demands he made upon himself on a wretchedly poor diet during the burningly hot summer. And now, here he was in a hospital bed, his left foot and leg in a plaster cast – with, it seemed, very little to look forward to.

But the situation was about to change. One day, the Air Officer Commander of Malta, Air Vice Marshal Keith Park, came to his bedside. The AVM congratulated him on his DFC and reported that there was something even better for him. He had been awarded the Distinguished Service Order. For a pilot officer to receive it was almost unheard of, and this must have kindled a feeling of warmth in the greatly stressed Canadian's heart. However, the rest of Park's news was less than pleasing to him. Instructions had been dispatched from the highest possible source in Canada that he was to return home. He was required to take part in a campaign to sell war bonds and in a recruiting drive.

As Beurling was apt to tell anyone who was prepared to listen (and this included the King at his eventual investiture), those months in Malta had been the happiest time of his life. The hardships and the dangers had meant little to him. This was the kind of place, and the kind of action, to which he belonged. His heel would recover quickly enough, and he could soon be back in a Spitfire's cockpit again. But take it all away: puff him up in some footling publicity campaign, and the prospect would be extremely unhappy.

There was to be no argument. On 1 November he boarded a Liberator *en route* to Gibraltar and thence, after a refuelling stop, to England and so to Canada. It was a journey that very nearly cost him his life. Among his companions on the flight was Group Captain Arthur Donaldson, who had been Beurling's wing commander during the latter months at Takali, and a fellow Canadian, Pilot Officer John Williams DFM, who had destroyed nine enemy aircraft and who was affectionately nicknamed 'Willie the Kid'. All told, there were eighteen passengers.

As the aircraft approached the Rock, a severe thunderstorm was raging. Visibility was down to almost zero and so, unfortunately, was the fuel supply. The pilot had to make a landing somehow – no matter how unpleasant the odds. It was not altogether surprising that he misjudged the touch-down, over-shot the runway, and ended up in the sea. The crew survived:

Beurling and Donaldson and one other managed to wriggle their ways to safety. All the others, including Pilot Officer Williams, died.

Beurling's return to Canada had been engineered by the Prime Minister, William Mackenzie King. The truth was that King needed a hero. He and his Liberal party were committed to a policy that opposed conscription. If it was to succeed, there needed to be enough volunteers, and recruitment was not going as well as the Prime Minister would have liked. Beurling would be evidence that it was possible to obtain fame and glory without actually dying. He received, as they say, the full treatment. Everyone, including King, said how proud they were of him. He was fêted wherever he went, surrounded by pretty girls, and accompanied by the strains of martial music. The press and radio subjected him to countless interviews: the stories made huge headlines. In Verdun, no fewer than 10,000 people crammed the local ice-rink to yell their approval.

Impressions of how Beurling withstood the experience vary. Some suggest that he loathed every minute of it (though could this have been explained by his ankle, which was still troubling him?). Others seem to imply that he rather enjoyed it. Whatever the case, he was never quite the same afterwards. The change was not for the better.

He was now a Flying Officer and still a member of the RAF. The latter situation bothered a lot of people. Why was not Canada's favourite hero in the RCAF – which led to the difficult question of why had they rejected him in the first place? This was clearly some sort of anachronism and it was about time it was put right. The RAF had no objection to parting with him, but these things take time. Six months were to go by until the transaction was accomplished. In the meanwhile, Beurling wanted to get on with the war.

When he had arrived in Canada, he was a physical and psychological wreck. His sleep was disturbed by fearful night-mares; only a brave (and, it must be agreed, handsome) face concealed whatever thoughts tormented him by day. But he was now fully recovered. The only reminder of his wounded heel lay in the dimensions of his feet. His right foot still took his customary size 11/12 shoe; his left had been reduced to accepting a size ten. It was apt to make life expensive: whenever he needed a new pair, he had to buy two pairs.

Eventually he was posted back to duty in England. During his publicity tour, he had met the widow of a bomber pilot – an attractive young woman named Diana Eve Gardner. She belonged to a wealthy Vancouver family and her parents, whilst applauding Beurling's exploits in the sky, did not see him as a suitable replacement for her lost spouse. When Beurling rang her up to invite her out to dinner, they opposed the idea. But opposition in such instances is futile. She accepted and the two became friends. Once he had left the west coast, fourteen months were to go by without a single letter. And then, out of the blue, he 'phoned her with a proposal of marriage. It may seem surprising, but she accepted.

He sailed for England in the *Queen Elizabeth* (then a trooper) on 5 May 1943. Once in London, he was called to Buckingham Palace, where the King formally invested him with the DSO, the DFC, and the DFM and Bar. The RAF was wary of him, and posted him to the Central Gunnery School at Sutton Bridge in Lincolnshire. No doubt his ideas on the matter of deflection could be put to good use. Perhaps they could, but he was bored. This was bad: it made him careless – an accusation that could not have been levelled at him before.

All told, he had three crashes during this period. The first was when a student, whose aircraft had been accidentally loaded with live ammunition, fired an all too accurate burst, and hit Beurling's engine. A fire broke out and, at 1,400 feet, he bailed out. By some oversight, he pulled the ripcord too soon. His parachute was damaged and it did not open until he was 600 feet from the ground. The matter was never discussed – he merely reported that his fuel tank had sprung a leak. Nobody questioned the explanation.

On the next occasion, he retracted his aircraft's undercarriage too soon: it collapsed and the Spitfire in question made a dismal belly-flop on to the ground. Finally, he had to make a forced landing on the shore of The Wash. He was rescued by a local boatman.

During this period, he has been described as 'lonely' and possibly he was. But his name continued to appear in the newspapers, and he was also criticized as 'arrogant' and as a 'headline hogger'. The arrogance may be explained by his solitary disposition; the headline business is not so easily dismissed. In some cases, fame is enduring and that may be very nice. But the kind of acclaim Beurling had received is ephemeral and conse-

quently dangerous. Afterwards, there is bound to be an anti-
climax, which is unpleasant. Having tasted glory, the appetite
does not sicken and so die – it wants more.

But the service had had its fill of Beurling's appearances in
the press. When, on 1 September 1943, he was transferred to
the Royal Canadian Air Force, an order was issued stating that
he must receive no more publicity. He was posted to 403
Squadron – part of 127 Wing, which, ironically, was commanded by an Englishman, James 'Johnnie' Johnson, who was to end
the war as Group Captain with a DSO and two Bars and a
DFC and Bar. Johnson was a decisive, no-nonsense, officer and
his own score of victims and medals was sufficient to render
him immune from the newcomer's reputation for heroism. He
tersely explained that, in his unit, there was only one rule: 'We
always fly as a team.'

Four-o-three Squadron was stationed at Headcorn in Kent.
On his arrival, Beurling was told to sharpen up the unit's
gunnery. He was not unsuccessful. With some ingenuity, he
built a scale model of an Me–109 as it would have appeared at
a range of 300 yards. He mounted it on a post: the student,
sitting in a chair twelve feet away, was told its speed. From this
he had to work out the angle of deflection.

The business in hand was somewhat different than it had been
when Beurling was last in England. Large formations of American bombers were making daylight raids on German industry.
The fighters' task was to protect them. During this period, he
added two more to his score. On the debit side was the occasion
when he suddenly broke formation, dived earthwards and shot up
just about everything in sight. It earned him a sharp rebuke from
Johnson, and he seems to have been suitably chastened. He
actually apologized.

In the second instance, he was seen to be falling out of the sky,
his aircraft inverted and apparently out of control. Over the radio,
he was heard to say, 'I've had it.' The rest of the squadron
returned to base. Fifteen minutes later, much to everyone's
surprise, Beurling appeared. It transpired that he was flying the
new Mark IXb Spitfire and had misjudged its considerable
power. He had gone down to attack a German bomber and was
flying low over the sea. Such was his speed that he blacked out
and, to make matters worse, the controls iced up. Somehow he
managed to regain level flight and struggle back to Headcorn.

Several of the rivets in his aircraft had popped and the skin had wrinkled. Any less gifted aviator really would have 'had it'.

The squadron moved to winter quarters at Kenley in Surrey. There were many days when the weather was too bad for operations. To fill in the time, Beurling borrowed an aircraft and indulged himself in the performance of aerobatics over the airfield. This was strictly forbidden. When he did it the first time, he was severely rebuked. Undaunted, he did it again. And, again, he received a mighty dressing down. Undiscouraged, he did it a third time – on this occasion, the ceiling was only 300 feet. This was too much: he was put under open arrest – with the threat of a court martial.

Possibly Mackenzie King himself was responsible. The point was that to fête a man as a national hero on day one, and to haul him up before a court martial on day two, is bad public relations. Somebody intervened, and the penalty was reduced to that of being grounded for a period. Eventually, he was transferred to Biggin Hill, where he scored his final victory when he shot down an FW–190 fighter.

All the while he was becoming more and more morose. Acting as sheepdog to a flock of bombers was not his idea of combat. He conceived the notion of acquiring four long-range Mustangs. With three carefully chosen wing mates, he would rove the skies of Europe, wreaking whatever havoc there was to be wreaked. 'Johnnie' Johnson liked the idea, but the authorities did not. He was told to forget it.

Beurling had had enough. A while later, he applied to be repatriated to Canada. His application was granted. On 8 May 1944, he arrived in Halifax.

What was to be done with him? For a while, the RCAF had the notion that he might be used as a ferry pilot. He was posted to No. 3 Training Command where, to gain experience, he was employed as co-pilot in a twin-engined Beechcraft that was running what might be roughly described as a small airline service. It was not a success. In the end, exasperated by circumstances, he resigned his commission.

Beurling's kind of war was over. Had he been in England for the Battle of Britain, he might have excelled himself. In Malta, he was brilliant – it was the kind of combat for which men such as he were designed. Curiously enough, when the fortunes of the Allies took a turn for the better, his took a turn for the worse. Or was it curious? George Beurling was not what would nowadays be called 'a company man'.

The rest of George Beurling's life was a shambles. He married Diana Gardner, but it was doomed from the very start. The two, to put it plainly, were incompatible (in fairness to his wife, it was not easy to be compatible with Beurling). For a year, he worked as an insurance salesman without selling a single policy. He tried barnstorming, but got into trouble with the authorities for carrying passengers when he had no licence to do so. In the end, he decided to offer his services as a mercenary. Any nation, apart from Russia, could apply. By devious means, the newly created state of Israel did so. In May 1948, he was in Rome, preparing to fly a Norseman – an eight/ten seater transport that could also be used to carry cargo. Twenty of them were at Nice on their way to Israel via Rome. One of them was to be flown on the last leg of its journey by Beurling assisted by a co-pilot named Leonard Cohen.

When the aircraft arrived, Beurling and Cohen were invited to take it up on a brief flight to accustom themselves to the controls. The Norseman behaved perfectly until it landed. As it touched the runway, it burst into flames and exploded. Beurling and Cohen were both burned beyond recognition.

The Italian inquiry into the accident was a lot less than satisfactory – indeed, it was a very shoddy piece of investigation. Thus the cause was never discovered – and never will be now. Beurling's father said, 'This is the way I expected his life to end – in a blaze of smoke from the thing he loved most – an airplane.' Perhaps: but his son was a perfectionist. This unexplained disaster does not seem to have been his style. To die in combat might have been acceptable. To die like this would not have been. The mystery remains unsolved.

4

Donald Bennett
THE PIONEER

Mﻗore than twenty years have gone by since I interviewed Air
Vice-Marshal Donald Bennett, CB, CBE, DSO. He was then a
man of about sixty, living in comfortable – affluent, perhaps –
retirement at Stoke Poges, Buckinghamshire. He was a patient,
friendly person, who took trouble to answer questions that he
must have been asked a great many times before. The purpose of
our meeting had to do with a children's book I was writing about
aviation over the North Atlantic.

In the meteorological sense, this may have been one of the
more stormy aspects of his remarkable career. In human terms,
however, it was comparatively uncontentious. The stresses that
might have sent the Bennett blood pressure soaring (though there
is no evidence that they did) were to come later.

As founder and commander of the Pathfinder Force, he did
very much more than most people to improve the accuracy of
Bomber Command. But this was not achieved without a struggle.
As his book, *Pathfinder* (published in 1958) makes clear, he fought
on three fronts: against the King's enemies, against the pettifogg-
ing ways of bureaucrats who seemed to oppose any form of
innovation, and against officers more senior than himself.

I am in no doubt that Bennett was often a difficult man, but he
got things done. He explored possibilities that had not been
considered before, and he inspired considerable loyalty among
those who served under him. By no means all his opponents were
little men in little jobs who niggled. His concept of the Pathfinder
Force was opposed by none less than Air Chief Marshal Sir
Arthur Harris, Commander-in-Chief of Bomber Command.
Harris disliked the idea of an elite unit, which would appropriate

the best of bomber crews, and argued that each group should find its own paths. The group commanders tended to agree with Harris, but Churchill liked the notion and, as usually happened, Churchill prevailed. By the end of the war, the squadrons under Bennett's command had flown more than 50,000 sorties. An assessment of the operations made by the *Luftwaffe* air staff in March 1944 contains these words: 'The success of a large-scale night raid by the RAF is, in increasing measure, dependent on the conscientious flying of the Pathfinder crews.' It may have been a grudging compliment, but it was a compliment nonetheless.

Donald Bennett was born on 14 September 1910 at Toowoomba in Queensland, Australia. His father was a cattle man, who also ran one or two agencies. By the time Donald was eleven, the family had moved to Brisbane, and three elder brothers were already displaying suggestions of achievements to come. Two of them qualified as barristers, a third as a doctor. Bennett Snr would have liked his youngest to go in for medicine, but Donald's results at Brisbane Grammar School were discouraging. He did well enough in physics, but his performances in the other disciplines were by no means satisfactory. The truth was, on his own admission, that he had been idle. After one particularly bad end-of-term report, Mr Bennett finally put his foot down. To spend any more money on his eduction would be a waste. He should join the agency business.

When it comes to choosing a career, a degree of self-knowledge is an excellent asset. Donald Bennett had no taste for business and the idea of toiling away in an office each day did not appeal to him. Instead, he went to work on a cattle station. He may have been short on industry at school, but the seeds of ambition were beginning to sprout. The life was pleasant enough, but where did it lead? The answer – in his case, at any rate – was nowhere. On the other hand, there was something making signals to him that were too strong to be ignored.

He had seen the Wright brothers when they came to Toowoomba to demonstrate their heavier-than-air machine. He had watched the arrival of Amy Johnson after her flight from England. He had also followed Kingsford-Smith's epic flight across the Pacific. Such exploits had appealed to his imagination. That must be where his future lay: in the sky. His father was less impressed; his mother dissented not only on account of the prevailing dangers, but also because she disliked the idea of his becoming an 'aerial bus driver'. One of his brothers joined in the anti-flying campaign, but to no avail. Donald Bennett's mind was made up. He left the cattle station, hitch-hiked his way back to Brisbane, and offered his services to the Royal Australian Air Force.

The authorities may have been sympathetic, but there was a snag that only time could overcome. To join the RAAF, you had to have reached a certain age. The eager young applicant had not reached it. He should call again when he had. There was nothing for it: he would have to adopt his father's original plan and join the business. He graduated from office boy to salesman, filling the evenings by attending Queensland University and plugging the gaps in his education. At last, in July 1930, he was old enough to report to the RAAF's Victoria Barracks in Melbourne. He spent his first week in the service square-bashing.

His difficulties were not yet over. Australia, like many places elsewhere in the world, was in the throes of an economic depression. The country could not afford a large air force. Consequently new recruits were required to volunteer for the RAF in England once they had trained. It was that, or nothing. He volunteered.

Training was carried out at Point Cook, which might be described as Australia's version of Cranwell. Among the aircraft at the base were two Southampton flying boats and five amphibians known as Seagulls. The course lasted for a year: at the end of it, he came second in the examinations – top in flying. Soon afterwards, he travelled to the UK by P&O.

After reporting at the Air Ministry in London, he was sent to Uxbridge and thence, after a period at the Flying Training School near Liverpool, to No. 29 Squadron at North Weald in Essex. At the flying school and at North Weald, he flew Siskins, an aeroplane over which opinions differ. It had been described as a 'superb aerobatic aircraft' and as 'one of the worst aeroplanes ever produced.' But the latter verdict may have been occasioned by its original engine which was, indeed, a disaster. Afterwards the power unit was replaced by something very much better, and the sight of two Siskins, flying with their wings lashed together, never failed to thrill the crowds at the annual Hendon air shows.

It may have been the memory of those Southamptons moored at Point Cook: at all events, after a year spent flying Siskins, he applied for a flying boat course. It took place at Calshot on

Southampton Water and lasted for six months. There was more to it than flying: seamanship was also involved. Once he had completed it, he was posted to 210 Squadron at Pembroke Dock. He drove there in an old Morris motor car he had acquired. His second major acquisition was more exciting. For the not altogether outrageous sum of £115, he bought a small aeroplane. Two and a half years later, he sold it for £130, which suggests a degree of business acumen.

One's impression of Donald Bennett in those years suggests a restless individual, constantly seeking new experiences – the more challenging, perhaps, the better. In 1934, he was given the opportunity to compete in an air race from England to Melbourne. One of the necessary qualifications was a First Class Navigator's Certificate. He did not have one: very few people did. For two and a half months, he studied hard. At the end of the period, he took the exam, passed, and thereby became the seventh person in the world to possess this precious piece of paper.

The race was less successful. The aircraft, which a friend was to pilot and he was to navigate, had an undercarriage that was apt to jam. It performed this diabolical antic to particularly ill effect at Aleppo – nearly writing itself off and completely writing off Bennett so far as the remainder of the race was concerned. He returned to England with an assortment of injuries including three crushed vertebrae, a stiff leg, trouble in one of his ears, and a wretchedly stiff neck and shoulders. Nevertheless, a fortnight later, we find him back at Calshot at the controls of a Southampton. He was now serving as an instructor.

Determined to increase his experience he took to putting in weekend work flying DH Dragons for Jersey Airways Ltd. The take-offs would either be from Heston, or Southampton, or Portsmouth. The time depended on the state of the tide at Jersey. Since there was no airfield on the island, the landings had to be made on one of the beaches. At high tide, this was impossible. The airline paid him nothing for three flights, nor did he ask for anything. It was a matter of accumulating hours in the sky. On the other hand, some Member of Parliament, whose name has long been forgotten, found reason for criticism. If members of the RAF were permitted to undertake such work, he argued, they were doing civilian pilots out of jobs. The practice should cease. It did. In its own small way, it had achieved something. When, in

August 1935, Bennett left the RAF, he had amassed 1,350 hours of flying, and had handled twenty-one different types of aircraft.

The reason for his leaving the RAF had nothing to do with dissatisfaction. He had enjoyed life in the service and he had accumulated a lot of experience. But his mind may have gone back to the days when he was working as a jackeroo in Queensland. What – in peacetime, at any rate – was the scope for advancement? The answer, he had to tell himself, was very little: it might be better to devote his considerable energies to commercial aviation.

At about this time, he married an attractive Swiss girl. Whatever storms his career may have encountered, they seldom penetrated his domestic life. He cannot have been an easy husband, but this does not seem to have blemished a singularly happy marriage. It was as well: even a man of such tough moral fibre as he required a refuge sometimes.

To combine a honeymoon with business, the couple set off for Australia. Before departing, he had visited the Pitman organization, which commissioned him to write a book on air navigation. He spent much of the outwardbound voyage working on it, and much of the trip back to England as well. Entitled *The Complete Air Navigator*, it amply justified Pitman's faith. It was still in print in 1957 and still selling tolerably well.

His target so far as employment was concerned was New England Airways. The managing director was enthusiastic. Yes, he said, they'd be delighted to take him on as navigation superintendent. The trouble, Bennett calculated, was that the salary would be about half of that paid to a first officer in Imperial Airways. And, again, the prospects were somewhat limited. The Bennetts returned to the United Kingdom.

One day in January 1936, he joined Imperial Airways. His stint as a first officer was commendably brief. Before very long, he was posted to Egypt with the promise of soon commanding a flying boat. The airline was as good as its word. Within a surprisingly short time – and after, one suspects, a good deal of manipulation – he was occupying the captain's seat in a Calcutta flying boat operating between Alexandria and Brindisi. Once they had set foot on the Italian mainland, the passengers continued their journeys to England by train.

The Calcutta was not the easiest nor, indeed, the most comfortable carrier from the crew's point of view. It was flown from open cockpits and its engines could produce a cruising speed of no more than 75 knots. This meant that when the forecast warned of strong headwinds the flight had to be delayed. On several occasions when he gave the weather the benefit of his doubt, he turned out to be sadly wrong. After two or three hours from the moment of take-off at Alexandria, he had to turn about and head back for Egypt. Had he continued, the aircraft would certainly have run out of fuel.

But there were newer and very much better flying boats coming into service – all part of a scheme to deliver mail by air to any point within the British Empire. No doubt Bennett's ability was again brought to the attention of management by the publication of another book. Its title was *The Air Mariner*, the subject was how to handle flying boats. He wrote it during a five-day stop-over in Brindisi.

Now the Empire flying boats were coming into service. These forerunners of the Sunderland were much bigger and more powerful than the Calcutta, and, given the right conditions, they were able to accomplish flights from Alexandria to the UK in one day.

By the early part of 1938, the crack German liners *Bremen* and *Europa* had brought an interesting innovation to the North Atlantic scene. Both ships were equipped with seaplanes. At some point in their voyages to New York, the aircraft were catapaulted from their upper decks, sped on ahead and delivered the mail before their parent vessels had so much as sighted the United States. In Britain, technicians were working on a more ambitious idea. There were two elements involved: an Empire flying boat named *Maia* and a seaplane called *Mercury*.

One of the problems of Transatlantic aviation was fuel supply. If an aircraft carried too much, its weight would become such that it could not get into the sky. On the other hand, the very act of taking off considerably increased the consumption. The answer, then, must surely be to cut out this part of the operation: to allow one aircraft to heft another off the deck, and, once airborne, to release it. The project was conceived by R. H. Mayo, General Manager (Technical) of Imperial Airways. *Maia* was selected for lift off with *Mercury*, as one might say, its passenger. The latter was specially built to carry mail. There was no room for passengers on board.

This development had come to the notice of Bennett, who applied for the post of *Mercury*'s captain. He was accepted and went into partnership with Captain A. Wilcockson, a veteran Imperial Airways pilot who would be at the controls of *Maia*. After rigorous testing, the 'Mayo Composite' (as it was called) was ready for action. The aircraft took off from Shannon.

'For take-off,' Bennett told me, '*Maia* was basically the master. The top half of the composite couldn't override the bottom. All I had to do was to keep the trims dead centre, to make sure *Maia* had a balanced load.' Once they were airborne, he called up Wilcockson over the inter-com and announced that he was ready to separate. Up to this point, *Mercury's* controls were locked and could be released only by Wilcockson. Once he received Bennett's message, he freed them. Bennett then pulled a lever that rendered the aerial divorce absolute. He went on to fly to Montreal non-stop in twenty hours, thus carrying the first commercial payload to fly Transatlantic. From Montreal he flew to Port Washington, New York, and so, via Botwood in Newfoundland, back home. Throughout their brief sojourn in Canada and the United States, he and *Mercury* were treated to a feast of publicity.

It could be seen as a considerable success, but some pundits, with their eyes on the cash ledgers, thought otherwise. Transporting mail and one or two other items (cans of motion pictures, for example) was not, they said, enough. For the project to be viable, passengers would have to be carried as well. Since *Mercury* had not been designed with this in mind, the proposition was impossible. As is the way with such matters, the accountants won. The business was brought to an end. Bennett afterwards used *Mercury* to break the record for a flight from Scotland to Cape Town (with an unscheduled stopover near the South African frontier to refuel). After the return trip, *Mercury* languished at moorings near Felixstowe in Suffolk, until she was bought by the Dutch Government for reconnaissance purposes. It was a sorry end for such a strikingly original innovation.

Sunderlands, derivatives of the Empire flying boats, were now coming on to the scene. Bennett was given command of one of them, an aircraft named *Cabot*. In August 1939 he took off from Southampton and thence, with refuelling stops at Shannon and Gander, to Montreal and New York. It was the inaugural two-way service of BOAC (which had succeeded Imperial Airways) across the Atlantic. On 3 September of that year, not long after Great Britain had declared war on Germany, he set off again. On the way, he received an SOS from the liner *Athenia* announcing that she had been torpedoed by a U-boat. The large ship sank in twenty minutes with the loss of 112 lives. But there was nothing Bennett could do about it. After the return trip, *Cabot* was ordered to Poole in Dorset and that, for the time being at any rate, was the end of BOAC's Transatlantic Service. When it was resumed, the circumstances were very different.

But many of the other services were continuing. Bennett carried out a flight to South Africa and another to Singapore, and he had the doubtful pleasure of being in Rome on the day that Italy declared war. Taking most of the BOAC staff with him, he escaped internment and flew back to Hythe on Southampton water. His next trip was to be considerably more dangerous.

On 20 June 1940 the Polish leader, General Sikorski, arrived in England from France and was taken to see Winston Churchill, who was now Prime Minister. Sikorski explained that the Polish general staff and members of the cabinet had reached some place near Bordeaux. He would be grateful if they could be brought to safety.

Since the object of the war had been to stop Hitler's invasion of Poland, and since Britain and France had responded to that invasion by doing nothing in particular, transporting Sikorski and his colleagues into honourable exile was the least anyone could do. A Sunderland flying boat was prepared for the operation; Bennett was given command of it. Accompanied by Sikorski, an aide, and a French colonel who was anxious to find his family, they headed towards Bordeaux and beyond. Eventually they came down at Biscarosse, a small place well to the south of the town. Bennett's instructions had been that, on the one hand, he should do everything he could to assist the General, and, on the other, that he should bring the aircraft back intact.

Nobody knew precisely what the situation was in France. The country had capitulated two days earlier. Consequently it was probably swarming with German soldiers. But had they swarmed as far south as Biscarosse? And, if they had, in what numbers? Bennett had devised what seemed to be a fair compromise. Before putting Sikorski and the other passengers ashore, he told them that he would wait at his moorings until first light next morning. If they had not returned by then, he would depart. Sikorski agreed. None of his party was armed with anything more substantial than a pistol. But, brimful of confidence, the General commandeered a car, and the three drove off in what anyone might have assumed to be the general direction of the German advance.

Bennett went to call on the seaplane base at Biscarosse to pick up whatever fragments of information he could. He learned that there were already sizeable forces of German troops in the vicinity. Most of them were mobile columns intent on rounding up French soldiers and taking them into captivity. The news was hardly encouraging: he never expected to see Sikorski again.

Once or twice during the afternoon, German aircraft flew over. But he had brought the flying boat close in to the shore, where it was reasonably well hidden by trees. Occasionally he and his crew heard the sound of tracked vehicles on the roads: they did not seem to be very far away. That night, they slept uneasily.

As soon as the first glimmerings of light appeared in the sky, he rowed ashore to see whether there were any signs of Sikorski and his henchmen. He was about to give up, when he saw the lights of four cars approaching. To his surprise and delight, he saw that the General was in the leading vehicle: the others were packed with Polish soldiers and politicians. He hustled them aboard the flying boat and, within minutes, took-off.

The only opposition they encountered was near the mouth of the Gironde, where a British cruiser opened fire on them. Quite why a warship that should have been friendly directed its guns on to a large flying boat with perfectly visible British markings is a mystery. But there you are: these things happen. Away to starboard they saw a number of German aeroplanes flying over the coast. Thankfully they went about whatever their business was and took no heed of the Sunderland. More disturbing were the sights of two ships, badly damaged and abandoned; three lifeboats – one of them with the bodies of dead men lying in it; and an enormous column of smoke climbing into the sky above Ushant – where the French had demolished an installation of oil tanks. In *Pathfinder*, Bennett wrote, 'On we went, very depressed at the fall of France and at the gruesome things which we had seen. I was then, as much as at any time in the war, thoroughly sick at the principle of international massacre which this world apparently regards as normal policy.'

On landing at Poole Harbour, the passengers were put ashore. Nobody seemed to know what the flight had accomplished 'but [Bennett's words] they seemed reasonably surprised that we had returned!' So far as he was concerned he had to report at BOAC's headquarters in London. One week later, he was given another special assignment. The destination, in this instance, was Lisbon.

For the Portuguese to have held an international exhibition at a time when much of Europe was occupied by Nazis may have seemed to be a trifle eccentric. Nevertheless, there was such an exhibition, and Britain was determined to be represented. At least it would display a kind of defiance: an exercise in public relations designed to show that the country was neither crushed nor cowered. To ram the point home, it was decided that the Duke of Kent should attend it. Bennett was given the task of taking him there and bringing him home. If you discount the fact that on the same floor of the hotel in which the aviators were quartered, the crew of a Lufthansa aircraft were also installed, the trip passed off quite peacefully. The return flight was made on 2 July 1940. It was the last that Bennett made on behalf of BOAC.*

At the beginning of the Second World War, President Roosevelt took great pains to emphasize how neutral America intended to be. But, a year later, such pious protestations did not prevent the United States from providing Britain with aircraft. It was now possible to fly the Atlantic with land-based aeroplanes: in this instance, the Hudson bomber and the Liberator. For anyone who had time in which to consider it, the future of post-war Transatlantic aviation was already apparent.

There were rules that had to be obeyed. The Hudson, for example, was manufactured at Lockheed's plant in California. It had to be brought to Canada by an all-American aircrew. There was also a kind of formality about crossing the frontier. The aeroplanes landed in a field some miles to the south of Winnipeg, where horses towed them over an invisible line dividing the USA from the British Dominion. The pilots were then free to take off again and to continue the journey. But their responsibilities did not extend to crossing the Atlantic. The British had to make their own arrangements for that.

One day in the late summer of 1940, Bennett was asked to call at the Ministry of Aircraft Production in London, where he met Lord Beaverbrook. He was invited to take on the job of Flight

*Neither of Bennett's illustrious passengers on these two flights survived the war. Sikorski was killed on 4 July 1943, when the Liberator in which he was supposed to be flying to England crashed after take-off at Gibraltar. The Duke of Kent died when a Sunderland assigned to take him to RAF establishments in Iceland smashed into a mountain in Sutherland. Ironically, like Bennett, the pilot of the aircraft on this occasion was also an Australian. Neither loss has ever been properly explained.

Superintendent for the ferrying of these aeroplanes to the UK. It transpired that his old friend Captain Wilcockson was already in Montreal, working as assistant to the general manager. The idea appealed to him: he accepted and a few days later was on his way westwards across the ocean in a Canadian Pacific liner. The ship was crammed with evacuees. She was not, however, sailing in convoy, nor was she afforded an escort. It was assumed that her speed would be sufficient to out-perform any U-boat that might show an unhealthy interest.

The choice of shipping line was appropriate for, as he discovered once he had arrived (without incident) in Montreal, Canadian Pacific was ready to play a very useful part in the operation. Indeed, to begin with, the project was known as the Canadian Pacific Air Service.

Donald Bennett was nothing if not thorough. Before any aircraft could fly to Britain, they had to be brought to Canada from Lockheed's. One of his first actions was to travel to Los Angeles to make arrangements. The people at Lockheed may have envisaged his arrival as something of a formality. But they did not know Bennett. Acting as his hosts, and putting him up at the Beverley Wiltshire (probably the best hotel in town), were not enough. The Hudsons had to be tested, and he intended to be on the flight decks of the first batch, recording his own figures and making his own observations. One of the latter was that they were inferior to their estimated performance by eight per cent. Put another way, they required extra fuel capacity to make a crossing of the North Atlantic.

Lockheed's should be given credit for the fact that they acted very promptly. Overnight, each aircraft was fitted with an extra tank inside its fuselage. In a hurry to get back to Montreal, Bennett hitched a lift in one of the aeroplanes that had to be delivered. It was not a very comfortable journey. The pilot insisted on sticking strictly to the prescribed airways no matter what. If there happened to be a thunderstorm raging, there was no question of flying round it. He pushed on through it, regardless of its fearful strength and the way in which it hurled the aeroplane and its luckless occupants about the sky. There was also the peril of a crowded airway monitored by a not yet very sophisticated system of air traffic control. Under the circumstances the risk of a collision was considerable. However, they got to Montreal in the end – here to find 'Wilkie' Wilcockson battling with problems of recruitment.

Beaverbrook had offered American pilots very high rates of pay to encourage them to volunteer for the service. Such munificence did, indeed, generate a lot of applicants, but most of them turned out to be rejects from various United States airlines. One of them actually admitted that he had been thrown out of every airline in America for drunkenness. But, he boasted, 'I'll show you how to fly the Atlantic.' Again, it was all very well to offer big money to Americans, but Canadians, Australians and Britons were given less generous terms, and this caused a good deal of ill feeling. As Captain Wilcockson once told me, many of these early pilots were 'adventurers and rogues'. But, he emphasized, they were good fliers – even if their knowledge of navigation was minimal.

The first trip in which seven Hudsons were to be ferried from Gander Airport, Newfoundland, to Aldergrove, Belfast, was scheduled for 10 November. Gander had no more than a field to offer: a control tower and three superannuated railway carriages to serve as accommodation. Bennett arrived there on the 9th, using one of the Hudsons as transport. Each of his aircrews consisted of a pilot, a second pilot, and a wireless operator. There was, you'll note, no navigator. For want of any bettter solution, he decided that they should cross the ocean in close formation – with himself in the leading aircraft. Once his Hudson had taken off, he handed over the controls to the second pilot, a genial Texan named Clauswitz, who wore cowboy boots with fancy leatherwork (for luck apparently): thereafter Bennett applied himself to finding the way to Northern Ireland. His only tool was a sextant. The meteorological facilities at Gander were unreliable. None of his pilots had ever flown the Atlantic before, and nobody had flown it as late in the year as this.

He had to accept the possibility that, somewhere along the route, an aircraft might become separated from the rest. The eventuality was provided for by a detailed briefing and the issue to every pilot of a flight plan covering every possibility he could think of. With its assistance and a bit of luck, the stray aircraft (or aircraft in the plural) might arrive safely at the other end.

November 11th was Remembrance Day. Anticipating it, the airport manager's wife (she was the only woman there) issued each airman with a poppy. It was a nice thought, but they would need more than poppies to see them safely over the long tracts of the Atlantic. Not least a good deal of hard work was necessary at the very outset, for winter had set in and the wings, the fuselages, and the tail planes of the Hudsons were covered with half-inch layers of ice. They had to be carefully hacked away before there could be any thought of flying.

The aircraft took off one after the other, each circling the aerodrome, until all the little flock was airborne. Then, with their station-keeping lights shining, they set off towards Belfast. All went well until they had completed about three-quarters of the journey. It then transpired that the met. authority had put a front in the wrong place and they flew into dense cloud. Even at 22,000 feet, where the icing would have been less severe, they were unable to climb over it. It was a situation that Bennett could well have done without. Nevertheless, all was very far from lost. Five of the aircraft touched down at Aldergrove according to plan. Another arrived later, and the seventh pilot landed somewhere else. But never mind: he, his crew and his Hudson were all in one piece.

From Aldergrove, the aeroplanes flew to an airfield near Blackpool, where they were serviced before moving on to their appointed squadrons. The crews returned to Canada by ship to collect another consignment. Bennett, seeking some cover story that might disguise his role, let it be known that he was travelling to Canada for winter sports. It did not go down very well with the other passengers, who considered that this apparently fit thirty-year-old might have been better employed serving King and country.

There were, of course, problems. Among the deliveries were a number of Catalina flying boats. These were to travel by way of Bermuda, but on one occasion somebody got it wrong. Instead of putting down in the calm sea surrounding this delightful island, it turned up at Halifax. Now it goes without saying that a flying boat requires water on which to land. There is plenty of water around Halifax; but, in winter, it is frozen. This happened in the darkest days of mid-winter, and the result was predictable. The catastrophe was followed by a chain reaction of rows. The Ministry of Air officials tried to blame Canadian Pacific, and then switched their attack to Bennett who, as it happened, was innocent of any mistake. Eventually there was the inevitable re-organization – with Bennett retaining control of the technical and operational sides, and Wilcockson taking charge of training.

On the fourth flight, one aircraft crashed on take-off, and another had to turn back early on with technical trouble. At another time, an aeroplane flown by a Captain Mackey went missing on its way to Gander. Bennett had been at San Diego, testing the latest version of the B24 (Liberator). By the time he got back to Montreal, forty-eight hours had gone by with no word from the absent pilot. Donald Bennett was a practical man who respected facts and had a knack of interpreting them correctly. But he had heard many stories about wives who, in similar circumstances, had rightly believed their husbands to be alive. This had aroused a feeling that there was probably something to be said for telepathy. He picked up a telephone, rang Mrs Mackey, and asked her whether she believed her husband had survived whatever had taken place. She replied that she was convinced of it. That was enough: climbing on to the flight deck of a Hudson, he set off immediately for Gander.

The search had been the responsibility of the Royal Canadian Air Force. The ferry pilots were supposed to play no part in it; but when he arrived at the Newfoundland airfield he found that many of them had taken-off of their own accord to have a look round. He loaded his aircraft with blankets and other comforts and joined in the hunt. At last, they came across some tracks in the snow; a small figure leaning unhappily against a tree; and a message stamped out in the white ground covering. It said THREE DEAD. They dropped the supplies. As they were about to depart to launch a rescue operation, somebody noticed two men and a sledge hauled by dogs making for the spot.

Back at Gander, a DH Moth equipped with skis had arrived. There was, in fact, no need for it. By the time it was over the scene of the crash, the solitary, tree-reclining figure had gone. He had been taken to safety by the men with the sledge – and yes, he was Captain Mackey.

At last Beaverbrook had been compelled to agree that delivering aircraft across the Atlantic in closely knit batches was not the right way of doing it. Better by far that each should be provided with a navigator and consequently have a degree of independence. The idea was that RAF personnel, who had been trained in Canada, should provide the facility. In their case, they would make only the one trip. The pilots, on the other hand, would be permanent. Some civilian navigators were also employed. This, of course, meant that, having delivered their aeroplanes, the pilots had to return to Canada. The question was: how? With the ocean infested with U-boats, the prospect of the sea voyage was a lot less than attractive. The answer lay in the formation of the Return Ferry Service, which was run by BOAC.

The workhorses of the service were Liberators, with the passengers (which included a number of less than very important officials who had business in Canada) travelling twenty-four at a time in the bomb bays. It was uncomfortable, damnably cold (one passenger actually succumbed to frostbite and lost all the fingers of one hand), but at least it was reliable.

With the entry of the United States into the war in December 1941, the United States Air Force undertook all the deliveries to Montreal, and the Atlantic Ferry Organization took over the bit from Gander to Belfast. The Canadian Pacific's role in the operation had withered and so died. As for Bennett, in the restructuring, a number of political ploys rendered him redundant. As a reward for services rendered, he was given the rank of acting Group Captain in the RAF. It did not escape his attention that, once he had gone, there was a grievous number of disasters on what had been a virtually disaster-free route. It transpired that somebody had re-written his rule book and produced the wrong advice.

In London, nobody seemed to know what to do with him. For want of any better idea, he was demoted – first of all to Acting Wing Commander and then, briefly, to Acting Squadron Leader. At this rate, it would not be long before he was reduced to Pilot Officer. It seemed to have occurred to nobody that, a while previously, he had been asked to call at the headquarters of Bomber Command. It seemed that whilst the then C-in-C, Sir Richard Pierse, was deluding himself that his employees' bombs were falling in the right places, the Directorate of Bomber Operations were under no such illusion. This suggested certain shortcomings in navigation and, as a very experienced navigator, Bennett's views would be worth hearing. He treated them to a homily on the art; pointed out that pilots on their own were not enough; and outlined an idea that was eventually to be adopted as the Pathfinder concept. But all this was for the future. For the moment, he was unemployed.

Six weeks after his return to England, he was appointed second-in-command to an establishment in Eastbourne. Housed in what, during peacetime, was Eastbourne College, it was a school intended to give preliminary training to 2,000 men who, or so it was hoped, would become navigators. He may have had some satisfaction in seeing that the remarks he had addressed to the Directorate of Bomber Operations had not been entirely disregarded. On the other hand, he was less pleased to hear that his rank was to be that of Squadron Leader. You did not trample over Donald Bennett – or, if you did, it was a mistake to think you'd get away with it. He kicked up a fuss with the result that he was inched up a notch to Wing Commander.

He helped to get the first course under way and then felt restless. A trip to Bomber Command, he decided, would do no harm. The commanding officer of the school was very reasonable about it, and even suggested a personnel officer who might be sympathetic. After all, Bennett did have a great deal of flying experience.

Thus he was given command of 77 Squadron, which was equipped with Whitleys – a type of bomber that he had wrongly assumed to be obsolete, but which, as time passed, earned his respect. The squadron was stationed at Leeming in North Yorkshire. On his arrival, the station commander gave him one piece of useful advice. He should make at least two flights as second pilot before taking over command. He chose the two most junior sergeant pilots. The experience taught him little about how to do the job, but it did give him valuable insight into the natures of the young men who were going on operations and who would be in his charge. He tightened up the squadron's ability to navigate and he insisted that photographs should always be taken to show exactly what had happened to the bombs they so hopefully released. The squadron carried out raids on the North German ports, on industrial targets within Germany, and on the Renault works at Paris. On one occasion, they spent an hour and forty-five minutes over the target, intent on getting it right. When they landed, the Whitley's fuselage and wings had fifty bullet holes in them. He reckoned that between four- and five-per-cent casualties was about par for a raid.

Can one foresee the future? One of his young pilots told him that he expected to be shot down before very long. When this happened, he hoped his squadron commander would dispel any notions his parents might have about his being taken prisoner. The possibility simply did not arise. He was quite cheerful about it and Bennett agreed to his request. Some weeks later, the youngster was indeed hit by flak and, true to his prediction, he was killed.

In mid-April, Bennett was given command of 10 Squadron (also stationed at Leeming). The unit was equipped with Halifax bombers which, with their four Rolls-Royce engines and their longer ranges, were an advance on the Whitleys. He had not been with it for long, when he was briefed for an uncommonly exacting mission. The target was the great German battleship *Tirpitz*, sister of the *Bismarck* (sunk in May 1941), and now moored in the Aasfjord near Trondheim. She posed a constant threat to convoys on passage to Murmansk in northern Russia; indeed, her very presence had been sufficient for one to scatter – with catastrophic results.

The great warship was moored close to the shore of the fjord, which sloped down towards the water. Spherical mines, each weighing 1,000-lbs, had been produced. The idea was that if they were dropped on land close to the water's edge they would roll into the fjord and explode underneath *Tirpitz*'s hull. This, it was assumed, was her vulnerable spot. Twenty-six Halifaxes and ten Lancasters were earmarked for the operation. It may have sounded excellent in theory, but the plan overlooked the very considerable anti-aircraft defences. Also, as Bennett wrote, 'Such an operation would be quite possible with a helicopter, but to do it with a four-engined bomber was, to say the least, a little difficult.'

Later that month, the units detailed for the raid moved up to Lossiemouth in Scotland. The mines, effective as they might be, were very much more bulky than bombs. When you crammed five of them into a Halifax, the bomb doors wouldn't close properly. But this seemed to be a matter of minor importance. On the night of 27 April the aircraft set off.

Crossing the sea posed no problems at all. Once they were over the Norwegian coast, however, the reception was devastating. Just about every flak weapon in creation seemed to open up at them. To add to the difficulties, the target was hidden by a canopy of white smoke, through which only the battleship's masts and part of her superstructure protruded.

Bennett's Halifax was hit several times. The tail-gunner was wounded and the starboard wing was set on fire. He ordered the mines to be dropped in what he regarded as roughly the right place, but, with the wing blazing away, there could be no thought of returning to Britain. Instead, he flew on eastwards towards the sanctuary of neutral Sweden. He did not get very far. The inferno was worsening; the aircraft became impossible to manoeuvre. He gave the order to bale out.

It was wonderfully well disciplined. The flight engineer, Flight Sergeant Colgan, went to the rear of the aircraft and released the injured tail-gunner. Bennett, who was doing what he could at the controls to make things a mite less difficult, suddenly realized that he was not wearing his parachute. Again, the admirable Colgan came to the rescue. Having found it, he brought it to the flight deck, and clipped it on to his commanding officer. It was not a moment too soon. The aircraft had been losing height, and Bennett was within a few yards of the snow-wrapped ground before the 'chute opened. But it was enough to break the impact of the fall, and he struggled to his feet unharmed.

Five bombers were lost that night. It would not be long before German troops mounted a hue and cry, which was every reason why Bennett should get out of the vicinity and proceed towards Sweden as fast as he could. Although he was in poor training, his adrenaline had lost none of its zip. To begin with, he made amazing good speed. The countryside seemed to be unpopulated: there was just this huge expanse of snow broken by well-drilled regiments of trees. At some point he saw somebody approaching him. He always carried a small automatic pistol on operations. Now, as the figure came closer, he debated whether, should he be confronted by a German soldier, he would have time in which to use it. But the man raised his hands.

It was a fine, clear, moonlit night and it did not take long for the two to realize that they knew each other; that they had, not all that many minutes ago, been sharing the inside of a very sick Halifax bomber. For this was Sergeant Forbes, the aircraft's W/T operator. They decided to continue the journey together. The immediate problem was crossing a mountain torrent.

Climbing to a higher point, they found that it narrowed and became more shallow. With assistance from a long stick, Bennett managed to negotiate it and Forbes followed. It was now nearly first light.

After a lot of walking, during which Bennett contracted frost-bite in one of his feet, they came to a house. The door was opened by a man who, to begin with, regarded them with suspicion. Assisting an Allied serviceman on the run was a crime with the probable punishment of death. The Norwegian's initial reaction was that they might be Gestapo agents keen to increase their tallies of arrests. But, as soon as he had identified them, he invited them inside. They were given a good meal and somewhere to sleep close to the kitchen stove.

The Norwegians had wanted no part in the war; but, now that it had been thrust upon them and their country occupied by Nazis, most of them treated Allied evaders with rare kindness and courage. Bennett and his companion were taken by one young man to a mountain cottage, where he handed them over to another. Shod with skis, the newcomer (they never discovered his name: merely that his initials were JGM) took them high above the tree line on to an immense plateau. About five miles away there was a mountain ridge. That, or so they gathered, was Sweden.

As Bennett wrote, 'He then left us, and skied off back down to his own house. I was terrified that he would be arrested for assisting us.' The evidence, after all, was plain enough: the tracks of a pair of skis and two sets of footprints marring the pristine surface of the snow.

The frontier was marked by a line of cairns. At last, and now in poor shape, they reached a ski resort in Sweden. An amiable Swedish officer named Captain Skoogh arrested them. The next day, they were taken to an internment camp.

It would have been foolish to have expected Bennett to sit back in resignation. He intended to get back to Britain – and to get back quickly. After an appeal to the British legation in Stockholm had met with a somewhat flabby response, he was taken in hand by a gentleman named Ake Sundell, the general manager of a firm set up by the Swedish Government to produce carbon gas as an alternative to petrol for cars. Sundell suggested that he should make contact with Count Bernadotte in the Foreign Office at Stockholm. It was good advice. Bernadotte was sympathetic and, happily, influential. Within a month of their arrival in Sweden, Bennett and Forbes were on their way back to the UK, passengers in a civilian version of the Hudson that was manned by RAF personnel from Leuchars in Scotland. It transpired that two other members of the crew had already returned home. Three, including the injured tail-gunner, had been taken prisoner.

On his return to the UK, Bennett was admitted to the Distinguished Service Order. The award presumably took into account his record of service. An RAF officer's standard decoration for escape or evasion was the Military Cross (since such adventures had nothing to do with flying, a DFC would, one assumes, have been inappropriate). Some received nothing at all. In any case, his journey to Sweden and his consequent repatriation had not been particularly difficult as these things went.

He returned to Leeming. In mid-summer he was about to be posted to the Middle East when he was called to Bomber Command headquarters. The special force that he had envisaged as an aid to more accurate bombing was about to be created. He was to assume command of it. To begin with, it was sometimes referred to as the Target Finding Force, but eventually it became known as the Pathfinder Force. It had not come about without a struggle. Harris had firmly opposed the idea – not least, or so he believed, because the 'creaming off of the best crews of all the groups in order to create a *corps d'élite* in a special group ... could be calculated to have a bad effect on morale in the Command as a whole.' The group commanders agreed with him. But Churchill would have none of this. Through the Chief of the Air Staff, he made it very clear that such an organization should be created – and quickly.

Bennett had every qualification for the appointment: his resolution, his brilliance for navigation, and his technical knowledge. He was immediately promoted to Group Captain, and invited to set up his command wherever he liked. He chose Cambridgeshire.

So far as aircraft were concerned, he chose Mosquitos and Lancasters – with a preference for the former. Dead reckoning or the use of a sextant were no longer the only means of navigating to the target. It had all begun with a system known as Gee, which employed radar. It was valuable, and particularly useful on the return trip, when it guided bomber crews faultlessly to their home aerodromes. But it was not sufficiently advanced to make precision bombing possible under poor conditions. The scientists were working on this, and they eventually produced H2S and, later, Oboe. These devices enabled crews to drop bombs through thick cloud in the very reasonable expectation that they would land on the prescribed objectives. Since the Germans, and Hitler in particular, believed this to be impossible, the effect was nothing if not dramatic.

Methods had to be found by which the Pathfinders, hurrying on ahead of the main force, could mark the targets, and there was also the question of the bombs themselves. The heavier they were, and the more that were carried, the less the aircraft's range would be. Consequently pilots had a habit of jettisoning some into the North Sea on their way out. The idea was to ensure that, having reached their goal, they would have enough fuel to take them home. This was a matter that demanded attention – preferably in the form of lighter versions.

As for the crews, Bennett insisted on having none but the best, and he was going to make considerable demands on them. The normal tour of duty was thirty operations. In the case of the Pathfinders, it would be sixty. Heavy casualties had to be expected – especially as German technicians could be expected to find counter measures to the new navigational aids. But counter measures can, themselves, be countered. One such system, which was very effective until the opposition found a way round it, was 'Window'. Basically it consisted of strips of tin foil. Dropped in considerable quantities, they confused the radar on the ground. They left the operators in a state of uncertainty about what was a formation of aircraft and what was not. The experts believed that its large-scale introduction would probably reduce bomber casualties by one-third.

Bennett was involved in all these matters and others, too. The meteorological forecasts were by no means accurate. It was understandable. With Germany occupying such a large part of the European land mass, there was no means of obtaining weather reports. He overcame this problem – partially, at any rate – by sending unarmed Mosquitos on daily flights over Germany and enemy-occupied territory. Their purpose was to find out what, exactly, the weather was like. In time, cutting through red tape as was his way, he more or less took over the met. side of operations. By January 1943, the Pathfinder Force became a separate group – No. 8 (PFF) Group – and he had been promoted to Air Commodore.

He had, of course, made enemies within the RAF. The first raid to be led by Pathfinders was a fiasco, which is really no discredit to them. Having grudgingly sanctioned the creation of the system, Harris was in a hurry to use it. The result was that he sent it into action before it was ready. Bennett realized this, but he was in no mood to dissent. The target was Flensberg, a submarine base to the north of Kiel. None of the new navigational equipment was ready, and the crews were not yet properly trained. To add to the troubles, the weather turned out to be the opposite of that forecast (bad rather than good). Result: nothing more than mild inconvenience to the enemy. The critics were delighted. Bennett was philosophic.

In a raid that should have bombed the living daylights out of Saarbrucken, they mistook the objective and bombed the living daylights out of Saarlauten. The unfortunate town had some industrial importance, but nothing like that of the intended target. It was not what Harris had in mind, though it did show that bombs could be directed to some purpose, and not scattered vaguely upon the soil of the Third Reich. Over Hamburg they were more successful, and the Pathfinder group was used to particularly good effect over Peenemünde, where the deadly V1 and V2 missiles were being manufactured.

Harris was eventually convinced of the Pathfinders' contribution and was responsible for devising their distinctive emblem: the eagle from the RAF officers' cap badge worn on the flap of the top left-hand pocket. Bennett, who went about his business firstly in an old Hurricane and then in a Beaufighter, was eventually promoted to Air Vice Marshal – as became a group commander. But, by this time, he had more than shown that it was as well to listen to him, and that to ignore his advice was often to court disaster. A very good example of this is afforded by a raid against Nuremburg.

The idea has been attributed to Churchill. It was Nuremburg's misfortune to be selected as the target, for the real purpose probably had little to do with the Bavarian town. Indeed, on the face of it, there were reasons not to attack it. It lay in the very heartland of Germany and the invaders would be exposed to all the wrath the Germans could hurl at them for an uncomfortably long period. Furthermore, the chosen route would take the bombers over the *Luftwaffe*'s night-fighter assembly beacons at Aachen and Frankfurt. It was also close to the interceptor bases in the Ruhr. Bennett was vigorously opposed to it, and he said so. He was ready to plot a much more acceptable way, but nobody paid very much attention. There were, of course, to be several diversionary raids, but the Germans seem to have anticipated these – just as the main force flew into what can only be described as an ambush. When it was all over, 95 bombers were lost; 10 more were severely damaged (one of them beyond repair) on return to England; and a further 70 were so badly mauled over enemy territory that they were out of action for anything from six

Who really shot down Douglas Bader?

SIR — Iain Duncan Smith (report, Aug. 4) states that Douglas Bader was captured by the Germans after colliding with a Messerschmitt 109. The truth of what happened in the skies over St Omer on Aug. 9, 1941, is cloudier.

The records show that Bader's formation lost two Spitfires that day and shot down six aircraft from Adolf Galland's wing, based at Abbeville. No one saw what happened to Bader and, after the war, he insisted that he had bailed out after a collision.

There the matter rested until, 39 years later, Galland told my astonished father, P. B. "Laddie" Lucas, that there had been no collision reported and Bader had been shot down by a lowly sergeant pilot, Oberfeldwebel Max Meyer.

By coincidence, the next year Bader went to open an air show in Sydney and was introduced to Meyer, who had gone to live in Australia after the war. Meyer said nothing to Douglas about shooting him down, but the next day the Australian papers were full of his story.

The likelihood is that Bader was shot down and mistook the sensation of being hit by cannonfire from the rear for a collision — an experience reported by other pilots. However, questions remain: why did Meyer's story take so long to emerge, and why didn't the Nazis take advantage of such a propaganda coup?

As Bader, pugnacious and defiant to the end, exclaimed: "My dear boy, if a sergeant pilot had shot me down, they would have had him goose-stepping down the Unter den Linden."

David Lucas
London SE23

**. Robinson and
.J. Gwillim**

ngagement is announced
en Paul, son of Mr
obinson, of Tickhill,
Yorkshire, and Mrs
obinson, of Stapleford,
ridge, and Elizabeth,
aughter of Mr and Mrs
rey Gwillim, of Pluckley,

**.R.S. Manks and
.R. Davidoff**

ngagement is announced
en Hamish, son of Mr
rs David Manks, of
tchurch, New Zealand, and
, daughter of Mr and Mrs
ence Davidoff, of East
on, West Sussex.

**.R.P. Macmillan and
.K. Munro**

ngagement is announced
en Marcus Richard Piers,
gest son of Mr and Mrs
rd Macmillan, of
inebleau, France, and
Katharine, eldest
ter of Mrs Camilla Good
tepdaughter of Mr David
, of Kintbury, Berkshire.

J.L. Buxton and

DOLLAR.—On July 4th, 2001,
to MILLIE (née Dare) and RICHARD,
a daughter, Effie Louise.

DRUMMOND.—On May 3rd, to
ROBERTA (née Palau) and NICHOLAS,
a daughter, Davina Francesca.

DRYSDALE.—On August 2nd, 2001,
to SARAH (née Gardiner) and TOBY,
a beautiful daughter, Emily Margaret,
a sister for James.

HARDWICK.—On August 1st, 2001, to
GILLY (née Meth) and COLIN, a son,
Maximillian Guy.

HEWLETT.—On August 7th, 2001, in
Ireland, to EMMA (née Gordon) and
MARK, a son, Joshua Nathaniel Lucien.

JOHNSON.—On August 7th, to
SOPHIE-JANE (née Treherne Pollock)
and RICHARD, a son, Antony Benedict
(Ben) Thewlis.

KEMP.—
See St. Pierre.

NORTHWOOD.—On August 1st, 2001,
to CAROLINE (née Vartan) and JEFF,
a son, Patrick Thomas Jonathan.

RAWLINGS.—On July 27th, 2001, to
SALLY (née Bentley) and COLIN, a son,
Tobias (Toby) Charles Percy.

STACEY.—On August 7th, 2001, to
JANE (née Dinwoodie) and GUY, a son,
Thomas Christian.

STEENBERG.—On August 7th, to
SOPHIE (née Fryer) and AXEL, a son,
James Ingwe.

ST. PIERRE.—On August 4th, 2001, to
SARAH (née Kemp) and BRIAN, a son,
Patrick Gerard. Deo Gratias.

TURNER.—On July 28th, to IONA (née
Leaver) and JONATHAN, a daughter,
Emily Hannah.

Anniversaries

Golden weddings

Rushden, Northants, tel: 01933 312142.

BLACKMORE.—Peacefully on Friday,
August 3rd, 2001 at Chyraise Lodge,
Millpool, Penzance, Cornwall, KEITH,
aged 88 years of Fraddam, Hayle,
Cornwall, formerly of Holyport,
Berkshire. Funeral service on Tuesda
August 14th at Penmount
Crematorium, Truro, Cornwall at 11
a.m. Family flowers only, donations,
lieu if desired for the Sunrise Appeal
Treliske Hospital, Truro c/o the
Funeral Director, W J Winn, 69 Fore
Street, Hayle, Cornwall TR27 4DX.
01736 752124.

BOHANE.—BARBARA MARY (née
Tolhurst), died at Rosset Holt
Residential Home, Tunbridge Wells,
August 6th, 2001, aged 96 years. Dear
wife of the late Edgar, much loved
mother to Michael, Paul, Margot, An
and Elizabeth, grandmother and grea
grandmother. Requiem Mass on
Tuesday, August 14th at 10.30 a.m. at
Augustines R.C. Church, Crescent
Road, Tunbridge Wells. Flowers can
sent c/o J. Kempster and Sons, 2 & 4
Albion Road, Tunbridge Wells, Kent
TN1 2PE, tel: 01892 523131.

CHOWN.—BARBARA ALICE, died
peacefully in The Royal Berkshire
Hospital, Reading on Monday, Augu
6th, 2001. She will be remembered
lovingly by her husband Dick and
daughter Susan and all who knew her
Funeral service to take place on Fri
August 10th at St. John the Baptist
Church, Kidmore End at 10.30 a.m.
Donations in Barbara's memory.
payable to "Tomalin & Son", this is
be split between Adelaide Ward
Equipment Fund and Leukaemia
Research Fund, c/o Tomalin & Son,
Reading Road, Henley-on-Thames,
Oxon RG9 1AG, tel: 01491 573370.

COATES.—SPENCER, on August 5th,
2001, peacefully at Clapham Lodge,
his 90th year. Late of Storrington,
Sussex and Leigh, Kent. Funeral
service at Worthing Crematorium
Monday, August 13th at 10 a.m. Fam
flowers only.

COOPER.—KENNETH, on August 7th,
2001, peacefully at St. Barnabas
Hospice, aged 73 years. Former
Consultant Obstetrician and
Gynaecologist. Beloved husband,
father, father-in-law and grandfath
Private cremation, donations, if
desired for St. Barnabas Hospice c.
H.D. Tribe Ltd, 130 F.

hours to six months. But this was not the sum of the disaster. All told, 108 RAF aircraft were destroyed that night: 745 crewmen were either killed or injured, and 159 were taken prisoner.

What went wrong? The weather did nothing to help: it favoured the night-fighters. Nevertheless, there were those who felt that the *Luftwaffe* had received advance warning of the raid – possibly by intercepting radio signals. Was, then, the operation intended to bring the opposition to battle, and, by opposing, to end it? If this were so, it was a hopeless miscalculation. The bombers had no fighter cover, and when Mosquitos swooped on the fighter bases with their 4,000-lb 'Blockbuster' bombs, they found nothing there. The aircraft were all in the sky, knocking hell out of the stoic bombers that droned their ways to Nuremburg. Harris omits all mention of the disastrous venture from his memoirs. Churchill dismisses it with a paragraph or two: paragraphs that really tell us nothing. Documents have gone missing from the Public Record Office. The whole thing, indeed, is a mystery – and one that begs the question of why, if they had to bomb Nuremburg, didn't they ask Bennett? Or, at least, listen to him?

The end of the war found Donald Bennett far from flushed with success, and greatly disillusioned. A CBE (1943) and a CB (1944) had been added to the display of medals on his chest, but these awards did nothing to lessen his feeling that Britain was sinking into the very slough of moral delinquency that had cost the country so many lives. He briefly represented Middlesbrough West as a Liberal MP in the House of Commons, and between 1945 and 1948 was employed as chief executive to British South American Airways. After three aircraft had been lost with no survivors, a change of policy was considered essential and the venture was taken over by the British Overseas Airways Corporation. The time had come for Donald Bennett to retire. He died in 1986.

5

PACIFIC ACES USA

Somebody who should have known better once said that the Japanese pilots were 'short-sighted, poor shots, and flew inferior aircraft.' This, of course, was balderdash: a statement almost to be compared with that of some idiot who, before the *Blitzkrieg* of 1940, advanced the idea that German tanks were manufactured from plywood. The United States in company with Great Britain declared war on Japan on 8 December 1941. But, whilst America was a newcomer to the Second World War, the Japanese had been engaged against China ever since 1937. There had been plenty of time in which to develop experience, not only in the art of fighter combat, but also in the construction of aircraft. To take only one example, the carrier-based Mitsubishi A5M interceptor had been in service throughout that Chinese conflict and had achieved very good results. Its successor, the famous Mitsubishi A6M Zero-Sen, had been in production since the middle of 1940. Nor were its bombers hastily conceived to meet expediency. The Mitsubishi G4M and the Mitsubishi Ki–46 had both been in existence before the Second World War (Japanese/USA version) had broken out.

As for the Japanese crack fighter pilots, 2nd Lieutenant Hiromichi Shinohara, who scored fifty-eight victories in Manchuria and thereby shot his way to the top of the tree, was already dead by 1941. He'd been killed in combat over Manchuria on 27 August 1939. But there were others who were far from dead – men such as Saburo Sakai (one of the few who survived both wars), Tetsuzo Iwamoto (188 victories in the Second World War and 14 in China), and Hiroshi Nishizawa (190 victories in the Second World War). For those of lesser talent, but with nevertheless a consuming desire to die for the Emperor, there was a vehicle such as the Yokosuka MXY–7 Ohka, which was cheap and easy to build, and intended for one-way trips. The Germans did these things rather better. They produced such missiles as the V1 and V2, which went on their lethal ways without assistance from pilots. The MXY–7 took a human being with it when it exploded on its target (or when it exploded having missed its target, come to that). To take part in these Kamikaze attacks against warships, you either needed a very high degree of patriotism, or else an intense world-weariness.

Opposing the Japanese over the Pacific was largely the business of the United States. Of the aviators involved, a number stand out – initially for their ability to shine in deplorable circumstances. Six hours after their attack on Pearl Harbour, the Japanese turned their attention to the Philippines – in particular to Clark Field on Luzon, which is situated sixty miles to the north of Manila. The population of Clark Field was ill-prepared for any attack. Even the best of the aircraft (the P–40Es) were regarded by many as obsolete. Many had not even been prepared for combat. The situation, in short, was not one to bring a worried frown to the brow of even the least confident Jap pilot.

When the first attack was made, the field was littered with 90 B–17 Fortresses and 20 P–40 fighters. A staff meeting was in progress at the time, and four American fighters of the 3rd Pursuit Squadron were about to land on the runway. On the other hand, four fighters of the 24th Pursuit were taking off – to relieve them on patrol. They were the only survivors of an assault that accomplished everything its perpetrators had hoped.

Led by Lieutenant Joseph H. Moore, the intrepid quartet made for the bombers. This, naturally, attracted the attention of the Zeros assigned to cover them: their pilots dived steeply to put a stop to what they regarded as unwarranted interference. Moore accounted for two of them, and 2nd Lieutenant Randall Keaton dispatched a third. But this put paid to any illusions about the inferiority of Japanese aircraft (or eyesight, come to that). The Zero turned out to be extremely manoeuvrable and those who flew them certainly knew how to do so. Its two 20-mm cannons brooked little argument; any ideas of dogfights the Americans may have entertained were almost literally shot to pieces. It wasn't like that at all. They also realized that the aircraft currently at their disposal were no match for those of their opponents. The only option, for the time being at any rate, was to engage the Japs at top speed, squeeze off a few bursts of ammunition, and then run. Anyone who failed to appreciate the fact was probably doomed to die.

Moore, incidentally, survived the fray and eventually rose to the rank of Major General in the United States Air Force. Somebody credited him with five kills, and he was admitted to the ranks of the aces. But he always denied this, claiming only those he had destroyed that day over Clark Field. The official records confirm this.

One who deserved better of fate was Lieutenant Ed Dyess. Dyess was present when the first round in the battle for the Philippines came to an end. General Douglas MacArthur had already removed himself to a safer place, but 70,000 Americans, including Dyess, remained. They were herded into captivity and sent off on the notorious 'Bataan Death March'. It was rightly named. Sixteen thousand of them died by the wayside: some of them from illness, some after their captors had beaten them up; and some the victims of Japanese drivers who deliberately ran over them in their vehicles.

Dyess was among the 54,000 who reached their grim destination. In April 1943, he achieved the remarkable feat of escaping (very, very few got away from Japanese captivity). He eventually returned to the USA, where fate revealed how vile it can be when it chooses. One day, he was flying a P–38 (a long-range interceptor and escort fighter with twin tail booms – more commonly known as the Lightning) over Burbank, California. The aircraft went out of control, crashed, and Dyess the survivor of so much, was killed. But that was sometimes the way of such things: when combat failed to accomplish what fate had in mind for an individual, it found some other way to do it.

Waiting in the wings, so to speak, to make their respective debuts on the Pacific stage were two pilots about whose qualifications to become aces there was no possible shadow of doubt. One of them was Richard Ira Bong, the son of a Scottish mother and a Swedish father. The other was Thomas McGuire. Majors Bong and McGuire were fighting a war against the Japanese with laudable determination. They were also, as a sideline, fighting each other. The object was to determine who of the deadly duo should be top-scorer. Bong won in the end with forty victories, which made him the top American ace of any war.

McGuire clocked up thirty-eight, but he was at a disadvantage. On 7 January 1945 he was killed during a sweep over the Philippines.

In 1941 Richard Bong joined the United States Army Air Corps. He was twenty-one, shortish, fair haired, and in appearance almost the prototype young American hero such as motion pictures used to feature. During his training he revealed above average ability as a pilot – to such an extent that as soon as he had qualified he was given a job as an instructor.

This was all very well, but it was not quite what the future ace had in mind. His reason for joining the Air Corps had been to fly fighters against one or the other of his country's enemies, and nothing less than this would satisfy him. He was not one to wait patiently until authority stirred itself. If he wanted something, he went after it relentlessly – whether it was chasing a hostile aircraft or badgering officialdom. As was his way, he won. In September 1942 he arrived in Australia with the 49th Fighter Group of the 5th Air Force. It might be argued that he came at just the right time. Also arriving in Australia was the first batch of P–38s: aircraft that, at last, were to achieve parity with the opposition and which, in the right hands, could kill very effectively indeed.

German fighter pilots dubbed the P–38 the 'Fork Tailed Devil' and yet, despite this sobriquet, their aces did not find it too difficult to shoot down. The crack Japanese aviators were inclined to agree with them – until this somewhat unusual aeroplane revealed its secret. The thing about it was that you had to use high-speed tactics. Men like Bong and McGuire realized this. It was a truth that anyone ignored at his peril. Flying the P–38, it did not do to hang around.

It says somewhere that only ten per cent of Japanese pilots survived the war, but there is nothing to show whether this proportion includes those who were not intended to survive, i.e. the Kamikaze warriors. In many cases these men were given no more than a week's training: enough to take off, maintain an aircraft in flight, and then dive to destruction. Diving was the hardest part. Either the pilot approached very steeply from a high altitude, making the aeroplane difficult to control and liable to miss its target, or else he came in at a low level, exposing his machine to the hazards of anti-aircraft fire and fighter attack. Initially, the Kamikazes achieved results; but, before very long, the US Navy found out how to avoid them. Nevertheless, inexperienced pilots were still sent on these missions – not least because there were no survivors to report the failures.

The talents of the United States pilots obviously varied. That great survivor Saburo Sakai (sixty-four kills) attributed his longevity to poor air-to-air shooting by Americans. Time and again, he professed, he should have been blasted out of the sky; time and again he had escaped from situations that he had regarded as certain death. As he saw things, this was not necessarily due to his own skill, but to bad marksmanship. He obviously never encountered Dick Bong – and nor, come to that, Tom McGuire.

Bong, like Beurling (see Chapter 3), was a past master of the deflection shot. He was also a very able tactician. He realized the importance of protecting his flanks, and it is significant that his wingman was always the most experienced and capable flier available. On one occasion, however, he got it wrong.

As he admitted afterwards, there was really no excuse. He had already scored twenty victories and could hardly have been described as a novice. A Japanese bomber formation accompanied by fighters came into view. He prepared himself for what, hopefully, would be a tidy massacre. But then he became aware that the aircraft flying beside him was not that of his usual wingman. It was, not to mince matters, a Zero fighter.

Bong briskly went into an aerobatic routine intended to shake off this intruder into his private world. At 15,000 feet, he levelled off and looked into his mirror. The Zero was still there – though just too far away for its pilot to shoot with any accuracy. More aerobatics followed until he was only a few feet above the sea. The Zero had been unable to keep pace with his P–38 and was now about a mile away. However, Bong's next manoeuvre brought him into the midst of a cluster of nine other Zeros. Their pilots were clearly unanimous on one point: Dick Bong's career should be cut briskly and painfully short.

It is something of a cliché that the best form of defence is attack. In this instance, it happened to be true. He flew, head-on, at the lead Zero and gave it a short squirt of fire. It was beautifully aimed, and the Japanese fighter exploded in mid-air. Having seen their leader destroyed, the others seemed uncertain of what to do. Their missiles sped into space well wide of the mark, and Bong was quick to cash in on their obviously reduced morale. He selected a second victim, blew it to smithereens, and climbed

Edgar James Kain (known as 'Cobber'), accounted for seventeen German aircraft before his untimely death in June 1940.

Safe home again – Guy Gibson (with pipe) with members of his crew after a bombing raid on Berlin, 1943.

George Beurling – the famous 'Screwball' of Malta. Next to fighter aircraft, Beurling enjoyed the company of beautiful women.

Donald Bennett (centre front) with the Path Finder Group in 1980. Leonard Cheshire is on his left.

Richard Bong (left) and Thomas McGuire, two of America's top fighter aces, in the Philippines in 1944.

'Sailor' Malan, 'a crack shot' and 'a brilliant aerobatic pilot'.

Leonard Cheshire, one of the RAF's leading bomber pilots, took command of 617 Squadron after it had won fame for the 'Dam Busters' raid.

Adolf Galland (left) and Werner Mölders, among Germany's top fighter aces and famous rivals, discuss tactics during the Spanish Civil War.

Werner Mölders with Hermann Goering.

Adolf Galland.

Douglas Bader with two of his pilots of No. 242 Squadron, Ball (left) and McKnight. The Hurricane's cowling shows the squadron's emblem, Hitler being kicked in the pants.

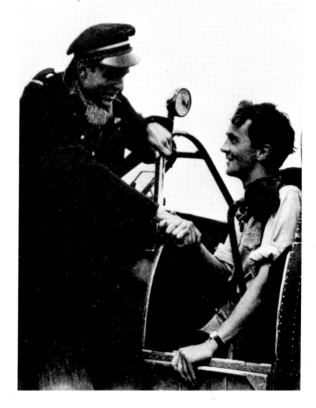

French fighter pilot Pierre Clostermann (left) when serving with No. 602 Squadron.

Air heroes Douglas Bader and Adolf Galland exchange copies of their books on the Battle of Britain.

upwards with all the power his two Allison V–1710 engines could give him. As he ascended, he treated a third Zero to a quick burst of fire. This aircraft did not transform itself into a ball of fire. Its health, however, had clearly been damaged: it slowed down, parted company with the others, and gave every indication that, merry though its life may have been, it was doomed to be a short one.

Thereafter, Bong did not hang about. Flying at full throttle, he raced away from the bewildered opponents and eventually landed safely at base. You had to be a man of Dick Bong's calibre to get away with such things. There had been no time in which to scratch one's head thoughtfully and wonder what to do next.

After he had landed in Australia, Bong had gone through a three-month period of working-up. Come Christmas 1942, and he was ready for action. It did not take long for him to show his mettle. On 27 December he shot down a Zero and a 'Val' dive-bomber (the Allied code-name for the Aichi D3A – a most formidable aircraft, examples of which had, in 1942, accounted for the British aircraft carrier *Hermes* and the cruisers *Cornwall* and *Dorsetshire*). By the following March his score had risen to nine, and by the end of July it stood at sixteen. He was then sent back to the United States for a period of rest and recuperation. Doubtless he spent much of his leave with his fiancée, a girl named Marge. In a sense, Marge was with him all the time: his P–38 was named after her. It was a nice romantic touch from a man one might not have suspected of such sentimentality. But, then, perhaps his outward attitude was misleading. He was essentially modest: a man who was certainly not given to describing his emotions.

Once his leave came to an end, he was sent on a course at the Air Force Gunnery School. If, as seems possible, the authorities had intended this as a preliminary to voicing fresh overtures on the matter of making him an instructor, they were to be disappointed. Before very long, he was back in action over the Pacific.

But the course, in his opinion, had certainly not been a waste of time. As quoted by Raymond F. Toliver and Trevor J. Constable in *Fighter Aces of the U.S.A.*, he remarked afterwards: 'If I had known as much about aerial gunnery on my first tour as I did when I came out of gunnery school, I might easily have scored eighty hits.' And: 'The Jap fighters I failed to down escaped mainly because I just did not know enough about the mechanics and art of air-to-air shooting.' Since he had already scored a good many more hits than most people, this may seem rather surprising. But that was Bong all over: self-critical, as quick to spot what seemed to be faults in himself as he may have been to notice virtues.

Now and then, one comes across an example of perfect teamwork. That of Dick Bong and Thomas J. Lynch is just such an instance. Lynch, in his own right, was no mean performer: by the time he had done, he had chalked up twenty victories. When flying with Bong, the two men's co-ordination was so masterly that there seemed to be some kind of telepathic communication between them. Depending on the circumstances, one would almost automatically assume the role of attacker, whilst the other would guard his tail. On one occasion, the two of them, accompanied by Lieutenant Delman Moore and another pilot, were 200 miles from their base and in the thick of a contest against a number of Japanese fighters. One of the engines on Moore's P–38 was hit and put out of action. Bong immediately ordered him home. But the poor fellow needed help. Such was the determination to run up a large score of victories, that the others might have left him to stagger back through an unkind sky as best he could. But not a bit of it. Bong and Lynch covered his retreat and, having driven off the enemy, shepherded him back to base flying at single-engine speed.

Despite his determination to be top of the ace list, such consideration was by no means untypical of Bong. That was no doubt what made him such a good leader. Men trusted him; they knew that if they were in a fix Bong would somehow get them out of it. Nevertheless, he was intent on being top-scorer, and any time spent away from combat was an opportunity for his rival, Tom McGuire.

McGuire (described as 'a slight, steely-eyed extrovert') was a member of the 475th Fighter Group, otherwise known as 'Satan's Angels'. He may have been as good as Bong, but how do you measure such things? With a score of thirty-eight to his credit, he was obviously in the same league and very nearly at the top of it. But then things went disastrously wrong for Major McGuire. On 7 January 1945, he was leading a section of P–38s over the Philippines. Unashamedly, he was seeking out enemy aircraft with the intention of beating Bong's substantial score of forty. McGuire was, after all, due to go home in February: there was not all that much time left.

The mission had been arranged quite casually. McGuire and some other pilots had been standing outside a tent on Leyte Island when this intensely ambitious man suggested, 'How about going out in a four-plane sweep tomorrow?' There was no lack of volunteers. In the end, McGuire chose Lieutenant Douglas S.Thropp Jr, Captain Edwin R.Weaver, and Major Jack B.Rittmayer to accompany him. Take-off was scheduled for 6.15 next morning – round about dawn.

Such opportunities as there were to be found would be to the west of the island, and it was in that direction that they headed. The weather worsened: soon they were flying through thick cloud. This was clearly a place to be avoided. The pervasive darkness made it plain that far above them the anvil tops of massive thunder clouds were approaching: clouds that generated such energy that no aircraft could survive in their midst. McGuire and his companions came down from 10,000 feet to 6,000 feet.

The signs were that they were alone in the sky. Visibility, admittedly, was awful, but the VHF radio might have given some clue. It was silent.

Silence can, of course, be misleading, and so it was on this occasion. Somewhere in that cloud mass were two Japanese aircraft: Ki–43s, which were code-named 'Oscar' by the Allies. One of them was flown by Warrant Officer Akira Sugimoto, the other by Sergeant Mizunori Fukuda. They had been detailed to seek out an American convoy that, or so they had been told, was bringing reinforcements.

McGuire had been instructed that he could do whatever he liked against enemy aircraft in the sky; but, for some reason, there must be no ground-strafing on this occasion. Consequently, when he brought the small formation down to 1,400 feet, when the cloud cleared and he could make out a landing strip down below with fifteen fighters parked on it, he was unable to do anything about it. Nor did the people down below seem inclined to do anything about him. He and the three others circled the field for five minutes, and then set off for another landing ground on the far side of the island. The radio still had nothing to say.

The fact that the radio was deceiving them became all too clear when Edwin Weaver spotted an aircraft 500 feet below and about 1,000 yards away. It was Sugimoto's 'Oscar'. The warrant officer had seen no signs of any convoy, but here was an opportunity to win a spot of glory. He went into the attack. His action was noticed by Fukuda who, at that very moment, was on the approach path preparing to land. He immediately retracted his landing gear, put on full throttle, and went to the support of his comrade who was beginning to show signs of distress.

Sugimoto was not a flier to be dismissed lightly. He was putting up a tremendous fight, surviving hits that should have destroyed him, and showing no signs of giving up. McGuire was doing his best to train his guns on the stubborn Jap, when he misjudged a manoeuvre. His P–38 stalled and plunged 200 feet into the ground below. Weaver heard an explosion and saw fire break out. He knew that one of the flight had crashed, but he did not yet know who it was.

The P–38s were now scattered over the sky. But Sugimoto was in the kind of trouble he could no longer ignore. He abandoned his attack. Nursing his badly damaged 'Oscar' carefully, he found a flat piece of land on which to make a forced landing. Immediately, six Philippino guerillas came out of the jungle, fired six bullets into the unfortunate Japanese, stripped him of his clothing and possessions, and retired quietly back into the bush.

But the battle up above was continuing. Fukuda saw McGuire crash and made haste to get in on the act. He was quickly rewarded with the sight of Jack Rittmayer's P–38. He did what had to be done at once. Rittmayer plunged to earth on the edge of a village. There was a big explosion followed by a mushroom of smoke. There were now only two members of the flight left. They decided to go home.

But Fukuda had not come through unscathed. Weaver had got in some well-placed shots, which, among other things, ensured that only one of his 'Oscar's' two sets of landing gear would lock down in the correct position. On landing, the aircraft cart-wheeled on to its back, and the sergeant had to be dragged from the wreckage. There were twenty-three bullet holes in the fuselage.

Fukuda survived the war. Thirty years after the engagement, and signing himself 'Former Flying Sergeant of the Japanese Army', he sent this letter, which he asked to be circulated among all members of the 475th Fighter Group. Laddie Lucas published it in his *Wings of War*:

We fought each other in the nightmare of war, but after thirty years it is my pleasure that we, Americans and Japanese, lead the world in our own way, and I hope to help each other with mutual understandings ever after. I hope you, the former members of 475th Fighter Group, will take an active part in world peace with good health.

With McGuire dead, there was nobody left to challenge Bong's supremacy. In any case, had there been, he was in no position to do anything about it, for Dick Bong was on his way back to America. He had flown more than 200 sorties, and he must have achieved some sort of record for the number of awards he had received. They were: The Congressional Medal of Honour, the DSC, two Silver Stars, seven DFCs, and fifteen Air Medals. Now, with a bit of luck, he could marry Marge and settle down in relative safety.

But that capricious entity fate didn't see it quite like that. To provide him with gainful employment, he was posted to Burbank to test fly the Lockheed P–80 jet fighter (it was more popularly known as the 'Shooting Star'). One day, during take-off, the aircraft suffered an engine failure and crashed. Major Richard Ira Bong was killed.

The P–80 went on to enjoy a long and tolerably successful career. The last order for it was placed in 1959 and here, had he lived, Bong might have found scope for his sense of irony. The customer was the Japanese government.

6

Adolph Gysbert Malan
'SAILOR' IN THE SKY

It was just after midday on 21 May 1940. The sky above the Dover Strait was blotched with lumps of cloud. Over in the direction of Calais, the anti-aircraft guns were producing a chorus of explosions. There was a more than reasonable chance of German aircraft in the vicinity. At 17,000 feet, six Spitfires broke cover. They were flying in perfect formation. Had there been a cameraman with them, his film might have been used at RAF training centres. 'This,' the instructor would have said, 'is how it should be done.'

The guns at Calais were still barking away. The fighters' section leader was crossing the peak of a bulky pile of vapour, when he nearly collided with an He–111. It was a close thing, but he swerved, climbed steeply, and then went into the attack. The He–111's pilot was obviously going to make for the concealment of more cloud – about 100 feet below. Carrying out a steep banking turn, the man in the Spitfire let fly with his guns. The bullets made a very fair job of carving up the Heinkel. Smoke billowed, fragments spun off into the sky, and the undercarriage flopped down. As the unfortunate aircraft sank into the cloud, it seemed unlikely that its crew would live to fight another day.

Not long afterwards, a Junkers 88 flew into view. It was slower than the He–111 and consequently an easier target. At 500 yards, some rounds from the Spitfire struck home; at 150, the score was a lot more. The Junkers, flames about to consume it, fell out of the sky. 'Sailor' Malan had scored his first two victories. The accountancy of kills is imprecise, but it seems fair to suppose that they were the forerunners of thirty more – thirty-three, if you take into consideration three more that he shared with others.

'Sailor' Malan was serving with 74 Squadron, sometimes known as the Tiger Squadron. In the other war, the 1914–18 business, Mick Mannock had flown with it. His score was about sixty-eight. He was rewarded with the DSO and two Bars, the Military Cross and one Bar (they had not yet invented the DFC), a posthumous VC and a grave in France – after his death on 26 July 1918. Mannock was mean: a killer to his finger tips. When he heard of von Richthofen's death, he smiled and said, 'I hope he roasted the whole way down.'

Malan took a scarcely more charitable view. When a reporter asked him how he felt after shooting down an enemy, he replied, 'I try not to know . . . I think it's a bad thing. You see, if you shoot them down, they don't get back and no one in Germany is a whit the wiser. So I figure the right thing to do is to let them get back. With a dead rear gunner; a dead navigator, and the pilot coughing his lungs up as he lands . . . I think if you do that it has a better effect on their morale.'

He also went on record as saying, 'They called me a cold, ruthless, calculating killer.' Perhaps they did: you don't get far in war if you have qualms about blood-letting. What's more, every killer goes about his business in danger. After all, somebody might kill him. Malan was the first to admit that 'We were not without fear. The fellow who wasn't didn't live for long.' But this was by no means the only occupational necessity. 'A pilot,' he said, 'has to be cold when he is fighting. He must have an aggressive nature. He must think in terms of offence rather than defence.'

Adolph Gysbert Malan was born on 3 October 1910 on a farm not all that many miles from Cape Town. His father, Willie Malan, was descended from Huguenots – with a generous dollop of Afrikaans blood added. His mother came from Southsea in England. Before they married in 1909, she had taught in a kindergarten school. There was a sizeable gap separating the Afrikaans-speaking members of the South African white community and those who spoke English. It was a situation that the Malans' first-born came to abhor. He took pains to make friends on both sides of the divide. The fact that he was virtually bilingual helped.

When he was seven – or, possibly, eight – his father presented him with a shotgun. He suggested that he might go out and shoot something 'for the pot'. Unfortunately, he omitted to give any instructions about how the thing worked. As a result, his son fired both barrels simultaneously, which did nothing for the pot and bowled him over backwards with the force of the recoil. On trying to reload, he jammed one of the cartridges in the breech and blundered indoors seeking advice. When his mother found herself regarding the business end of a loaded (or almost) gun, she expressed herself with exquisite candour, and that seems to have been the end of that episode. It did not, however, diminish young Malan's liking for these weapons.

Moored a quarter of a mile offshore from the naval base at Simonstown, there was a very old cruiser originally named *Thames*. She was, they said, 'too weak to fight, and too slow to run away.' But these deficiencies didn't much matter. After the First World War, she had been bought for a knock-down price by a gentleman named Mr T. B. F. Davis . Mr Davis had not decided that he needed a navy; but, rather, that South Africa could do with a training ship. He spent a lot of money equipping her for her intended role, and it was decided to rename her *General Botha*. She was not required to go to sea, which was probably just as well. The idea was to teach such nautical requirements as mathematics, seamanship, signalling, gunnery and drill. You joined at the age of fourteen and left at sixteen.

Quite why young Malan decided that he would like to join the *General Botha* is something he never fully understood. He had not seen the ship and really knew nothing about her. Mathematics were never his strong point – nor was he aware of any particular ambition to go to sea. Nevertheless, by the time he was thirteen he had made up his mind – and committed himself to what sounds like a pretty passable imitation of hell. He signed on (if that is the correct expression) in February 1924 – one of an entry of sixty new cadets and, or so it was estimated, the second smallest boy on board. Because he was uncommonly good looking, and because he looked virtuous, he was quickly nicknamed 'Angel Face'. But to appear angelic was no great advantage, and certainly did not provide immunity from the two most favoured punishments: a stroke or two from the end of a rope (administered casually for minor misdemeanours), and caning (carried out with a grim formality by the master at arms).

The cadets were occasionally allowed ashore, but a term lasted from February to December without any interruption by such trivialities as holidays. Consequently, he saw little of his parents who, in any case, had plenty with which to occupy themselves. Other little Malans were being (or had been) born – bringing the score to five. As for Willie, he was in the throes of a personal economic depression that eventually caused him to give up the farm.

'Angel Face' seems to have had few complaints to make about life aboard *General Botha*. In the passing-out exams, he came top in seamanship; but, as was his wont, he did rather less well in mathematics. His parents were advised that if he wished to be considered by a shipping company he should stay on for another six months. At the end of the period, his work had improved sufficiently for him to be taken in by the Union Castle line as an apprentice. His first voyage was in a freighter named *Sandown Castle* from Cape Town to New York.

A picture begins to emerge of Malan as he was and, in some respects, as he was to remain. He was quiet, conscientious, rather shy perhaps, and very self-contained. Others might pour out their hearts on occasion, but he never did. In New York, whilst other youngsters may have preferred to live it up in the bars and brothels, he used to frequent the British Apprentice Club. Founded in 1921 by two ladies who wished to repay the hospitality afforded by the British to American servicemen in the First World War, it was designed as a kind of home-from-home. The atmosphere was genteel and kindly – just the kind of place to allay the fears of any mother who might be concerned about the perils of the land as well as those of the deep.

He seems to have been a reasonably cheerful young man – not much given to reading, but a tolerably deep thinker. He enjoyed discussions and, to those who penetrated his reserve, turned out to be something of an idealist. He was always immaculately dressed and, yes, people liked him.

Malan's life was, you might say, scripted for him by circumstances. In a better world, he might have become a successful officer in the mercantile marine – probably ending up with a command. But, come the thirties, the world was plunged into a recession. The merchant fleets were hit as badly as anything else; there were cases in which men holding masters' certificates were only too glad to sign on as deck hands.

In nine years he had served in nine ships. He had taken (and passed) the exams that led to a master's certificate. He had joined the Royal Naval Reserve: at a shore establishment in Devonport, and at sea in the battleship HMS *Malaya*, he had shown an aptitude for gunnery. To be fair to Union Castle, the company did not abandon its officers in the bad economic climate. On the other hand, and apart from those employed on the mail steamer service between England and South Africa, it had not a great deal to offer them. For a while, Malan was employed as a watchman in ships laid up at Southampton. Now and again, he augmented his small income by working in coasters trading between Britain and Hamburg.

For a young man of reasonable ambitions, this offered little hope for the future. On his trips to Hamburg, he spent a good deal of time talking to harbour officials, seamen, and suchlike. The drift of their remarks suggested to him that war was inevitable. Might it, then, be a good idea to offer his services fulltime to the Navy? He thought not. He found the attitude of RN officers to those of the RNR and RNVR less than congenial. He deplored the great divide that separated the inhabitants of the wardroom from the lower deck. The RAF, he decided, might be a better proposition. Fighters, he told himself, would be his *métier*. As he remarked to somebody, he wanted 'something to throw about'. Whether the senior officers of the Royal Air Force would have approved of the idea of their aircraft being 'thrown about' is another matter.

On the face of it, he was just the kind of person the service was looking for. Not all that long ago, he would have been refused entry on account of his age. But the limit had recently been raised to twenty-five and so that was all right – he could qualify with a few weeks to spare. Furthermore, applicants from the Dominions were especially welcome. When he told them about his seafaring career, that more or less clinched it. He had only to pass the medical, and he was in. He passed.

His first posting was the flying school at Filton. Just as he had worried on the eve of taking his various exams for the merchant navy, so did he now feel anxious about his ability as an up-and-coming aviator. Other pupils seemed to get the hang of things more quickly. At last he managed to bring an aeroplane back to earth without bending anything, and his instructor pronounced him ready for his first solo. Perhaps he was not a natural flier: a report on his progress observed that 'This pilot is inclined to be heavy and impatient at the controls.' It was, however, nothing that time and practice could not cure.

From Filton, he was moved to No. 3 Flying School, Grantham, with the rank of Acting Pilot Officer. By now, he was more self-confident and he found the aircraft, Gloster Gauntlets – one of the last generation of biplanes – much to his liking. With his seafaring associations, he became known as 'The Admiral'. But then a former officer from the Royal Navy arrived. He pointed out that whilst an RN officer might deserve such a nickname a former RNR person did not. He urged that Malan should be demoted to 'Sailor', and the motion was carried. When, at about this time, he married, his wife always called him 'John'. Adolph had become the exclusive property of Hitler, and he was welcome to it.

He did well at Grantham, earning himself a 'special distinc-tion' and moving on with commendable speed to No. 74 Squadron, which was stationed at Hornchurch as part of the defences guarding Greater London. He and his Gauntlet got on splendidly together. It was, indeed, an aircraft that you could throw about. In terms of aerobatics, there was seldom anything more nimble. By 1937, he had progressed to the rank of Flight Lieutenant and was in command of the squadron's 'A' Flight. One of his duties that year was to contribute to a flying display at Aldergrove, Belfast, to mark that now defunct celebration – Empire Day. The object was to thrill the spectators with a few loops and rolls and then return to Hornchurch.

But he and his friend, Paddy Treacy, commanding 'B' Flight, decided to depart from the text and stage a mock dogfight attended by flick half-rolls and all sorts of fancy stuff. To put in a spot of practice, Malan flew out over the sea, where his aerobatics would escape attention. Coming back, he flew into a bank of fog that nobody had foreseen. He lost his way, nearly ran out of petrol and made an unscheduled landing on Lord Antrim's private golf course.

The display itself was a huge success with the crowd, but his commanding officer was furious. He and Treacy had exceeded their briefs: such aerial hooliganism was not to be tolerated, and the two officers should consider themselves under close arrest. Later, this was amended to open arrest, which was better but still not good. On the following morning, however, the matter was unknowingly resolved by a reporter from the *Belfast Telegraph*. In the opinion of this scribe, the Malan/Treacy act had lifted the show from the ordinary to the excellent. Clearly it would be absurd to discipline the two officers for a display that had won such lavish praise. The CO relented and there was no more talk of any kind of arrest.

In 1938 the squadron collected its first Spitfires. Malan said it was 'like changing over from Noah's Ark to the *Queen Mary*.' Certainly, the Spitfire had style such as had seldom been seen before. It was also, he said, 'a perfect lady. She had no vices.' You really could throw her about the sky and she never protested, never faltered. This, of course, assumed that you were on the right side. If you were not, she tended to be lethal. The eight Browning .303 machine-guns delivered a devastating fire power: the best range, Malan decided, was 250 yards. (The original Spitfire had only four Brownings – the number was doubled on the instructions of Hugh Dowding, head of Fighter Command.)

September of that year put Britain and France through the stress of the Munich crisis. At Hornchurch, anyone who could find a paint-brush directed his energies to transforming the recently arrived aircraft into carefully camouflaged machines that would not attract unnecessary attention. The squadron also began to fly patrols in formation and, generally, to put itself on a war footing.

In 1937 Malan had married Lynda Fraser – a young lady who lived at Ruislip, and whom he had met on one of his shore leaves in the Union Castle days. He was by no means a fluent correspondent and letters to his parents in South Africa were rare. But on 4 September – the day following Britain's entry into the war – he really let himself go. '. . .The biggest factor is that I have had 18 months of complete happiness and blissful content-ment with one of the sweetest women in the world, and thank God for that. It probably seems a strange thing to say but I am more ready to enter the conflict having had those eighteen glorious months.' It may seem odd that (assuming this was the case) he had taken so long to tell Willie Malan and his wife about the marriage, but that was 'Sailor' Malan all over. He believed in the importance of communication. On one level, he was a very good communicator, but when it concerned his personal life, he was awful. It was as if he surrounded himself with barricades. Was it, perhaps, significant that whilst his fellow officers could lap up a good deal of beer when they were thirsty (which was often), he could spin out a pint to make it last an entire evening. Didn't he like the stuff, or was he afraid that it might loosen his tongue, opening doors to a realm that concerned no one but himself?

Some clue to his demeanour at this time is to be found in a book by one of the controllers at Hornchurch, a veteran of the Royal Flying Corps named Ronald Adams. Entitled *Readiness at Dawn*, and published in 1941, Adams, using the pseudonym of 'Blake', describes the early days of war at Hornchurch. The characters are imperfectly disguised, and nobody would have had much difficulty in identifying 'Sailor' Malan as 'Bosun' Spritt. 'The nose was straight,' Adams wrote, 'the eyes very direct and head exceedingly powerful. "Tough customer to fall out with," Roger thought, and then Bosun smiled and the whole face crinkled with geniality.'

The so-called *Sitzkrieg* yielded to the no less aptly named *Blitzkrieg*. Business at Hornchurch perked up. The aircraft took off three or four times a day and some of them never returned. Dowding once said, 'The life of a military aviator consists of hours of idleness punctuated by moments of fear.' Malan's version was, 'I don't know which is worse, being perpetually bored or perpetually scared.' In fact, the summer of 1940 demolished the bit about boredom. Contrary to the beliefs of many members of the Army, the Spitfires found plenty to do in the skies above France during the German offensive of those inglorious months May and June.

One of the troubles was that the fighters were either flying too high for their exploits to be witnessed by an audience at ground level, or else they had to perform too low to operate to the best advantage. There was also the problem of fuel. The early Spitfires guzzled it. This was all very well on the short-range operations for which they were designed, but when it came to covering the evacuation at Dunkirk, it was stretching things. As Malan told his biographer, Oliver Walker (*Sailor Malan*, 1953), 'The only way we could fly to Dunkirk and have enough juice to spend a few minutes over the battle area was by coasting and flying at sea-level up from Boulogne.'

As if this were not difficulty enough, the Spitfires and the Hurricanes were severely outnumbered. Dowding had won his point that at least twenty-five squadrons should be kept in reserve against the inevitable onslaught that would follow what now appeared to be the equally inevitable fall of France. Malan's personal policy was economy – in terms of pilots and of machines. On one occasion he was informed that somebody's engine had been hit and that the pilot would have to abandon his aircraft. 'No you don't, you so-and-so,' Malan snapped back. 'You'll make a decent forced landing.'

It needed no feat of navigation to find Dunkirk. You could see the smoke rising from the bombed and burning oil tanks near the harbour. The sky, of course, was cluttered with German aeroplanes. On 24 May, Malan and eight others were patrolling the French coast near Calais and attracting a lot of flak in the process. Suddenly over the R/T, he was informed that a large force of German bombers was busy over Dunkirk. The formation divided up into three units and came down to sea level. The pilots were soon able to discern tight formations, each of twenty or so aircraft, leisurely circling the docks, offloading their bombs, and then being replaced by other formations. 'I could not see the beginning or the end of them,' he said.

The Spitfires climbed to attack, whereupon a covering force of Messerschmitts came down to greet them. There could be no planned and co-ordinated assault: it was a free-for-all in which the British pilots shot at anything that bore enemy markings. Malan sent an He–111 hurtling groundwards and then found himself in trouble. An ack-ack shell modified his starboard wing; rounds from a Messerschmitt cut his electrical leads and snipped a piece off one of his flying boots. With uncommon skill, he regained control and managed to get home. It was a difficult trip – not only for himself, but also for his companions. His friend, Bertie Aubert, was killed. Two others were wounded, and Paddy Treacy's aircraft was so badly damaged that he had to bale out. When he came to earth just beyond Dunkirk, French troops fired on him. He landed in a pigpen – the home of a large boar that resented the intrusion. It charged him. A wise man does not pause to argue with angry boars; Treacy fled and, in doing so, badly twisted his ankle. Now limping and in a good deal of pain, he found temporary cover in a cluster of bushes. Inevitably, the French soldiers discovered him, but he managed to convince them that he was British. Their attitude immediately became less hostile: they assisted him as far as the coast, where he managed to get on board a British destroyer.

Malan took part in ten operations over French soil. On 11 June he was awarded a DFC; eight days later he achieved one of his less predictable victories, and one which the designer of the Spitfire had never envisaged. He was standing outside the mess on a beautiful moonlit night, when he became aware that bombs were falling not all that far away. Searchlights were fingering the sky, now and then illuminating one or another of the intruders. The anti-aircraft fire was so intense that it was judged to be unwise for any fighters to join in. But this was too much: he asked his commanding officer for permission to take off, and the CO granted it.

Seldom had any departure been organized more quickly. Within a remarkably short time he shot an He–111 out of the sky – the range was so close that oil from the mortally damaged bomber spattered over his screen. He went on to destroy another He–111, which crashed on the lawn of a vicarage near Chelmsford. That was enough fun for one evening. He returned to base.

On 8 August he was given command of 74 Squadron. Three days later he was awarded a Bar to his DFC. According to Wing Commander H. R. ('Dizzy') Allen in *Battle for Britain* (first published by Arthur Barker in 1973, and this extract reprinted in Laddie Lucas's *Wings of War* – Hutchinson, 1983): 'The other squadron (No. 74) was . . . under the command of the redoubtable South African, "Sailor" Malan. He made his pilots live . . . like Boer farmers in their wagons. He even made sure they went to bed at 10 pm each night although, presumably, he did not actually close their eyelids for them.

'He was tough, strict, a martinet and, operationally, it paid off. I doubt if there was a more successful squadron commander in 1940 than Malan . . . He was so long-sighted that he could see a fly on the great wall of China at five miles.

'He was a crack shot, a brilliant aerobatic pilot, but, above all, he was utterly determined. He even won a dogfight against the German ace, Mölders . . . If Malan had had decent armament instead of the puny battery of eight .303 Brownings we were equipped with, Mölders would never have got back to his base at Wissant.' (Later versions of the Spitfire were armed with two 20-mm Hispano cannons in addition to the machine-guns).*

In 1938 'Sailor' and Lynda Malan visited the Battersea Dog's home where they bought a mongrel puppy that seemed to be in the terminal stages of distemper. It cost them the large sum of 2s 6d (12½p). They lovingly nursed their acquisition back to health, named him Peter, and wherever 'Sailor' Malan went Peter was

---

*The brush with Mölders took place on 28 July. The German ace was flying a Messerschmitt of Bf 109E–3. It was a close fought thing: when his opponent departed in a hurry for Wissant, Malan claimed a probable, but this was later disproved.

sure to go too. The togetherness stopped short only at the cockpit of an aeroplane. In June 1940, when she was living at Westcliff-on-Sea in Essex, Lynda gave birth to their first child – a boy they named Jonathan. It is some measure of Malan's success that when, just over a year later, the boy was baptized, Winston Churchill agreed to become one of the godfathers and posted off a silver mug. He might even have attended the ceremony, too, but he was engaged in business with Roosevelt on the far side of the Atlantic. Instead, he asked his brother, Major Jack Churchill, to be there as his proxy. Lynda, by this time, had left Westcliff. She returned to Ruislip for a while and then moved to Norfolk. It was just as well. Two days after her departure, the roof of the Ruislip house was blown off.

Malan once said, 'The sky's very small when you want to hide.' No doubt, but he wasn't much inclined to conceal himself. The Battle of Britain saw his score steadily mounting – and, indeed, that of 74 Squadron as well. To take only one example, on 11 August 1940 the squadron was involved in no fewer than four different fights between dawn and 7 pm. At the end of it all, they had dispatched thirty-eight enemy aircraft at a cost of only two pilots. Between August and December of that year, they had accounted for eighty-four hostile aeroplanes and many more severely damaged. Again, in return for small losses – but that was one of the things about 74 Squadron: it hung on to its pilots. Much of this was due to its impeccable teamwork. It was small wonder, then, that on Christmas Eve 1940 Malan was invested with the DSO. He received a Bar to it in August of the following year. At the investiture, the King told him, 'I'm very glad to see you again.' But he may have said this to other pilots, too. The real satisfaction, so far as Malan was concerned, must have come when his personal score had reached thirty-five (if you include shared victories) – at a time when the toll of that ace of aces, Douglas Bader, was twenty.

Tough though he undoubtedly was, even Malan could not go on at this pace forever. There comes a time, and there are many instances to prove it, when aerial combat is addictive. This is the dangerous period: some of the essential coolness has gone, and a pilot is liable to make mistakes. Paddy Treacy's time came when he was killed, not by hostile guns, but in an avoidable mid-air collision. Malan, fortunately, saw the warning light in August 1941, when he led an attack against a formation of German fighters. It may have been in the best tradition of British bravery, but, rather like the charge of the Light Brigade, his calculations were wrong and it had the makings of a disaster. As he said afterwards, 'You don't get the chance to make mistakes like that more than once.' And 'I knew I had made a mistake – a mistake I wouldn't have made if I had been fresh.'

He needed a rest and luckily received one – brief though it was. For three days he enjoyed the peace and quiet of a cottage in Kent. 'It was queer – and salutory,' he said. 'I heard the birds for the first time, and smelt flowers. I did a bit of rabbit shooting, looked at the scenery, heard people talking about ordinary things, and suddenly I knew how really clapped out I was.'

On 10 March 1941, he was posted to command the Wing based on Biggin Hill in Kent. But then it occurred to somebody high up in the hierarchy that men of Malan's calibre could put in some useful war work without firing a shot. America had yet to enter the hostilities, and it seemed in no hurry to do so. If three fighter aces and three crack bomber pilots were sent on a tour of the United States, it might have some not inconsiderable propaganda value. Thus on 29 October of that year, a party that included himself, Wing Commander 'Bobbie' Stanford Tuck, DSO, DFC, and Group Captain Harry Broadhurst, DSO, DFC (later to become Air Vice Marshal Sir Harry Broadhurst), settled themselves in the not very comfortable interior of a Liberator and set off for New York.* They were all wearing civilian clothes out of respect for America's neutrality. Had they been in uniform they could, in theory at any rate, have been interned.

Whatever their effect on the Americans, the Americans do not seem to have impressed Malan very much. He wearied of the apparently endless invitations to 'have a highball', when he considered there were more important things to be done. In New York he went to earth on a sentimental visit to the British Apprentice Club (no highballs offered there). At one aerodrome he went to, the station commander told him that his pilots were all up aloft practising tactics. Could he, Malan wondered, go up and join them? His host agreed, put an Aircobra (a single-seat fighter) at his disposal, and promised to warn his men about his impending arrival. He had never flown an Aircobra before, but

*The Bomber Command representatives included Wing Commander 'Taffie' Edwards, the Australian who had won both the VC and the DFC in a single month.

this seemed to be no great handicap. Within four minutes and fifty-two seconds of taking off, he had 'shot down' all twelve aircraft in the sky with his camera guns. In his opinion, the tactics being used had been discarded by the RAF way back in 1937. He found the experience depressing.

He and Stanford Tuck returned to the UK by way of Canada, where they turned out to be disappointing microphone fodder. When interviewed, they showed greater interest in the campaign in Libya than in questions about their visit to the United States – in the Air Training Scheme (it produced over 100,000 air crews) than about how it felt to be an ace. On the whole, they seemed glad that the razzmatazz was over, and that they could soon return to the serious business of destroying Germans.

In Malan's case, the more active side of combat would have to wait a while longer. It seemed wrong that such skills should be the province of one man. They should be disseminated. He was accordingly posted to command the Central Gunnery School at Sutton Bridge in Lincolnshire. It was here that he produced his celebrated 'Ten Commandments'. They were:

1. Wait till you see the whites of their eyes before opening fire. Fire short bursts of about one or two seconds and only when your sights are definitely 'on'.

2. When shooting think of nothing else. Brace the whole body with feet firmly on the rudder pedals having *both* hands on the stick. Concentrate on your right sight.

3. Always keep a sharp look-out even when manoeuvring for, and executing an attack, and in particular immediately after a breakaway. Many pilots are shot down during these three phases as a result of becoming too absorbed in their attack. Don't watch your 'flamer' [i.e. victim] go down except out of the corner of your eye; in fact, 'keep your finger out'.

4. If you have the advantage of height you automatically possess the initiative.

5. Always turn and face the attack. If attacked from a superior height wait until your opponent is well committed to his dive and within about 1,500 yards of you. Then turn suddenly towards him.

6. Make your decision promptly and smartly. It is usually better to act quickly and decisively when attacked or evading, even though your action is not necessarily the best possible.

7. Never fly straight and level for more than 30 seconds at any time whilst in the combat area or at any time when enemy aircraft are likely to be encountered.

8. When diving to attack always leave a proportion of your formation above to act as top guard.

9. Initiative: Aggression: Air discipline: Teamwork: are words that mean something in air fighting.

10. Get in quickly, punch hard, get out smartly.

He had much else to add to these precepts, but these were the cornerstones of his philosophy. Indeed, there's little doubt that the Malan influence lingered on at the school long after he had departed. He was there for about a year – until 1 January 1943, when he was posted back to Biggin Hill as station commander. The appointment brought with it promotion to Group Captain, a rank that carried the privilege of wearing 'scrambled egg' on the peak of the cap. The trouble was that, immediately, he couldn't find any such headgear. He asked the advice of the Senior Air Staff Officer who, it transpired, had one left over from his previous rank. He was, he said, prepared to do business. A shop in Regent Street, London, had a razor the officer particularly wanted. For some reason (lost in the quagmire of history) the assistant wasn't prepared to sell it to him. If Malan, with his charm and array of medals, could obtain it for him, the cap would be his. Malan was successful; the cap less so. It was a size too small.

He went on several operations, but claimed no victims. He had, one must assume, learned something from his hell-bent-for-glory fiasco of August 1941. More junior officers may have been expendable and many of them were, indeed, expended. As the padre at Biggin Hill said, 'Most of these lads died all too soon to win reputations or many decorations.' Malan had survived and won both. His life was now too precious to be squandered in the slaughterhouse of the sky. When, on 15 May 1943, Biggin Hill Sector scored its 1,000th victory, the event was later celebrated in the grand manner – by a ball at Grosvenor House Hotel in Park Lane, London. Fifty London cabbies gave their services for nothing – driving the guests to and fro. Some weeks later, Malan did the decent thing, and entertained the drivers at Biggin Hill. They came bearing gifts. One of them was a clock that the donor insisted should be stopped on the day war ended.

For Malan, this was a double celebration: a few hours before the ball got under way, Lynda gave birth to their second child – a little girl.

If El Alamein had been 'the end of the beginning' (Churchill's words), 1944 was the beginning of the end. Malan was moved from Biggin Hill and given the job of preparing No. 20 Fighter Wing for D-Day and the invasion of Normandy. During the operation itself, he led a section of 340 Squadron, escorting the Albemarles that were towing Horsa gliders. Thereafter he flew over Normandy twice a day to see how things were going. He was not actually looking for trouble, but any German pilot who cared to engage him could be assured of a scrap he would never forget (or never have the opportunity to remember). Nobody took advantage of it, but the conditions were now so remarkably changed since those days of 1940. Then the skies of Western Europe had been filled (or so it seemed) with German aircraft. Now, you had to look for them – unless you were a bomber pilot operating over Germany, but that is another matter.

Malan's ability as a fighter pilot has become legendary. But he was also a very good teacher, and, once the invasion was firmly established, which is to say in July 1944, he was given command of the Advanced Gunnery School at Catfoss in what is now Humberside (it used to be part of Yorkshire). Among the instructors who came and went were Richard Bong (enjoying a respite from the turbulence of combat over the Pacific) and that most difficult of aces, 'Screwball' Beurling. On the day that Pierre Clostermann came to the school, he noticed a strange figure in the officers' anteroom. He was badly turned out, wore no badges of rank, and had a couple of women's stockings wrapped round his neck. His lanky figure was lounging in an armchair: he appeared to be unwilling to speak and he was clearly in no hurry to do anything else.

Suddenly the anteroom silence was broken by a rebuke that would have done credit to a sergeant-major in the Guards. 'Who are you?' the voice exclaimed. 'Stand up! What the bloody hell are you doing here?' The speaker was Malan, but the ungainly stranger must have been unaware of the fact. He replied with two words, one of them containing four letters. This produced the kind of explosion to which the earlier sentences, however crisp, had been no more than a mild prelude. Malan concluded with, 'Get out of here and come back when you're properly dressed.'

Picking up a grubby cap, Beurling slunk off. Afterwards, Malan told Clostermann, 'It is better that it should have happened on the first day, in private. He'll know now that he has got to behave himself here. But don't get him wrong. He really is a remarkable type.'

The war was coming to an end. In 1945 Malan attended a course at the RAF Staff College, and there seemed to be no reason why his career should not continue – and, indeed, flourish. But, for some while, other things had been niggling at his mind. He was afraid that in the peace to come fighter pilots might become members of a lost generation. There would be work in civil aviation for the surviving pilots of Bomber Command. After all, many of the immediately post-war commercial airliners were derivatives of bombers (the Lancastrian and the York could trace their ancestries to the Lancaster, the Halton to the Halifax, and so on. Even the Constellation had originated as a transport used by the US Navy). But what was there for fighter pilots? The question worried him.

He was also anxious to return to South Africa and settle down there. This, as it turned out, was not difficult. During his time at Biggin Hill, he had been entertained on several occasions by a man who lived in some style at Sundridge, a village just a few miles from the RAF station. His name was Abrahams and he was head of the Diamond Trading Company – an organization that handled the sales of De Beers diamonds. *Chez* Abrahams, he had met Sir Ernest Oppenheimer, the chairman of De Beers and his son, Harry, who had served with the 4th Armoured Car Regiment in North Africa. Malan and Harry had become friends. Their conversations often turned to the state of South Africa at the time. It was not a happy situation: the villain, ironically, was a very distant relation of Malan – Dr Daniel Francois Malan, the former leader of the Nationalist Party who was soon to become Prime Minister. Dr Malan was a bigot of the worst type: he was anti-semitic, anti-black, anti-pretty-well-anything except the fortunes of the more narrow-minded Afrikaaners. At one stage during the war, he had openly sided with Hitler – listing among the dictator's supposed virtues the fact that, emerging victorious, he would give South Africa the status of a republic.

If 'Sailor' Malan needed South Africa, it was clear in Harry Oppenheimer's mind that South Africa needed Malan. He offered him a loosely defined job, and the aviator accepted.

Turning his back on the service in which he had done so well, and which still seemed to offer so much promise, he resigned his RAF commission. In 1946 he and his family sailed for Cape Town in the *Caernarvon Castle*.

He worked for a while in the De Beer offices and was then given one of the company's farms near Kimberley. He also became very active in politics, eventually being elected national president of Torch Commando – an organization that stood for everything that his namesake did not. He was trying to create in South Africa the kind of world for which he had fought. Ever a believer in teamwork, he felt that the country should become one – regardless of race, creed, and whatever. As others discovered, it was less than easy – especially in an environment so ridden by those prejudices piously fostered by Dr Malan and his like.

Nor did 'Sailor' Malan have all that much time at his disposal. In 1963, after a long illness, he died. He was only 53. It was a sad ending to a remarkable life – and a waste of some kind of wisdom.

7

Leonard Cheshire
THE PERFECTIONIST

An eminent Harley Street neurologist once said that Leonard Cheshire was fearless but not courageous. The point, of course, is that he who has no fear needs no courage with which to overcome it. In fact, this seems to me rather too much of an over-simplification. Cheshire was not one to storm into battle, a reckless daredevil who, either from lack of imagination or else from stupidity, never counted the possible cost. He was (and still is) an extremely intelligent man, sensitive, a brilliant organizer, and a stickler with a nice sense of detail. These, perhaps, are some of the reasons for his success – and, indeed, for his survival. When he was in trouble, he might take an apparently outrageous way of getting out of it, but he was determined that if trouble there should be, it would be of the enemy's making and not his.

There were some who disliked him – or, rather, the idea of him; for these were people who knew his reputation, but did not know the man. Anyone who came into really close contact with him (his aircrews, for example) regarded him with a respect that stopped only a few millimetres short of idolatry.

Whoever believed that he really knew Leonard Cheshire was rash. During the years of his evolution, one sometimes wonders whether he completely understood himself. This is not to his discredit: there are so many facets to this complex character, some in contrast to others, some overlapping. During the Second World War, he was awarded the Victoria Cross, the DSO and three Bars, and a DFC. More recently, he has been admitted to the Order of Merit, a society so exclusive that its membership is limited to twenty-four. To win the VC is achievement enough, to be invested with the OM as well is amazing. I may be wrong, but I cannot find a record of anyone else accomplishing it.

Leonard Cheshire was born on 17 September 1917, the son of an Oxford don who, at the time, was serving with the Royal Flying Corps in France. Dr Cheshire was not one of those glamorous and all too mortal young men who patrolled the sky and became involved in dogfights. Confined to a basket suspended from a balloon, his job was to observe whatever was going on down below. It was uncomfortable and damnably dangerous. By good fortune he was recalled to England shortly after his son was born and, because his subject was jurisprudence, he was given work of a less hazardous nature within the service. A year or so later, a second son, Christopher, was born.

To do justice to Leonard Cheshire in a few thousand words is impossible. It would take at least three books. Some of them have already been written: *No Passing Glory*, by his friend Andrew Boyle, is the most comprehensive, taking us through his youth, the war years (in excellent detail), and so to the creation of the Cheshire Foundation. Russell Braddon has contributed *Cheshire, V.C.* Among books by Cheshire himself are *Bomber Pilot* (which is incomplete: the story stops in 1943, when it was published) and *The Hidden World* (1981), a moving account of the Cheshire Foundation's origins and its development. But there is, one suspects, another unwritten story that might elaborate on certain aspects of his life. If Evelyn Waugh were alive, it would suit his talents admirably. But, then again, perhaps he has already written it – not about Leonard Cheshire, but concerning a world that, briefly, one of his several selves inhabited.

His father, Geoffrey Cheshire, had few doubts about the plan his firstborn's life should follow: a conventional education, a degree in jurisprudence obtained at Merton (his own college – though he later became Bursar of Exeter), and then the Bar. Had it not been for the war, events might have followed these lines. He attended The Dragon School in Oxford, and won a scholarship to Stowe (a quite recently established public school in Buckinghamshire which, under its then headmaster, J. F. Roxburgh, treated boys as individuals – this was in contrast to the fashion of kneading them into a corporate mass, compelling a kind of individuality to flare up in the minds of those who wished to survive the experience). At Stowe, he accomplished all the right things, such as becoming a prefect, the head of his house, the captain of lawn tennis, and attaining the sixth form. Furthermore, wrote Mr Roxburgh, 'There was something about him – was it perhaps a kind of moral dignity? – which made it inconceivable that he would think of doing anything which was below top level.'

Between school and the University, his parents sent him to lodge with a German family at Potsdam for four months. The head of the household was Admiral Ludwig von Reuter, who had commanded the German fleet during its internment at Scapa Flow after the First World War, and had given the order to scuttle it. With a quaint fancy, he had named each of his three sons after a German warship: Derflinger von Reuter, Emden von Reuter, and Hipper von Reuter. The Admiral was undoubtedly a martinet, but he appears to have been a pleasant one, and his little eccentricities appealed to his guest. Indeed these four months did two things. Firstly, they showed young Cheshire's ability to settle into whatever set of circumstances he encountered – to such an extent that when his parents came to fetch him home he departed with reluctance. The second was to instil in him a considerable enthusiasm for motor racing. He was frequently to be found watching the cars zoom by on the Avus circuit near Berlin. Given the money and the encouragement, he would doubtless have taken part. For want of either, he had to remain a spectator, which was probably just as well. But it did implant in him a love of fast cars – notably Bentleys, which were to become his standard means of personal locomotion.

His period at Oxford might be described as the 'Waugh Years'. He was inclined to disagree with his father about law as a career that would suit him, but he did sufficient work to take a good second-class degree in jurisprudence (to the displeasure of Cheshire Snr who would have preferred something better); he also discovered that life had many pleasures to offer – especially if you were rich. He was not, but this did not deter him. There were frantic trips up to London to visit this or that nightclub. There were days at the races, which enriched the bookies and added to his mounting pile of debts. He found a vehicle called a Squire lying dismantled in a garage, and bought it. It was a wonderful 1½-litre sportscar. Had he assembled it and stashed it away, it would be worth a fortune nowadays. Out of the 12 laid down, only ten were completed. But he was seduced by an offer of £25 plus an old MG for his acquisition. He sold the MG for £100, and used the lot as a down-payment on a 1931 supercharged Alfa-Romeo that he'd seen in a dealer's window. He was doubtless very fond of it, but this was not apparent in the thrashings he gave it.

A more praiseworthy outlet for his high spirits and sense of reckless adventure was the Oxford University Air Squadron based at Abingdon. The RAF had posted Flight-Lieutenant Charles Whitworth to it as instructor. Cheshire had been inexcusably rude to him on their first encounter, and Whitworth was determined to have his revenge when he first took the aspiring pilot into the sky. He performed just about every aerobatic manoeuvre that might be calculated to turn his passenger into a nausea-ridden wreck. At the end of it, and considerably to his dismay, he found Cheshire jubilant and eager for more. That was his first surprise. The second surprise came when he allowed his pupil to fly the aircraft. Such was his aptitude that it required all Cheshire's powers of conviction to assure him that he had never flown before. Whitworth had, it seemed, a natural aviator under his tutelage.

Along with most other members of the squadron, he joined the Royal Air Force Volunteer Reserve – hoping, among other things, that the war, which now seemed inevitable, would break out in time to absolve him from having to take his jurisprudence finals. It didn't. The escapades continued. When three Fairey Battles (a three-seater, single-engine, light bomber) came to Abingdon, he conceived a stunt that, he felt sure, would make him a much needed fortune from the national press. The idea was that he should stow away on one of them. When they were flying in formation, he would emerge, climb out on to the wing, walk to the edge and jump across to the aircraft flying next to it. He would then move on to aeroplane number three and repeat the performance. Happily the pilot he propositioned managed to convince him that the stunt was a) impossible and b) suicidal. He did, however, as a kind of final flourish at the University, spend a night on the top of Merton College tower, and he also, at considerable discomfort, won a bet that he could travel to Paris from an Oxford pub in one week at an expenditure of only 15s.0d. (75p).

True to its promise, the war came. In early October 1939, as a pilot officer in the RAF, he presented himself at the 9th Flying Training School situated at Hullavington in Wiltshire. On 15

December he received his 'wings'. His report described him as 'average', but insisted that '. . . if he can check his tendency to over-confidence, should become Above Average.' He was also impatient and, in all honesty, inclined to seek whatever limelight was there to be sought. He had, one feels, a sense of the theatrical – a sense that, in the long run, made him almost as many enemies as it did friends.

By mid-April of 1940, he had returned to Abingdon, which was now the location of No. 10 Operational Training Unit. Here he was introduced to the Whitley bomber. The station commander, an old friend of his father's, was inclined to think that his mentality was more that of a fighter pilot than of a bomber captain who had to endure the long slog over enemy territory night after night. In the general opinion, he was either destined for an early death or a brilliant career. Luck, of course, plays a decisive part in any undertaking. But, given this precious commodity, his passing out report suggested that he might achieve the latter. It described him as 'Exceptional day and night'. He was the first pilot from 10 OTU ever to reach this category of excellence. He took pains to ensure that as many people as possible should know about it. Was this conceit? In a less complex character this might have been the reason, but in Cheshire's case it could equally well have been some private joke. He enjoyed acclaim for its own sake. He certainly didn't need it to reinforce a flabby ego – nor was he reluctant to laugh at himself.

His first raid was something of a non-event. It took place from Driffield in Yorkshire; the aircraft was a Whitley; the target was a bridge at Abbeville; and Cheshire was flying as co-pilot. By the time they arrived, the bridge had already been destroyed. There was no opposition. Indeed, none of the first four trips gave any suggestion of the hazards to come, but Cheshire was taking no chances. He had already arranged with his parents a code that he would use in his letters should he be taken prisoner. If he wrote the date in Roman numerals, it was a signal that a hidden message was waiting to be deciphered.

During these apprentice days, he was fortunate in his captain: a patient New Zealander named 'Lofty' Long, who was one of the first members of Bomber Command to be awarded the DFC. The two men got on famously together, and Long spent much time coaching him on such matters as wireless, navigation, bomb-aiming, and all the other essentials. Whenever he had time to spare, Cheshire borrowed one of the aircraft and flew it until he could sit relaxed at the controls – and until instrument flying was (his words) 'no more tiring than reading a book.'

He became accepted by the others. They even began to understand his somewhat individualistic sense of humour. There was, for example, the occasion when somebody exclaimed, 'Good God!' Cheshire overheard it and said, 'You really must not take my name in vain like that. Please address me with more reverence in future.' It may not have been wit as Noël Coward understood the word, but it amused.

The airfield at Driffield was bombed by the *Luftwaffe*. The squadron was moved to Aldergrove in Northern Ireland, with Cheshire now in charge of his own aircraft. They spent most of the time looking for enemy submarines: a task that he found uncongenial. On the morning of 5 October, he was ordered aloft to search for a convoy that had gone missing. A storm was raging, in his haste he overlooked the precaution of taking parachutes, and Desmond Coutts, the co-pilot, could not be found. Thus, with only his navigator and the wireless operator to keep him company, he flew off on what might be a fruitless errand.

With such atrocious weather it followed that visibility would be virtually nil. They found the convoy, but this was the least of their problems. Cheshire and his companions now had to apply themselves to the more difficult task of finding their way back to Aldergrove. At some point they were informed that they were over the coast and that the only sensible thing to do was to jump for it. Since they had no parachutes, this posed a number of snags. Eventually, with only ten minutes' supply of fuel left, they managed to make out a glimmer of lights marking the flare path. It had been a very near thing. Far from returning to a hero's welcome, Cheshire was rebuked for a number of faults: not least the folly of setting out on such a parlous assignment without taking parachutes. His crew, on the other hand, saw no reason to criticize him. They had already carried out three raids and ten Atlantic patrols under his command, and they had absolute faith in him. Coutts, who had followed the event from the safety of the control tower, said, 'Leonard, you're damned lucky! If you fell down a cesspit, I swear you'd come up with a gold watch and chain round your neck.'

At the end of the first week in October, the squadron was ordered back to Yorkshire, where they settled in at Linton-on-

Ouse. They returned to the business of bombing (or trying to) the living daylights out of Germany.

They were now confronted by very much stronger opposition. A visit to the sky above Lunen in the Ruhr produced five direct hits on railway sheds on the credit side. On the debit, there was the fragment of shrapnel that pierced the Whitley's belly and broke the bomb-sight. There was the desperate evasive action that Cheshire had to take against the flak: action that stretched the aircraft's durability to its limits. When at last they landed back at Linton, there were more than a hundred holes and rents in the wings and fuselage showing how close they had come to extinction.

Worse was to come on 12 November when they set off by night for Cologne. Somewhere over the city centre, the gunfire from below suddenly ceased – which suggested that a night fighter was unhealthily close to them. Seconds later, there was an explosion in the front turret. Cheshire was stunned by it and the aircraft lurched out of control. But this was where the bit about luck came in. The shock was no more than momentary. He pulled back the control column and somehow got back on course. The Whitley responded – as if to show that although it might have been wounded it was by no means maimed. The real casualty was the wireless operator, an eighteen-year-old sergeant named Davidson who was making his first trip. The young NCO was preparing to release a flare, when a second shell exploded just above the port wing. It set fire to the rest of the pyrotechnic assortment, dreadfully burning Davidson. Nevertheless, he insisted upon being carried to his seat, where he tried to resume his duties.

The intercom system had been shredded and, with so much else to think about, Cheshire nearly forgot to offload the bombs. Having got rid of them, and briefly noticing that they seemed to be making a contribution to the inferno below, he turned for home. The Whitley hobbled through the sky back to Linton. Davidson was hurried off to hospital; the others attended the debriefing. That afternoon, Cheshire and two other members of the crew drove to York, where they watched a Fred Astaire and Ginger Rogers film. A day or so later, Cheshire was informed that he had been awarded the DSO. For such an honour to be accorded to a young pilot officer was unusual: indeed, he was the first junior officer in Bomber Command to be so decorated.

Leonard Cheshire was not one to keep his thoughts to himself, unpopular as his ideas may have sometimes been. To those who

flew with him, however, he was skipper next to God. This applied
no less to his ground crews, one of whom helped him to restore a
rather too experienced Bentley he had acquired. His one-time
co-pilot, 'Taffy' Roberts (quoted in *No Passing Glory*), said, 'My
lasting impression of Cheshire . . . is the absolute faith he inspired
in us. Other crews regarded him as the Elizabethans might have
regarded Drake: "You're cutting it a bit fine, old boy," is a rather
polite way of putting it. Yet we would have followed him anywhere.'

Some of this was due to his obvious ability and his talent to
survive, but it went beyond that. He took considerable interest in
the lives and activities of those who assisted him in the air and on
the ground; was never in too much of a hurry to smoke a cigarette
and drink tea with them. After the first raid from Linton, he told
somebody to paint a bomb on his Whitley's nose. There was to be
one for each succeeding sortie until the score reached ten. Then,
he promised, he would take them to York for a party. He was true to
his word. The rendezvous was an establishment named Betty's
Bar, which was out-of-bounds to Other Ranks. When a senior
Army Officer complained about the intrusion of NCOs, Cheshire
politely, but in words that brooked no argument, told him to amend
his attitude. The party went ahead and a very good one it was, too.

At this distance in time, people are apt to forget (or do not know)
what these young bomber crews endured. The conditions were
dreadfully cold and, sometimes, wet. It was not until the long-
range Mustang came into service, that it was possible to provide
any fighter cover (which was why the RAF went about its business
by night: the casualties of daylight raids had been horrific).* Even
with the concealment of darkness, there were perils enough.
There was also the long flight to the target and back again: an experience that niggled incessantly at the nerves and sapped the
stamina. And, when the ordeal was almost over, there were the un-
certainties of the weather – that most treacherous of circumstances,
which could wrap an airfield in fog and make the coming down
more uncertain than the going up. Whose side was it on, anyway?

There was also, had they realized it, the question of whether
their work was actually doing anything to confound the enemy.
When cameras were introduced in the summer of 1941, they
revealed some startling shortcomings. During a period of

*US bombers made daylight raids over Germany without fighter cover. But the Boeing
B-17 Fortress was more heavily armed than, say, a Lancaster. Despite this, however, the
casualties were horrendous.

eighteen months, out of every three bomb loads released, only one landed within five miles of the target. Since the idea had been to make precision attacks on individual installations, this was nowhere good enough. For want of any solution, the Air Council had to change its policy. Henceforth, the raids would be used to disrupt the enemy's transport system and to terrorize civilians. Put another way, the outlook that had deplored the *Luftwaffe*'s depredations of London, Coventry, and suchlike, now had to do a double-think and adopt a similar policy. But that, surely, was all right. After all, the Germans had initiated it.

Whatever their perils and discomforts, Cheshire seems to have enjoyed most of these excursions into German air space. By this time he was flying Halifaxes, which, with their four engines and larger bomb loads, were a decided improvement on the Whitley. He was content to go on flying them, but the Halifaxes were suddenly grounded for modifications. On the other hand, there was another assignment that was not unappealing. Volunteers were needed to ferry Hudson and Liberator bombers from the United States. Every pilot in the squadron (No. 35) applied. The matter was settled by the adjutant putting their names into a hat. Cheshire's, that apparently most fortunate of individuals, was drawn out. He set off for Montreal in a Norwegian ship in which the discomforts of the accommodation were compounded by the roughness of the ocean. The voyage took two weeks. Among the other passengers were six pilots from Coastal Command.

There could be no question of simply grabbing, say, a Hudson and flying it back to England. Before anything could be done, Cheshire had to carry out a conversion course as a co-pilot. Nobody seemed to be in much of a hurry to make use of him, and for about thirteen weeks he enjoyed an above-average period of leave in the United States. During it, he met an actress named Constance Binney. She was considerably older than himself: whatever talents she may have lacked as a performer were more than redressed by the size of her income. Some strange chemistry must have been at work. She had been twice married already and now it was Cheshire's turn. Everything about it seems tinged with the improbable. She was a prominent New York socialite, unaccustomed, one must consider, to any great hardship (or to any small hardship, come to that). How, then, would she adapt herself in the transformation from the razzle-dazzle of New York's smart set to the life of an RAF wife making ends meet in the austerity of wartime Britain? And how would she, so accustomed to being the centre of attraction, accept the role of coming second to the RAF in Cheshire's design for living? For, make no mistake about it, this was what it amounted to.

Nevertheless, a marriage was arranged. At the end of those thirteen weeks, Cheshire was judged fit to pilot a Hudson to the UK. The flight from Gander to Prestwick, in which he was accompanied by two sergeants, took ten hours. Constance's arrival in her new country took rather longer, but she got there in the end.

He returned to 35 Squadron at Linton. Many of his old friends were missing, and he applied himself to working up a new crew. It cannot have been an easy time. His parents – understandably, perhaps – disapproved of his excursion into wedlock: they did not see the former Constance Binney as a suitable daughter-in-law. On a Berlin raid in which they were both involved, his brother Christopher was shot down and taken prisoner. During an attack on Magdeburg, he attempted to deceive the enemy defences by 'feathering' the engines. He had tried it before under less perilous circumstances, and it had worked perfectly. When it came to restarting them, they burst into eager life as if they'd enjoyed the brief rest.

Over Magdeburg, they were less co-operative. As a ruse, it seemed to work well enough. After the Halifax had lost 2,000 feet, however, Cheshire pressed the starter button on one of them. The engine coughed politely and did nothing else. The aircraft became out of control. Several more efforts brought the two starboard motors to life, but those on the port side remained obdurate. The German flak gunners were now giving them a lot of attention. With shells bursting all around them, Cheshire succumbed to his only recorded moment of panic. He ordered the crew to bail out. The wireless operator, 'Jock' Hill, was not of the same persuasion. As quoted by Andrew Boyle, he said, 'For God's sake, Chesh, pull yourself together. You can do much better than that if you try.' Luck, it seemed, was the handmaiden of self-confidence. Lose the latter, and the former went, too. Hill's words had the desired effect. Cheshire pulled himself and the Halifax together. The ground-ward spin was corrected: at 2,000 feet the port engines stopped sulking and woke up.

Back at Linton, Cheshire was severely chided for his near-fatal experiment. The squadron commander might have been harsher; but he, like several others, had noticed a change in Cheshire since his return from the United States. Far from exuding the happiness that newly weds are supposedly to exude, he seemed to be deeply depressed. Action against the enemy, even ill-judged action, seemed to be the only palliative.

Despite his state of mind, he was promoted to Squadron Leader, awarded a DFC, and (with money supplied by Constance) treated himself to a good second-hand Bentley. Constance eventually arrived in England with thirty-six pieces of baggage, having been given passage in a troopship bound for Liverpool. As a diversion, he was given the task of flying the C-in-C of Bomber Command, Air Marshal Sir Richard Peirse, on a tour of inspection to the Orkneys. The Air Marshal impressed him by his skill at navigation; indeed, the two seem to have got on very well together.

For living accommodation, Cheshire had acquired an old railway carriage, which was brought by road from York and parked on grassland near the officers' mess. It may not have been the sort of thing to which Constance was accustomed, but they managed to make it reasonably comfortable and even to use it for entertaining. To augment their rations on these occasions, it was sometimes possible to pick off a hare or a brace of pheasants for the pot. The household was enlarged by the coming of Simon, a poodle to which they had taken a fancy, and which accompanied Cheshire on his daily rounds. Simon was not allowed to fly – though, had he been, one doubts whether anyone would have been surprised.

Cheshire never told Constance anything about his life in the RAF – any more, one suspects, than he told the RAF more than it needed to know about Constance. It was not the ideal relationship; but, for a while it seemed to work. Later she would resent what seemed to be a division of loyalty. She was almost certainly jealous, and one is bound to feel sorry for her. How can you hate an entity such as the air force as you can another woman? How can you resent your husband's devoted performance of his duties in the way that you can resent adulterous dalliance? Under these circumstances, a vice may be preferable to a virtue. Not being a woman, I can only guess at the intensity of the problem, but it does not require a psychologist to realize its existence.

His worries increased when he was moved to Marston Moor – to serve as chief instructor converting pilots to the ways of the Halifax. He found the work dull – despite two interruptions in the routine. On 30 May 1942, the Commander-in-Chief produced the great Harris spectacular: a raid in which 1,046 bombers were supposed to converge on Cologne. Nine hundred reached the target and devastated 600 acres – with a loss of only thirty-nine. Since pretty well anything that could fly was required to make up the number, Marston Moor was ordered to contribute. Cheshire took with him a crew of trainee sergeants. On the next big outing (to Essen), he was joined by the station commander. On this occasion, however, the target was obscured by low cloud and by the haze that was the constant canopy of industrial cities. It is doubtful whether more than a handful of bombs fell anywhere near the Krupp factories, which were the real objectives.

Meanwhile, the business of running the conversion unit continued without any more welcome interruptions such as the big raids over Cologne and Essen. Eventually, he was allowed to return to fulltime operations by being given command of 76 Squadron at Middleton St George (not far from Darlington). Christopher had flown with it, which was more than sufficient recommendation. Whenever he could, he accompanied his pilots – earning a Bar to his DSO in the process. These missions took place without inflicting too much unacceptable drama on himself and his crew, but something else was now troubling him. Arthur Harris, who had taken over from Peirse as C-in-C of Bomber Command, believed that the war could be won by saturation bombing – in other words, by smashing civilian morale. Cheshire – like Bennett, whom he had met on his trip to North America – was convinced that better results would be obtained by precision bombing; by hitting targets that were vital to the German war effort. To carry out such a policy with accuracy, the aircraft should fly as low as possible.

This tour of duty came to an end, and, despite his excursions over Germany, his duties as a Squadron Leader kept him on the ground for more time than he enjoyed – which was helpful in his task of assisting Constance to settle into what was an unfamiliar environment. But he disliked paperwork, and he particularly disliked the writing of letters to the next of kin of crews who had failed to make the return trip. To fill in odd moments, he wrote *Bomber Pilot*, which sold very well and was serialized in the *Sunday Graphic* (which gave him the headline treatment he enjoyed, but which some people found distasteful). He was sent back to Marston Moor as Station Commander. He had every reason to be satisfied with himself. Within three years of being permanently commissioned in the RAF, he had risen to the rank of Group Captain, had been awarded two DSOs and one DFC, received so much publicity that he had become something of a legend, and developed opinions that were listened to with respect by more senior officers. Finally, he had completed sixty operations without excessively damaging his aircraft and incurring no damage to himself.

But he was by no means happy. There were aircrew members who would have given a good deal to be absolved from the need to go on operations. The more extreme cases were labelled as 'lacking in moral fibre' and became outcasts. If other methods failed, they were demoted to AC2s (the lowest rank in the RAF) – unhappily aware that the reason for their demotions would be made clear to all and sundry. Cheshire had encountered a number of such cases when leading 76 Squadron and took what he deemed to be appropriate action. An airgunner who flinched from the fray was locked in his room until he could be removed from the station. It was, somebody said, as if Cheshire regarded it as an infectious disease that might spread to other members of the squadron. On another occasion, his treatment was more moderate. A youngster – who had, as it happened, only recently been decorated – protested that he was unable to continue. Cheshire, feeling that in this instance a display of trust might work, switched him to his own crew. It was a near thing, but the remedy was successful. On the whole, however, he was less than sympathetic to this state of mind.

He himself suffered from what might roughly be called the opposite of it. Put him in the pilot's seat, send him on some unholy mission, and he would be happy after his fashion. But leave him on the ground, burden him with paperwork, and he became fretful. At this stage in his career, such was the situation that led to further promotion, but he would gladly have dropped rank to get back into the air.

Hearing that Guy Gibson had been removed from the famous 617 (Dam Busters) squadron, he flew over to its base at Scampton to see whether there was any chance of taking it over. He was told that the vacancy had already been filled. In any case, his informant explained, the appointment would not have suited him. Six-one-seven Squadron was in 5 Group, and 5 Group was commanded by Air Vice-Marshal Sir Ralph Cochrane.

Cochrane's reputation was as a somewhat rigid figure; somebody with whom Cheshire, a flexible opportunist, would not have been compatible.

Surrounded by, as he saw it, a sea of problems, his nerves became frayed – to such an extent that he feared the approach of a breakdown. One evening at Marston Moor, he and Constance entertained to dinner a Member of Parliament who was currently serving as an Army welfare officer. Their guest brought the conversation round to the matter of nerves, and how even the most stalwart could not live on them for ever. He had obviously noted that something was wrong. Afterwards, he drew his host to one side. 'If you'll let me, I can help,' he said.

His remedy was a method of thought-control. Cheshire adopted it, but it was not sufficient. The only sure cure, he was convinced, was to get away from his present duties and back into the sky. One day he complained of feeling unwell. It was no physical ailment, he explained – something to do with his nerves. It was agreed that he should see a specialist and, in this instance, he was fortunate. Sir Charles Symonds had, in peacetime, been an eminent Harley Street neurologist. He had worked at Guy's and at the National Hospital for Nervous Diseases. The RAF had taken him over as a consultant, in which capacity he had done much to explore the causes of so-called 'flying stress' ('lack of moral fibre' was a harsher description), and to develop forms of treatment.

Cheshire, knowing the answer already, asked him whether it was true that too much flying might bring on a state of anxiety neurosis. Symonds agreed that such, indeed, was the case, and that he was constantly trying to deal with such afflictions. Then, wondered Cheshire, was it equally possible that such a complaint might be brought about by doing too *little* flying? Sir Charles said that it was an interesting idea, but he had never come across such an example.

Cheshire then stated that this omission in his medical experience had at last been made good. He was talking to just such a case.

They discussed the matter at some length, and Symonds agreed to do what he could. He proposed no course of treatment. Yes, he said, he went along with the idea that his visitor (one cannot really call him a patient) would be better employed flying. And there the conversation ended.

The base commander at Marston Moor (he was responsible for three conversion units) was a very experienced Air Commodore named John Kirby. At first sight, Kirby was rather severe in appearance, but when you got to know him better, he was a reasonable, even kindly, individual. When Cheshire had been to see him with a plea to be excused his present duties and returned to operations, his reaction was unsympathetic. However, he was not entirely unbending and he proposed a deal. If the subject was allowed to lapse for the next six months and if, after this period, Cheshire's feelings remained the same, he would do something about it.

Six months later, on the dot, Cheshire presented himself at Kirby's office. The Air Commodore had been expecting him. Much as he may have disliked the work, Cheshire had been good at his job and his name had been put down for a course at the RAF Staff College. With this behind him, there was no end to the possibilities for promotion. Cheshire protested that he was not interested in promotion. All that he wanted to do was to fly aeroplanes against the Third Reich – even if this meant demotion. Kirby nodded. He was not surprised. As it happened, the command of 617 had again come on to the market. It would mean dropping back to Wing Commander, but how about it? Cheshire was in transports of delight. He made no mention of it, but he must have wondered whether Sir Charles Symonds had been busy somewhere in the background.

In fact he and Cochrane were very much more compatible than might have been expected. Nevertheless, the latter had noticed that the new squadron commander's experience of four-engine aircraft had been confined to Halifaxes. Since 617 was equipped entirely with Lancasters, he would need to attend a conversion course. There was just such a unit not far away at Balderton. Cheshire should go there immediately.

Cheshire demurred. Surely he could pick up the technique as he went along: he wanted to get down to business and not waste time. Cochrane refused to budge. The course it had to be, or else . . . In the end, Cheshire was grateful for his attitude. He fell in love with the Lancaster immediately, but he had to acknowledge that it had its own little ways, and that it took time to become accustomed to them. In fact, it took him three days, which was quick. But, then, he had a remarkable aptitude and he crammed in as much flying time as his instructor would permit.

The members of 617 Squadron were all volunteers: men who had seen a great deal of action and some of whom felt that there could never be another Guy Gibson. At first they watched their new squadron commander with some suspicion. Despite the medal ribbons that decorated his chest, he was clearly not another Gibson. Nor did the amount of publicity he had received reflect credit upon him. He was, they suspected, an egoist with a mighty good opinion of himself.

It took him one evening in the mess to demolish any such ideas, and his popularity with the ground crews was equally quickly aroused. Here, they decided, was an officer who was not governed by the drill book: someone with a sensible idea of priorities with whom it would be a pleasure to work.

Harris had, in the summer of 1943, decided to reserve 617 for what he described as 'special duties'. Bennett, with his Pathfinders, would, or so Bennett thought, be able to assist any unit on such missions. He was not entirely correct. Even if one disregards the fact that the degree of proficiency varied from one aircrew to another, there were certain generalities that could not be disregarded. Navigational aids had become greatly improved by 'Oboe' and 'H2S', but they had not achieved perfection. A great deal of thought had been applied to the production of target markers, but nothing could overcome the effect of high wind. You might release one in precisely the right place, but there was no guarantee that it would stay there. As some people saw it, if precision was required, there was little point at operating from, say, 20,000 feet. The only way was to get as close to the ground as possible: to see the objective and to do whatever was appropriate under the circumstances. This school of thought had been strengthened by the production of a new bomb sight. It was more accurate and was calculated to simplify the work of the pilot, the navigator, and the bomb aimer.

Hitler had a good deal of faith in his 'secret weapons': pilotless rockets that would reduce London to rubble. They were the V1 (which you could see coming), the V2 (which you could not see coming), and the V3 (which never came. Sometimes referred to as the 'high pressure pump', it was a kind of multi-chambered gun with a range of 175 miles. One or two rounds were fired during the Ardennes battle of December 1944. There is no record of their results, and the project was abandoned).

Before Cheshire joined 617 Squadron, it had been busy over

Peenemünde – the place on the Baltic shore where, with assistance from slave labour, these devices were designed and manufactured. According to one estimate, the operation set the production of the V2 rocket back by six months. Nevertheless, launching sites were being established in the Pas de Calais. Situated in thickly wooded country between Abbeville and Amiens, they were difficult to see.

The squadron had moved to Woodhall Spa, Lincolnshire. It was a pleasant enough place: the snag was that the officers' quarters were three miles from the airfield. By mid-January, Cochrane had agreed that 617 could go it alone without assistance from Pathfinders. This amounted to accepting Cheshire's convictions about low-level attacks – though the Air Vice Marshal stipulated 5,000 feet as the minimum altitude. In mid-January, they made two raids on the rocket launchers (they called them 'ski-sites'), and the photographs revealed very satisfactory performances. The results were, indeed, better than anything the squadron had accomplished with Pathfinder help.

An aero-engine factory at Limoges was next on the list. One of the employees had left the lights on, which helped. The idea was to do the maximum amount of damage to the plant; the minimum to the workers. Coming down to fifty feet above the rooftops (Cochrane would have been appalled), Cheshire made two swoops before being satisfied that the night shift had removed itself to a place of comparative safety. Then the Lancasters released their explosive hardware. All but one of the bombs fell smack on target. On this occasion, he took with him a member of the RAF Film Unit, an ex-operational pilot named Pat Moyna. Having told the other pilots that they could go home, Cheshire lingered over the badly mauled factory to let Moyna take his pictures. When he saw them even Harris was impressed. 'The very severe damage caused by so small a number of aircraft is most remarkable,' he observed.

One of the key features in the supply line on which Kesselring depended for his attempts to prize the Allied forces loose from their beach-head at Anzio was a railway viaduct at Antheor (between Marseilles and Genoa.) It was pushing the limits of a Lancaster's range too far. The night was pitch dark, and there was a great deal more anti-aircraft opposition than anyone had expected. Cheshire and that great exponent of low-level flying, 'Micky' Martin, arrived over the target five minutes before the rest to mark it. After three runs had been unsuccessful, Martin thought he saw an opportunity. Just as his bomb-aimer was about to release the marker, a 20-mm cannon shell hit the aircraft and killed him. This was the cue for every gun down below to open up. Martin was lucky to get away with his Lancaster and his life. After that, it was sheer, undiluted hell. Although no aircraft were lost, the result was not calculated to bring a happy smile to the collective face of 617 Squadron (nor to that of Cochrane, come to that). One 12,000-lb bomb fell reasonably close to the target. The others were very wide of the mark. Cheshire attributed the failure to inaccurate information about the enemy defences, and to the fact that insufficient petrol could be carried to satisfy the Lancasters' thirst.

During the first three weeks of March 1944, the Squadron fared rather better. Cheshire's briefs gave him more latitude which was just what operations of this kind needed. In another raid on an aero-engine factory, this time at Albert in North France, the auspices could hardly have been worse. The new bomb sight failed. During the delay occasioned by this, the marking flares began to go out and the target area had to be relit. Despite all this, however, every bomb landed in the right place. The plant's machine tool section was so badly hit that it was never used again. The output of the engine building department was reduced by nine-tenths. During the following week, on 10 March, the only bearings factory of its kind in France was attacked. The visibility was atrocious, and it required seven approaches to find it. And, even then, it needed several attempts before the aircraft got anywhere near the mark. On the flight back, the Squadron was despondent. It seemed to have been the waste of a clutch of perfectly good bombs.

But, when the photographs were developed, it transpired that 80 per cent of the bomb-loads had landed on target. A raid on the Michelin tyre factory, mounted on 16 March, was a very model of precision. About the only building untouched was the workers' canteen, and this was deliberate. Politically, the slaughter of French civilians would have done the cause no good at all. An explosives plant was literally exploded on 18 March. Soon afterwards, and after two false starts, an aircraft works at Lyons was put out of business.

Sometime earlier, Cheshire had been to see the guru of low-level tactics, Group Captain Charles Pickard. He found the conversation useful and was delighted when Pickard took him up in a Mk VI Mosquito. This, he felt sure, was exactly what the Squadron needed, and he applied whatever moments he could spare to acquiring it. His early attempts failed. The aircraft, they told him, was in short supply and there were none to spare for the likes of 617 Squadron. On the other hand, a visit to a friend at the Air Ministry assured him that, in fact, there were plenty available. He kept on lobbying until, after these March successes, he was informed by Cochrane that he could have two on loan for a month. There was no time for conversion courses: he just climbed into one and flew it as if it were the natural thing to do (which begs the question of Guy Gibson's last mission. It has been suggested that, had he gone to be tutored in the ways of the Mosquito, he might have come back alive. On Cheshire's evidence, this seems to be rubbish).

Cheshire once described the men of 617 Squadron as 'the toughest-looking bunch of fliers I ever faced in my life.' His personality was certainly not that of Gibson. He was quieter, more sensitive, more given to introspection. But his style of leadership prevailed. As a member of the ground crew put it, 'I'm not exactly a glutton for work, but I don't think I've ever worked harder in my life than I worked for Cheshire. And I can't remember a happier period in the service.'

The day was coming when Normandy would be invaded, and there were certain essential preliminaries. One of them was the disruption of the French railway system to prevent German reinforcements being rushed to the area. A prerequisite was, of course, that such disruption should provide no clue as to where that area would be. The venture was called TRANSPORTATION PLAN and, as it happened, there was no need to go anywhere near Normandy to carry it out. If marshalling yards in Belgium, in Paris, and along the Seine, could be hit, the effect would be more than adequate. Six-one-seven Squadron was ordered to act as a spearhead for two mass attacks on yards in the region of the French capital. Two hundred Lancasters from 5 Group were employed, and Cheshire was allowed two more Mosquitos. Both raids were carried out impeccably and inflicted little damage to houses in the vicinity.

Meanwhile, as mentioned elsewhere, a device named 'Window' had been produced to mislead enemy radar by the scattering of tinfoil. Immediately after D-day, it was used for what might be described as a double-bluff. Masses of the stuff was offloaded by 617 to mislead the German radar operators at Cap d'Antifer. The idea was to make them think that a convoy was crossing the north-west part of the Channel to somewhere north of the Normandy beaches. It was carried out in bright moonlight at a height of only 3,000 feet. One pilot's comment (a New Zealander named David Shannon, who ended the war with a DSO and two Bars, a DFC and one Bar), was 'Successful, but bloody browned off.'

There was still work to be done on the railways. A tunnel near Saumur seemed to be in need of attention – to block the passage of reinforcements from south-west France. Tunnels were apt to pose problems, but nothing, it seemed, was beyond the scope of Barnes Wallis's 'Tallboy' bombs – such as were later used to destroy the German battleship *Tirpitz*. They were also known as 'earthquake bombs', for that was what they simulated. Enormous craters were created; the tunnel's roof fell in; and the flow of German troop trains was stopped. Two raids on E-boat (the German version of the motor-torpedoboat) pens at Le Havre and Boulogne followed. Again 'Tallboys' were used: in the case of the Boulogne affair, the number of fatally damaged craft added up to nearly 100. Cheshire, who dived towards the target through a curtain of heavy flak, may have considered himself fortunate to have survived. The damage done to his aircraft was considerable.

Despite the early, rather parsimonious, attitude of the authorities towards supplying 617 Squadron with Mosquitos, these remarkable aircraft were exactly what were needed to mark the targets. There was only one problem: range. They had been designed to fly at high altitudes, where fuel consumption is least. Cheshire wanted them for low altitude operations. A member of the de Havilland family (their manufacturers) came to 617's base to discuss matters.

The immediate project was a trip to Toulouse to attack a factory that repaired airframes. De Havilland insisted that the project was possible, but only just – and then only if the aeroplanes were fitted with long-range tanks. The raid was eminently successful, assisted as it was by bright moonlight. It was just as well. Flying on such a low margin of fuel, there was no time to mess about.

Harris was obviously taking an interest in his 'special duties' squadron. On one occasion, Cheshire was invited to dinner at the Commander-in-Chief's home. They discussed the possibility of attacks on targets inside Germany. Had Cheshire, Harris asked, any preference? His guest replied without any hesitation: Munich. It was pushing things so far as this question of range was concerned, but Harris agreed. But he made sure to emphasize that it had been Cheshire's idea – not his.

According to Boyle, 'Cheshire still believes that the Munich attack was his greatest single triumph of the war.' Ninety per cent of the bombs exploded where the planners had intended. It has been suggested that, in this single night, 617 Squadron did more damage than Bomber Command and the American Air Force had achieved in four years. Cochrane was more sceptical. Yes: it had been a triumph, but, afterwards, other squadrons were even more successful. Nevertheless, he conceded, it had been Cheshire who had devised the low-level marking technique – he who had led the way.

One day in August of that year, Leonard Cheshire was summoned to Bomber Command Headquarters to see Harris. He searched his mind for any possible misdeed that might have incurred the inclined-to-be-testy C-in-C's displeasure. He couldn't think of any; nor need he have worried. The object of the interview was to tell him that he had been awarded the Victoria Cross. The tidings seemed to come as something of a shock to him, but this was typical. As Harris said, 'I have never known any recipient of the Victoria Cross not to be astonished at the news of the award – but I have sometimes met others astonished that they had not been awarded the Victoria Cross.'

In one respect, Cheshire's award of the VC was unique. Twenty-two members of Bomber Command received it – 13, alas, posthumously. In all but one case, it was a reward for a specific operation. The exception was Cheshire, whose achievements were described as 'various'. They included his service with 4 Group.

He had now completed more than 100 operations, and the strain was beginning to show. Cochrane insisted that he should resume his rank as Group Captain and move to a staff job in the Far East. Harris was in full agreement: much as Cheshire disliked the idea, there could be no appeal. Constance was to return to the United States. Her husband was to set off for Calcutta in a Sunderland. The journey would take a week.

The appointment in the Far East did not last long. Constance, having arrived in New York, had succumbed to a serious nervous breakdown. The doctors said that it was essential that Leonard should be with her. He was given immediate leave. After her recovery, he was appointed to the British Joint Staff Mission in Washington.

When two people who have very little in common get married, the outlook is not good. In the weeks that followed her breakdown, it became more and more clear that the Leonard/ Constance relationship no longer had any meaning. They simply did not relate, and the result was emptiness. The only sensible thing was to recognize the situation and to seek a divorce.*

The war against Germany was over; the war against Japan was approaching its conclusion. Whether it would have ended any more quickly if the atomic bombs had not been dropped on Hiroshima and Nagasaki has been a matter for endless debate. It is not the province of this book to examine it. In the third week of July 1945, Cheshire was sent for by Field Marshal Lord Wilson, head of the British Joint Staff Mission in Washington. Wilson had attended the summit conference at Potsdam, where the leaders had agreed that Japan should be the target for this latest and most terrible of weapons. The Americans had consented, not without argument, that a British scientist and a member of the RAF should be present on one of the raids. Sir William Penney had been chosen to occupy the former slot; Cheshire was to represent the RAF.

And so they came to the island of Tinian, where their immediate admiration of the American preparations was replaced by frustration when, contrary to the agreement, they were refused permission to fly. After many protests, and climbing ever higher up the ladder of command, the most they could achieve was the promise of the official reports once the operations had taken place. As a last resort, they decided to appeal to the Joint Staff Mission in Washington. The attack on Hiroshima duly took place. In the meanwhile Wilson had obviously been busy and, at last, word came from Washington that Cheshire and Penney could fly as observers on the Nagasaki raid.

At some point, the pilot of the Superfortress lost touch with the two leading aircraft in the formation, and assumed that something had happened to them. He was inclined to turn back, but Cheshire managed to discourage him. As he pointed out, they

*In 1959, he married Sue Ryder – later Baroness Ryder of Warsaw. Her work, dedicated to the dead of two wars, was not dissimilar to his during the post-war years.

were 20,000 feet higher than they should have been according to the briefing. When they were forty miles from Nagasaki, they saw a flash followed by the mushroom-shaped cloud. They spent an hour circling the scene of devastation. Cheshire made innumerable sketches of what he thought was happening – sketches that turned out to be remarkably accurate. Then they turned for home. They landed on Tinian at 6.00 in the afternoon of that 9th day of August 1945. They were all of them in a state of severe emotional shock; none of them could sleep and they argued about the effects of this monstrous weapon upon the new age that was about to begin. But Cheshire never had any doubts about the rightness of the action. The bombing of Hiroshima and Nagasaki had brought the war to an end. When he returned to England, he said as much to Clement Attlee, who had succeeded Churchill as Prime Minister. So far as Cheshire was concerned, the time had come to leave the RAF. He thought a career in scientific research might be a good thing.

But this was also the beginning of a new age – a new life, indeed, for Leonard Cheshire. The story of the Cheshire homes is beyond the scope of this book – as is that of his conversion to Christianity. It may be a pity, but these are tales of war; of experiences that, one devoutly hopes, will not be repeated. As Cheshire wrote at the end of his book *The Hidden World*:

> We need a vision, a dream.
> The vision should be the oneness, the essential and organic solidarity of the human family. The dream, that we each in our own way make our personal contribution towards building unity and peace among us.
> The only question is how?

Leonard Cheshire found an answer. Few of us are so fortunate. It was St Paul, not Richard Hillary, who defined death as the last enemy. But, before it strikes, there are others that have nothing to do with warfare, but which are no less awful. The achievement of Cheshire Homes, now to be found throughout the world, has been to mitigate their horrors by giving comfort to the suffering.

8

Adolf Galland
VIEW FROM THE
OTHER SIDE

Although he shot down 109 Allied aircraft (or thereabouts), Adolf Galland was not Germany's top-scoring fighter pilot in the Second World War. Who, after all, could compete with Erich Hartmann's 300*, or Heinz Bär's supposed 220? On the other hand, Galland was able to spend less time in what we might, perhaps, call the hunting field. With his talent for administration and innovation, and his charismatic personality, he was a natural commander. At the age of thirty, he was promoted to general major. Thereby he became the youngest German to achieve such rank. He received just about every award there was to be won; and, from time to time, he listened to the confidences of his supreme commander, Göring – and, indeed, to those of Hitler.

His friend and rival was that other ace, Werner Mölders: outwardly a more serious man, tight-lipped, and quieter. Galland, with his black moustache and high spirits, was more of a latterday buccaneer. On a routine journey from A to B in France, he might suddenly divert across the Dover Strait and bag a Spitfire for, so to speak, the pot. Mölders earned respect and, to some extent, affection. Galland was the stuff of legend. To take only one instance, he was a compulsive smoker of black cigars. Such was his passion for the weed that a special tray was installed in the cockpit of his aircraft. It contained all that the airborne cigar smoker needed, and the story goes that he used to puff away until he found it necessary to don his oxygen mask. Nowadays, it would probably be deplored by the vociferous anti-smoking lobby. In those days, it was the kind of eccentricity that got a chap talked about.

*An approximation. German claims tended to be greatly exaggerated.

Adolf Galland was born in March 1913. His family was descended from Huguenot stock. For the past 200 years, Gallands had served an important land-owning family. In his youth, his father was employed by this enclave of noblemen as bailiff. As he began to grow up, young Adolf (later, and more affectionately, known as 'Dolfo') decided he wanted to become a pilot. When he told his father, that gentleman was less than enthusiastic. The punitive terms of the Treaty of Versailles, which had cut back the German army and navy to mere shadows, had done away with the air force completely. Civil aviation was still more or less in its infancy. In short, the prospects for a budding aviator seemed to be very limited.

Like most problems, there were ways around it. A great many gliding clubs were established throughout Germany, and nobody could grumble about this seemingly innocent form of sport. There were ploys by which an aspiring warplane flier could be trained in Russia – and, with Mussolini and his Fascists in power, in Italy. There was also a flying school at Brunswick, where Lufthansa instructed its civil pilots.

During the latter part of his schooling, Adolf Galland took up gliding with an enthusiasm that stopped only marginally short of obsessive. There was no gainsaying his talent: one day he raised the endurance record for north-west Germany from forty-seven minutes to two hours, six minutes and five seconds. But Galland thought big. He was proud of his achievement, but one ambition was replaced by another. He determined to found his own club.

When he left school, there was the matter of getting into the flying school at Brunswick. Nobody pretended it was going to be easy. At a rough count, there were about 4,000 applicants competing for twenty places. To hedge his bets, he applied for an officer cadetship in the 18th Infantry Regiment, which was stationed at Paderborn.

The army accepted him and so, despite the intense competition, did the flying school. By a coincidence, both notifications arrived on the same day in the autumn of 1932. He immediately cancelled his request to join the infantry – which seems to have been received without protest – and made preparations for his departure for Brunswick. It was, of course, only a beginning. To be invited to join the course was one thing; to survive the very stiff curriculum was another. Many young hopefuls had been thrown out for failing to reach the required standards. Only a fool or an uncommonly self-confident student would consider his foothold in aviation as secure. Galland was neither. He worried a good deal; he worked extremely hard; and, as his gliding experience may have suggested, he was a natural pilot. He survived.

From Brunswick, he was sent to a school specializing in aerobatics – and, thence, to Warnemünde on the Baltic coast for flying-boat training. He enjoyed the former; was less enthusiastic about the latter. He found the instruction in seamanship rather dull. But flying-boats were not his *métier*. As he must already have realized, if fate had singled him out for one particular occupation, it was to fly fighters. He had named his record-breaking glider *The Vagabond*, which tells us something about him. The more he could roam the sky in search of prey, the better he liked it. He was, above all things, an individualist.

The plans to re-create an air force were continuing – though still clandestinely. You could learn to fly an aeroplane in Germany, but you could not receive any combat training. For this, in Galland's case, you had to go to Italy. Getting there was the problem. Parties of apparently innocent young German civilian males arriving at Italian air bases might have aroused suspicion in the minds of observers less than enthusiastic about the German-Italian link. Consequently, he and his companions were fitted out in the uniform of a Tyrolean mountain regiment, supposed to be carrying out manoeuvres in the Alps. Once across the frontier, they were given Italian air force uniforms and sent to an aerodrome down in the south – roughly between Taranto and Brindisi. Much to their disgust, they were treated as novices. As a protest, Galland took a training biplane into the sky and broke some sort of record by flying upside down for forty minutes. He seems to have made his point. Thereafter, they were tutored in combat flying, reliving the aeronautical manoeuvres of 1914–18 but with none of the dangers.

In the autumn of 1933, Galland returned to Brunswick where he was attached to Lufthansa. Twice a week he flew a Junkers airliner from Stuttgart, via Geneva and Marseille, to Barcelona – and twice a week, he flew back again.

January 1933, you'll probably recall, was the month in which Hitler became Chancellor. He made no bones about his determination to tear up the document that had resulted from the musings of the Allied statesmen at Versailles. Nor did he do anything to conceal his intention to re-arm Germany. The emerging *Luftwaffe* was taken out of its hiding places; the armourers contentedly prepared to thrive. Among them were Messrs Messerschmitt, Dornier, Junker and Heinkel.

At the beginning of 1934, Galland and many of his friends were asked, 'Do you want to be on the active list?' – which was to question whether they wanted to stay with civil aviation or to turn their talents to something more bloodthirsty. If they wished to take the latter route, a spot of military training was necessary. It was carried out in the 10th Infantry Regiment stationed at Dresden. The aviators became known as 'The Sports Gang'; their NCOs took a tolerant view of their lack of conformity. The experience, even if it seemed to be a waste of time, was not unpleasant. It helped to pass the days until, in April 1935, the *Luftwaffe* unwrapped itself – armed with Heinkel 51s, a new biplane of which a tolerably good performance was expected. Galland, now commissioned as a Second Lieutenant, was posted to the 1st Wing of the Richthofen Fighter Group II, which was stationed on an only partially completed aerodrome near Berlin. He spent many hours performing low-altitude aerobatics for flying displays and competitions. His enthusiasm very nearly put an end to his ambitions, for he had a habit of cutting things a little too fine.

His first crash occurred in October 1935, when, trying to pull out of a series of three tight rolls, he misjudged his altitude by 300 feet. The aircraft was sluggish in its response. Had he been where he thought he was, he might have got away with it. As things were, he plunged to earth and ended up with his head stuck in the instrument panel. The surgeons performed something not far short of a miracle. Nevertheless, they were unable to mend his left eye, which had been severely weakened by cuts and splinters. He was considered fortunate to have survived; but the rejoicing was somewhat marred by the doctor's verdict: 'Unfit for flying'. Still, if you play your cards right, there are ways around most tribulations. His commanding officer was a sympathetic gentleman who clearly disagreed with the medical opinion. The piece of paper that sentenced him to life on earth without the stimulant of life in the sky disappeared. Galland was able to climb back into the cockpit.

About a year later, he was on leave beside the Baltic, when somebody invited him to make a test flight in an Arado Ar 68 – a shortlived biplane that was under consideration as a front-line fighter. Coming in to land, the sun caught his eyes, the engine misfired, and he crashed into a light intended to warn pilots of another obstacle (a line of fruit trees on the edge of the aerodrome). The aircraft was a write-off and so, or thus it appeared, was Galland. But this underrated his remarkable powers of recovery. It also brought to the authorities' attention the 'unfit for flying' verdict. When he came out of hospital, he protested that he was perfectly well – that his left eye had recovered and that there was nothing he could not do as well as anyone else – possibly, better.

He was told that a medical exam would decide the matter. The doctors did their best to fault his body, but everything turned out to be in excellent working order. The difficult bit concerned that inadequate left eye. Despite his assertions, it was not as effective as it should have been. With his right eye covered over, he was instructed to go through the rigmarole of reading letters and numbers on a chart. Somewhat to the medical officer's surprise, he accomplished it without any apparent difficulty. But this was not the end of the matter. He was now told to go through the sequence in the reverse order. Again, he rattled it off without hesitation. What the medic did not know was that, some weeks beforehand, a friend had informed him of the sequence. Very sensibly, he had memorized it backwards as well as forwards.

The Spanish Civil War, which erupted in July 1936, provided the Germans, the Italians, and the Russians with a killing ground in which to try out their war machines. Germany raised the German Volunteer Corps in Spain – otherwise known as the Condor Legion. Applications for membership were invited: aspiring adventurers had to get in touch with an organization known as Special Branch W, which had its office in Berlin. Galland was one of those who sent in his name – and one of those who was accepted. He was given a set of civilian clothes and, with a good many others, directed to a run-down merchantman of 3,000 tons. She was berthed at Hamburg, flew the flag of Panama, and was supposed to be going on a cruise to Genoa.

It did not require a very astute eye to see that this was no cruise ship. Previously, her owners had been involved in gun-running. The accommodation was in her holds, the food was vile, and the weather did its best to emphasize the wretched vessel's short-comings. After a ghastly voyage lasting the better part of two weeks, she came alongside the quay at El Ferrol on the north-western corner of Spain.

Looking back on this most unhappy period of Spanish history, it is tempting to visualize the Loyalist forces as a band of peasants reinforced by idealistic and not very practical intellectuals. This is nonsense. The war did, after all, drag on for nearly three years. Indeed, Franco would have fared a lot less well if a fleet of German Ju–52 transport aircraft had not ferried troops to the pint-pot Fascist dictator-in-the-making from bases in North Africa. Two squadrons of the Condor Legion were equipped with Me–109 fighters. Galland's was not: it had to depend on the old He–51 biplane, which was no match for the Russian and American aircraft flown by the opposition. Consequently, the pilots were discouraged from provoking the so-called 'Reds' in aerial combat. Their role was to support the troops on the ground.

On arrival, Galland was instructed to take charge of maintenance. He was given the uniform of a Spanish officer and a rank one stage above that which he occupied in the *Luftwaffe*. He was now *Captain* Galland and eventually given command of Micky Mouse Squadron (the two with the Me-109s were known as 'Maribou' and 'Top Hat').

To begin with, he was stationed at a town named Vitoria in northern Spain with the object of supporting Franco's spring offensive of 1937. His first assignment was to silence the enemy's anti-aircraft batteries – thereby allowing the bombers to fly by without let or hindrance. The squadron's aircraft, flying with their namesake portrayed on their fuselages, were badly shot up, but the mission could be accounted a success. He may very well, indirectly at any rate, have helped to make possible the destruction of Guernica. But Galland argues fiercely in defence of this notorious raid. He protests that Guernica was not, as the press claimed, an open town. It was bombed, he insists, by mistake; and, in any case, there were masses of Guernicas in the Second World War. It was the sort of thing that was apt to happen in modern warfare – though, if we are to believe him, 'We did not like discussing it.'

A Condor pilot's tour of duty in Spain normally added up to six months – sometimes ten. Galland spent fifteen months there, carrying out more than 300 sorties in his old H51 – an aircraft for which he conceived an affection that was unashamedly sentimental. It should have been shot to blazes on many occasions. Every time, it delivered him back safely to earth, battered almost beyond repair, but always repairable. Some days they went up as many as seven times, always in support of the troops on the ground: aggressive, punishing an enemy that Galland never made the mistake of underrating.

He and the rest of the volunteers mostly lived on a train – a sort of camp on wheels. The life was free-and-easy and he enjoyed it. However, there had to be an end to it. Hitler was preparing to invade Czechoslovakia, and pilots of his experience were needed back in Germany. Three officers were sent out to replace him. The first was judged to be unsuitable. The second made the fatal mistake of colliding with another aircraft in mid-air. The third was faultless: his name was Werner Mölders. Shortly after Mölders took over the squadron, it was re-equipped with Me–109s. Its role was no longer confined to shooting up soldiers on the ground. It could engage the enemy in aerial combat, and its new commander thus engaged it. He became the top-scoring pilot of all the Germans who flew for Franco. But that was Mölders all over. He was apt to come top.

Reading through Galland's book, *The First and the Last*, one has the impression of a man who was politically naive. But so were a lot of Germans: how else could Hitler have won power and devotion? The truth, of course, is that he was simply an air force officer doing his job: a pilot fighting for his country which happened to be Germany, and trying to do it as best he could. He had strong views on the type of aircraft that should be used, and on how they should be used. One doubts whether he gave much thought to the matter of Nazism, or any other 'ism' come to that.

On his return to Germany, he was posted to the Air Ministry. He disliked it intensely: a pilot's job, he not unreasonably believed, was to fly an aeroplane and not to be pegged down behind a desk. In any case, air support against the Czechs was neither necessary nor possible. There was no opposition and the weather put an embargo on flying. Poland was another matter. The bulk of the Polish Air Force was destroyed on the ground during the first day of the invasion. But there was still the task of affording ground support. The Stuka dive-bombers were apt to crash in bad weather: fighters were more reliable. And this was how Galland had come to envisage the fighter's role – as a weapon of attack.

He was thankfully released from his chores at the Air Ministry and put back to where he belonged – in a cockpit. Among his early targets were the Polish staff headquarters and its adjoining infantry barracks. During twenty-seven days, his unit flew about fifty sorties with the loss of ten aircraft. On one occasion, Hitler came to visit them at their base to the south of Warsaw. He held court in a field kitchen, listening to their reports and enthusing about how well everything was going. By the end of the campaign, Galland had received the Iron Cross 2nd Class and had been promoted to the rank of captain (*Luftwaffe* version). That October, he was sent to Brunswick for a rest. The idea, it appears, was to train with paratroops. But this interlude did not last for very long. He was soon transferred to the 27th Fighter Group stationed at Kreffeld.

It seems probable that the *Blitzkrieg* against the Low Countries and France might have taken place earlier had not a *Luftwaffe* major been blown off course. He had been assigned to take the plan of operations from Münster to Bonn. Somewhere along the route, the weather turned nasty and the upshot was that he had to make a forced landing in Belgium. He was captured before he had time to destroy the aircraft or, more importantly, the document. Thus the proposed offensive became common knowledge and they had to begin all over again.

Galland was now in a position of some responsibility. 'Responsibility', in this instance, means administration. There were so many things to be done on the ground that he had to sneak off into the sky rather as a schoolboy may play truant. Nevertheless, on 12 May 1940, three days after the campaign had begun, he scored his first victory. He describes it as 'child's play'. It took place five miles to the west of Liege. He and another pilot were flying at 12,000 feet when they spotted eight Belgian fighters 3,000 feet beneath them. The Belgians seemed unaware of their presence; for Galland and his friend, it was all too easy. They had practised the routine on innumerable occasions: the dive, the short burst of fire, the readiness for a second attack, and so on. It was not until the two Me–109s had swooped to conquer, that the Belgian pilots did anything that might be calculated to avert the forthcoming disaster. When the first victim was brought down by Galland's companion, the other seven scattered – not very competently. Galland shot down a second, and then a third. The rest managed to escape. That afternoon, he made another kill. 'An excellent weapon and luck had been on my side,' he wrote. 'To be successful, the best fighter pilot needs both.' Surprisingly, he experienced no elation over what had to be considered a very satisfactory day – rather, a feeling of impatience at the Belgian pilots' inability to defend themselves. He might have described it as 'unprofessional'.

His introduction to the RAF took place over Dunkirk, where he accounted for his first Spitfire and a brace of Blenheim bombers. The second was shot down at such short range that when he landed at the airfield close to St Pol he found that his Me–109 was covered with oil. On another occasion, he was engaged in so close a combat with a French Morane-Saulnier fighter, that he damaged his airscrew, his under-carriage, and lost his aerial by hitting his victim's wing. Despite the damage, his Messerschmitt was still in good enough health to dispatch another. He did not actually see it crash: had he done so, it would have brought his official score up to thirteen. On 18 July 1940 he was promoted to major. Three weeks later, having destroyed seventeen enemy aircraft, Kesselring (then C-in-C of *Luftwaffe* operations in Western Europe) invested him with the Knight's Cross. The ceremony was carried out at Cap Gris Nez. During it, two Spitfires flew over as a considerable height. The Field-Marshal made some joke about the RAF being the first to congratulate him. Galland dutifully laughed.

With France defeated, and Britain clearly in no mood to make peace, Germany had three objectives. The first was to blockade the UK with the *Luftwaffe* working in co-operation with the German navy. The second was to achieve air supremacy as an essential preliminary to the invasion of Britain. The third was to defeat Britain by all-out aerial warfare. As Galland points out, they were more easily defined than executed. For one thing, according to his calculations, Germany had 2,500 warplanes available against 3,600 at the disposal of the RAF. For another, the Battle of Britain involved an area occupying only one-tenth of the United Kingdom. Beyond its limits, aircraft could be built and pilots trained without unwelcome interruptions. Furthermore, for no sensible reason, Hitler and the German General Staff had put a stop to all further research and development unless a project was able to produce military results within four months of its conception. Not the least of its effects was to delay the production of the Me–262 – a jet fighter that, had it been ready in time, could very well have changed the balance of power in the air and, possibly, the course of the war.

On 24 July 1940 the 3rd JG 26 was established near Guines

and Galland was given command of it. This was a group comprising about thirty aircraft. The appointment should have given him considerable satisfaction, but, as a fighter pilot pure and simple, he was well aware that there was at least one man he had to beat. His rival was 'Vati' Mölders, the officer who had taken over from him in Spain. He liked Mölders; he revered him; but in the competition between the two, no holds were barred. Once, when Göring had occasion to discuss matters with the two separately, the Reichsmarschall gave his word that he would not detain one a minute longer than he would detain the other. Each wanted to be back in the sky adding to his seemingly ever-increasing score.

One of Galland's earlier missions in the Battle of Britain was to escort a squadron of Stukas on a raid to the airfield at Detling in Kent. The bombs fell at 5.00 in the afternoon – when the mess halls were filled to capacity. As a result, sixty-seven members of the RAF were killed. Twenty-two aircraft were destroyed on the ground – and all at no cost to the Ju–87 bombers. This was no mean achievement. In Poland and in France the Ju–87, by plunging from the sky, had brought terror. But it was unsatisfactory in bad weather, and, against the more formidable RAF fighters, an easy prey. To take X number to a target, and to bring X number back, was a considerable feat. On paper, then, it all looked very satisfactory. In reality, however, Detling was not part of Fighter Command. To those who knew, it was a somewhat hollow victory.

The *Luftwaffe* headquarters at Cap Gris Nez was known as 'The Holy Mountain'. From time to time, Göring used to visit it in his luxurious train code-named *Asia* (its amenities even included bathrooms and wagons to carry any 'shopping' he might collect on his journeys.) On one of these occasions, he asked Mölders and Galland what they would most like. Mölders replied that he would be pleased if the Me–109s could be fitted with more powerful engines. Galland answered, 'I should like an outfit of Spitfires for my group.' He always protested that he had made the observation as a kind of joke. If this were so, the Reichsmarschall failed to see it. He stomped off in a huff.

In fact, Galland considered that the Me–109 compared very well with the Spitfire. It was more powerful, though it did have two shortcomings. The Spitfire had stronger wings, which meant that after a steep dive it could pull out and begin to climb more sharply. The Me–109 also suffered – in the early days, at any rate – from the limits imposed by its fuel capacity. The Spitfires and Hurricanes were fighting over their home ground, so this was the least of their pilots' worries. The Me–109s had to get there and, hopefully, to return. On one operation, Galland recalls, twelve of the fighters were lost simply because they ran out of petrol. Five of them made pancake landings in France; seven came down in the Channel. Each remained afloat for about one minute, which was little enough time. Nevertheless, most of their occupants were brought safely ashore by air-sea rescue launches.

Galland's relationship with Göring seems to have been somewhat ambivalent. For example, the Reichsmarschall, who had a liking for self-decoration, had the idea of creating what he called 'The Gold Fighter Medal'. There were two recipients: Galland and Mölders. It was presented to them on the occasion of their promotions to group commanders (something that Galland regretted: he felt that, as a more humble wing commander, he'd be able to spend more time in the sky). The ceremony took place at a conference at Göring's Karinhall residence. Under these circumstances it should have been a pleasant affair. But Göring was already aware that winning the Battle of Britain was not going to be the push-over he had expected. Having made the awards, he accused the fighter arm of lack of aggression. He insisted that the bomber crews should be able to see their guardians at all times – meaning that they should fly in close formation. The two arms of the service, he insisted, should get to know each other, working, ideally, as teams. This was entirely contrary to Galland's concept of fighter tactics. He believed that any such pilot should be a free-ranging opportunist, and not hobbled to some sacred cow of a bomber. But then, he reflected, the High Command seemed to be obsessed with the priority of bombers. As he put it, 'We felt like the Cinderellas of the German *Luftwaffe*, and that is what we were.'

It might have been better if this obsession had been supported by the right types of aircraft. The only thing the *Luftwaffe* even had to match, say, the Lancaster was the He–177. But this has been described as 'possibly the most troublesome and unsatisfactory aircraft in military history' (Bill Gunston in *Combat Aircraft*). In any case, it arrived too late in the day – even if it had been a better performer.

Sometimes it seemed as if the aircraft manufacturers were uncertain about what they had produced – or the High Command unsure of how to use it. The Me–110 was intended to make good some of the Me–109s shortcomings – notably that of range. It looked like a bomber. It could be used as a bomber: indeed, in the Polish campaign and during the *Blitzkrieg* in France, it had performed satisfactorily in a ground-support role. But, as a fighter, it was a disaster. Its manoeuvrability in no way equalled that of the Spitfire or the Hurricane. The result was that the supposed escort had to be escorted – by the very Me–109s to which it was supposed to be superior.

The Iron Cross was an award for valour with a history dating back to Frederick the Great. During the Second World War, they kept on coming up with additions for which there was a kind of tariff. For instance, there was the Iron Cross with oakleaves, which was awarded to any fighter pilot with a score of forty kills to his credit. Galland received his after a sortie over the Thames Estuary. Mölders (the competition was still flourishing) had been awarded it three days earlier. It was the highest military award on offer – if one discounts the Grand Cross that was available only to Göring who, needless to say, helped himself to it.

Galland travelled to Berlin for the investiture, which was made by Hitler in the Reichs Chancellery. They spent some time together. Galland, never afraid to speak his mind, criticized the attitude of the German press and radio to the RAF. 'I expressed my great admiration for our enemy across the water,' he recalled. He had expected contradiction, or even an explosion of anger. Instead, the Führer agreed with him. He had, he said rather sadly, a sympathy – even, admiration – for the British. The tragedy was that he had tried to bring the German and English people together. In this, he had failed. Claptrap or not, Galland was impressed.

Later, when they produced an even more supreme award (diamonds – he and Mölders were the only two to receive it), the situation degenerated into comedy. Hitler presented Galland with it. Immediately afterwards, Göring summoned him to a conference. Nothing was said that might advance the conduct of the war: the Reichsmarschall's only concern seemed to be this new decoration. Might he have a closer look at it? Galland unhitched it from his neck. Göring studied it carefully and presently pointed out that the diamonds were fakes. Hitler, he chortled, might know a lot about guns and tanks and battleships, but his knowledge of diamonds was nil. If Galland would leave it with him, he would see that the pretenders were replaced by the real thing.

Not very eagerly, Galland agreed. After his service in Spain, he had been given the gold Spanish Cross. Göring had demanded a sight of it, and Galland never saw it again. However, on this occasion, the Reichsmarschall was as good as his word. Some while later, he was called to Karinhall, where Göring handed him two decorations: the version that Hitler had given him and another in which the diamonds were perceptibly different, which is to say better. It was suggested that he might use one for weekday wear and the other for Sundays.

Hitler must have heard about this; for, on the next occasion when Galland was with him, he explained that his original presentation had been only temporary. He was now able to give him the genuine article. Would Galland please hand over the decoration. Galland, alas, was wearing what we might call the Göring version. Nevertheless, he did as he was told. Hitler glanced at the two, pointed to the medal his guest had been wearing and explained that they were just ordinary stones. What he was about to receive contained genuine diamonds.

'Dolfo' Galland was a winner; a master of his craft who, it seemed, never made mistakes. In fact, he made at least two. One of them occurred on 21 June 1941, when twenty-three Blenheims with a Spitfire escort attacked the airfield at St Omer. He and his fellow pilots dived through the screen of British fighters and set about demolishing the invaders. He accounted for one – was able to see smoke coming from it and the crew bailing out. Then he turned his attention to a second. He watched his bullets find their mark and the aircraft plunging downwards. Suddenly his inspection was cut short by a Spitfire's rounds smashing into his cockpit and into his radiator. The Me–109 had just sufficient life in it to take evasive action, but then the engine seized up. With a lot of good fortune, he crash landed on another field. The mistake, of course, had been to linger over his triumph. It needed only one unguarded moment to produce disaster.

The second occasion was over Boulogne, when he actually followed one of his victims down to see it crash. A Spitfire pilot made the most of this unexpected opportunity. His tracer ripped holes in the sides of the fuselage and tore into the fuel tank. All this happened at 18,000 feet. Galland was now wounded by splinters that sliced into his arms and into his head. Burning petrol was pouring over the aircraft: the odds against his survival had to be reckoned as considerable. Nevertheless, by some miracle, he managed to get things under control. After a struggle, he forced his way out of the cockpit. By a mixture of skill and luck, he was thrown clear of the aircraft. His parachute dutifully opened and he made a heavy landing in a nearby wood. His injuries, which turned out not to be serious, were treated in a field hospital. That night, he was back on duty. Yet again, he had been shown that a fighter pilot had no time to stand and stare. He did not make the mistake a third time. Still, there were compensations. He had not been feeling too ill to deny himself the pleasure of smoking one of his cigars when his wounds were being treated. It was his birthday, and he had just claimed his seventieth victim – which caused a signal to be sent from Hitler's headquarters. It read: 'I present you as the first officer of the German forces with the Oak Leaves with Swords to the Knight's Cross of the Iron Cross. Adolf Hitler! [*sic*.]' (Messages from Hitler tended to be concluded with an exclamation mark after his name.)

Galland viewed the German invasion of Russia with a marked lack of enthusiasm. He believed, as Hitler had once believed, that it was a mistake to wage war on two fronts. The Mölders/Galland rivalry had come to an end when the former was dispatched to the Russian front where he added another 100 aircraft to his score (or something like that. It is impossible to be accurate). Later in 1941, Mölders was appointed Inspector of Fighter Aircraft at *Luftwaffe* headquarters. To a man as astute as he, it must have been evident that all was not entirely well. Ernst Udet, the popular, colourful Director General of the service, was under fire from many quarters. Eventually, the pressure became so great that he committed suicide. They tried to cover up this sorry fact by announcing that he had been killed when testing a new type of aircraft. How many believed this lie can only be a matter for conjecture. Mölders was on a tour of inspection in the Crimea at the time. He was called back to Berlin where, on the strength of the test flight myth, Udet was to be given a state funeral. Bad weather caused the He–111 in which he was travelling to make an emergency landing. Next day, he ordered the pilot to carry on with the journey. The weather was still atrocious, and the pilot – Oberleutnant Kolbe, a veteran who had served in Spain – had extreme misgivings. But Mölders seniority brooked no argument. The He–111 took off.

One of the engines failed. Kolbe decided to land at Breslau. The visibility was virtually nil. Coming through cloud and fog, Kolbe realized that he had lost too much height. To redeem matters, he opened up the throttle in an attempt to climb out of trouble and try again. This was the cue for the second engine to pack up. The aircraft cleared a nearby cable railway and then stalled. Mölders and the mechanic were killed as the plane smashed into a field. Kolbe died on the way to hospital. The only survivors were Mölders' ADC and the radio operator.

Consequently, eight days after Udet's funeral, it was Mölders turn. Galland was among those in the guard of honour, when Göring suddenly called out his name. He came to the point immediately. Galland was to take over the now vacant post.

'I had been afraid of this, but I had not really counted on it,' Galland wrote. 'I have no recollection of my immediate reaction. I was never in my life happy at a desk. My group meant everything to me, and everyone who shared those difficult but wonderful times on the Channel coast will sympathize with me when I declare that I was numbed by the thought of having to leave it.' He took up the appointment on 1 January 1942. In November of that year he was promoted to Generalmajor. Aged only thirty, he was the youngest general in the German armed forces.

There were one or two highlights – as in the case of Operation Cerberus, which was the code-name for the dash up the Channel by the battlecruisers *Scharnhorst* and *Gneisenau* and the heavy cruiser *Prinz Eugen en route* from Brest to their home ports in Germany. It was Galland's job to provide fighter cover – a task he performed admirably, with relays taking off from Caen, Le Touquet, Schipol and Jever (near Wilhelmshaven).* But ventures such as this were the exception. He was still not happy at a desk. Nor, as Germany's fortunes began to flag, was he happy about the employment of the fighter arm. The situation was aggravated still more by the political in-fighting that went on. Jeschonnek (Chief of the Air Staff) and Milch (Secretary of State for Air and Director of Armament) were continually at logger-

---

*There is an amusing sidelight to this. In an attempt to mislead, somebody had the idea that the battlecruisers should be said to be proceeding to the Far East to assist the Japanese. The question arose of how best to disseminate the information. Hitler's notion was to inform Mussolini in confidence. Then, he said, it would reach the British Admiralty with the utmost expediency. But he may have been joking. One never knew with Hitler.

heads until the feuding reached a tragic conclusion. When Germany was forced on to the defensive, Jeschonnek became hopelessly out of his depth. The culmination was reached when aircraft from RAF Bomber Command raided the rocket establishment at Peenemünde. By a grievous mistake, Jeschonnek, ordered the Berlin flak to open fire on 200 *Luftwaffe* fighters – which, in any case, had been stationed in the wrong places. Jeschonnek put the blame, not on Milch (which was fair enough), but on Göring with whom he had also been in conflict. 'It is impossible to work with Göring any longer,' he wrote. 'Long live the Führer.' Then he shot himself.

Milch took over his duties in addition to his other commitments. He was eventually promoted to Field Marshal; but he, too, succumbed to the power struggle. On 1 August 1944 he was shunted off into a siding where he remained for the rest of the war.

Hitler never visited cities such as Hamburg and Frankfurt or Cologne and Munich – places that had been burned and battered by Allied bombs. Göring, to his credit, did and the experience brought naught for his comfort. He raged against the apparent inadequacy of the air defences, but he made little effort to improve them. He was, it seemed, completely in thrall to the Führer who, himself, was in thrall to an obsession. Far from strengthening the fighter arm, he insisted that the answer to everything was to bomb Britain into submission. It mattered little that he had already failed to do so. There were other weapons: the V1, the V2, and the never to be used V3. There had also been the possibility of producing an atomic bomb. This project depended upon the work of a heavy water plant in the Telemark Mountains of Norway which, after one unsuccessful attempt (the gliders carrying the Commandos lost their way in bad weather and crashed. Those who survived were interrogated and then executed by the Gestapo), was demolished by Allied special forces. Even the Me–262, which had such huge potential as a fighter when fighters were most needed, was looked at again and again for its possibilities as a bomber. The idea of disbanding the fighters was even considered.

All this put an increasing strain on Galland who, despite his dislike of desks, was proving to be a most competent young general. He managed to inspire his pilots when inspiration was most needed. He was quick to consider new technology, and he was steadfast in his support of his men. They needed it. Inevitably the depredations of the Allied bombers produced the need for scapegoats and, equally inevitably, that unhappy role fell to the fighter pilots. People at the top were quick enough to ask why they seemed to be failing in their responsibilities, but they were not sufficiently discerning to question whether they were being adequately equipped.

Row succeeded row until, in the end – which is to say January 1945 – Göring had wearied of his argumentative young general's convictions. He was dismissed from his post and given command of a unit of Me–262s. He was not altogether sorry. The sky might have its perils; but it was a cleaner place than the intrigue-infested corridors of power. As to the Me–262 – it was the aircraft he had wanted ever since he had seen the prototype fly in May 1943.

JV44, which was the designation of his new command, was formed in February 1945. To begin with, it was composed of forty-five top pilots – ten of whom wore the Knight's Cross and all of whom had proved themselves time and again. In the few remaining weeks of the war, Galland accounted for another seven victims until, at last, his luck ran out. On 26 April he was shot down near Munich by a P–51 Mustang and wounded in the knee. It was the last of more than 400 missions.

Despite its temperamental engines, the Me–262 was by far the best jet fighter to be produced in the Second World War. It handled beautifully and the hundred or so that flew on operations shot down more than that number of Allied bombers. It also had considerable possibilities as a ground support weapon. During the final days of the war, JV44 became a rallying point for other Me–262 units stationed in southern Germany. Free from interference from Berlin (where the supreme command had other things to think about), Galland was able to employ the tactics in which he believed, and for which he had fought with such fervour. But it was too late. As the American armoured columns advanced towards the base near Salzburg, he sent a message. He was, he said, ready to keep his force intact – ready to be captured. That wasn't good enough for the US commanders. They insisted that he should deliver the aircraft to them.

As it happened, the weather was not good enough for him to carry out the flight within the stipulated time. In any case, having made what he thought to be a generous proposition, he was in no mood to comply. Instead, he ordered the aircraft to be destroyed. As Laddie Lucas remarks in *Wings of War*, 'It is almost incomprehensible that with the Germans so far ahead of the Allies in the design and operation of jet aircraft, so dunderheaded a response could have been given to Galland's offer. The emotions of war can be bad counsellors.'

The columns arrived; Galland and his comrades were taken into captivity. But at least they fared better than that top-scorer of all time, Erich Hartmann. Having flown 800 sorties, crashed twelve times and bailed out once, the American unit that took him prisoner handed him over to the Russians. He was sentenced to twenty-five years hard labour (understandable, perhaps, when one considers the brutality with which the Nazis treated Russian POWs). He served ten of them before being repatriated in 1955. Both pilots took to the air again in the following year – when the *Luftwaffe* was reformed as part of NATO. But all was not completely forgiven. For some while, these officers were not allowed to wear their Second World War decorations.

9

Douglas Bader
LEGLESS INTO
THE SKY

One afternoon in August 1941, an encounter of singular interest took place. Adolf Galland, the *Luftwaffe* ace with a string of victories to his credit, entertained the legendary Douglas Bader to tea at his headquarters near St Omer in north-west France. The German ace sent his personal car to collect his guest, who was recovering from injuries after recently bailing out. To begin with, the conversation must have been somewhat stilted. Both Galland and Bader were determined to give away nothing that might benefit the other. In any case, Bader could speak only a very few words of German, and Galland could speak no English at all. Consequently, a German flight engineer had to act as interpreter.

As time went by, however, the two men became more relaxed – to such an extent that, when Bader asked whether he might sit in the cockpit of an Me–109, Galland assented. The German ace was less ready to oblige, however, when his guest wondered whether he might take off and fly a circuit of the aerodrome. England, after all, was not very far away. What a triumph it would be to come home from German-occupied territory – bringing with him an example of the enemy's latest fighter. Galland rightly judged his reasoning and politely declined. Nevertheless, some kind of understanding had been reached between the two men. When, ten years after the war, Galland's reminiscences were published in English, it was Bader who wrote the foreword.

Quite how Bader came to be brought to earth that day remains a mystery. Galland's opinion was that he had been shot down, and that the identity of the shooter mattered. To one of Britain's foremost pilots (or so Galland assumed) the idea of having been blown out of the sky by a non-commissioned officer would have been intolerable. There was no evidence that such had been the case, but the German commander was taking no chances. He nominated a bright young officer with an impressive record to fill the role of victor.

In fact, it seems improbable that anyone shot Bader down. More likely, another aircraft collided with his Spitfire. As he recalled, something hit him – after which, the aeroplane made no response to the controls and began to spiral earthwards. When he looked round, he saw that, aft of the cockpit there was nothing: no fuselage, no tail, no fin. With a good deal of difficulty, he managed to bail out. On landing, he blacked out. The next thing he knew was that he was in a car, and that three German soldiers were taking him to hospital.

Bader had considered himself to be indestructible and there were many who agreed with him. The fact remains, however, that he was tired that day. Innumerable hours in the sky had sapped his strength and his refusal to take any leave had done nothing to help the situation. Things had reached a point at which his adjutant, Flight-Lieutenant Peter Macdonald, MP, had nearly succeeded where even the likes of Air Chief Marshal Leigh-Mallory had failed. He had come very close to obtaining Bader's approval to a plan by which he would take the ace and his wife on a week's golfing holiday at St Andrews in Scotland. But it was all too late. Fatigue is the enemy of alertness and quick reactions. It could have been that, on that fateful day, Douglas Bader was not at the peak of the customary Bader form.

Douglas Robert Steuart Bader was born on 21 February 1910. His father was employed by the Indian civil service: he and his wife were on leave in London at the time. Young Douglas attended a prep school in Eastbourne, and later won a scholarship to St Edward's School, Oxford (anticipating Guy Gibson by eight years). In 1928 he was awarded a prize cadet-ship at the RAF College, Cranwell. He was commissioned as a pilot officer on 25 August 1930 and posted to 23 Squadron at Kenley.

He had already gone some way to establishing the pattern for his future. As his academic record suggested, he was intelligent. He was extremely good at any form of sport that aroused his interest; and, at Cranwell, he showed himself to be a pilot of uncommon promise. But, most of all, he was a young man of immense determination for whom the constraints of discipline were not enough. He needed responsibility as well.

Number 23 Squadron was equipped with Gloster Gamecock fighters – a rather tubby looking biplane with a top speed of 155 mph and a remarkable agility. Consequently, it was a star performer in the aerobatics show at the Hendon Air Display (an annual RAF event that used to attract crowds of up to 175,000). Bader was picked for the Squadron's two-man team appearing in the 1931 display. They delighted the spectators with an apparently death-defying performance, which caused *The Times* to remark that he and the team leader (Flight Lieutenant Harry Day) 'provided the most thrilling spectacle ever seen in exhibition flying.'

He was excelling in other areas, too. His arrival at Kenley coincided with his being chosen for the RAF's cricket team, and his appearances with the Harlequins rugby football club were impressive enough for him to be marked as a future 'cap' for England. All in all, he had much to be grateful for. He expressed it by trading in his ancient Austin Seven motor car for an MG. Since he was involved in several accidents, one has to assume that his driving was not as faultless as his flying. Nevertheless the MG, Bader, and the other people involved, survived these little incidents with only rather minor injuries.

The Squadron was the last in the RAF to be equipped with Gamecocks. The time came when it, too, had its aircraft updated – in this instance to Bristol Bulldogs (top speed 174 mph and without the Gamecock's manoeuvrability). It was an aeroplane that did not forgive easily, and with which it was unwise to take such liberties as doing rolls at too low an altitude.

On Monday, 14 December 1931, Bader was amusing himself by performing aerobatics at 4,000 feet, when he noticed two Bulldogs taking off from the aerodrome. He identified the pilots as a couple of his friends who had decided to fly to Woodley Aerodrome near Reading. The brother of one helped to run the flying club there. Since it was a pleasant morning with a great deal more sun than cloud, he decided to join them. The time was 10.00.

The flight was short and uneventful. In the clubhouse some young pilots were drinking coffee, and the threesome from the RAF joined them. The talk turned to aerobatics – a subject on which, with his performance at Hendon still remembered, Bader's views were in demand. One of the young hopefuls went further: he suggested that Bader should give them a private demonstration by beating up the airfield.

Bader pointed out that a Bristol Bulldog was by no means the same creature as a Gloster Gamecock and that low level antics in the former were almost suicidal. He thanked the young man for his invitation and declined it. The subject was dropped until they were on the point of departing. Then this tiresome apprentice pilot raised it again – with the same result. He (or it may have been somebody else) made some ill-judged wisecrack to the effect that Bader was 'chicken'. It was impolite, ridiculous, but it succeeded in its purpose. Bader became quietly angry, climbed into his aircraft, and took off. When he was far too few feet above the ground, he began to execute a roll. You could do such things in a Gamecock but not in a Bulldog. One of the wing-tips touched the grass. The nose dropped – the crash was inevitable. All that Bader was aware of was a great deal of noise.

He was vaguely conscious of somebody offering him a swig of brandy and replying that he did not drink (even on the most boisterous of guest nights in the mess, he consumed nothing but orangeade – his intake of alcohol was confined to one or two glasses of champagne, and then only on very special occasions. It was a duty, you may say, rather than a delight).

He was taken to the Royal Berkshire Hospital at Reading where, by a fortunate coincidence, Leonard Joyce, one of the country's top surgeons, was about to go home. Joyce cancelled his immediate plans and went to take stock of the new patient. He found that he had two broken ribs, a tooth had pierced his upper lip, his right leg had almost been removed, and his left shin was in a very sorry condition. To add to all this, his pulse was so weak that it seemed unlikely that he would last out the night.

During the operation that followed, Bader's right leg was removed at a point just above the knee – later, his left leg was amputated six inches below the knee. During the latter surgery, his heart actually stopped beating, but the anaesthetist, a retired naval surgeon commander named Parry Price, brought him back to life.

Those days were a very good imitation of hell as it might be. His right leg (or, rather, its absence) gave him no trouble, but his left gave him considerable pain – so considerable that even generous doses of morphine did little to relieve it. At one point, his condition, as he saw it, seemed to have improved. He felt warm, at peace, feeling that he had only to relax and the whole ordeal would be over. Even his left leg was not producing its usual agony. His reverie was interrupted by a woman's voice on the far side of the half-open door. 'Sssh!' she said. 'Don't make so much noise. There's a boy dying in there.' It was, indeed, perfectly true, but the boy heard the words and decided that he was not going to die. With the decision, the pain returned. Everything came back into sharp focus, and the battle for survival was resumed. Nevertheless that short journey down the path towards death had one beneficial effect. Thereafter, Bader was never afraid of dying.

His condition began to improve. On 15 January he got up for the first time, but then Joyce decided that one or two modifications were necessary. The after-effects of the operation were not pleasant. The old agony returned and his general condition deteriorated. But Bader was a fighter: he fought the pain. He fought the often dismal prognoses. He fought the depression that the prospect of going legless into the world produced. Nature would not obligingly grow him a new pair of legs, but there were artificial limbs to be had and people spoke well of them. It was, perhaps, a matter of adapting and Bader, normally rather inflexible, was determined to adapt. This was not to admit defeat. On the contrary, it was the only way in which to achieve victory.

They gave him a stump that at least regained some sort of contact with the ground, and a pair of crutches to go with it. When he was fit enough, they discharged him and sent him to the RAF hospital at Uxbridge. By this time, he had worked out how to drive a car. The stump worked well enough when it came to depressing the clutch, the hand throttle (cars had them in those days) stood in for the accelerator, and the handbrake for the footbrake. He had not been at Uxbridge for long before he and two kindred spirits were going out on drives around the countryside in a Humber belonging to the RAF. Quite by chance, they stopped for tea one day at a café near Bagshot. It was called The Pantiles. To say that Bader fell in love with the waitress at first sight would be to overstate the matter. Just the same, he and his friends – on his insistence – continued to patronize The Pantiles at uncommonly frequent intervals. In time, Bader was to discover that the girl's name was Thelma Edwards, that her step-father was a lieutenant-colonel, three of her cousins were officers in the RAF, and that she had taken on the job of waitress to distract her mind from the grief she had experienced when her pet dog died.

Meanwhile, Bader was taking his next step towards mobility. An inventive individual named Marcel Dessoutter had lost a leg some while previously in an air crash. This had turned his attention to the manufacture of artificial limbs. In partnership with his brother, he set up an establishment in the grounds of the hospital at Roehampton and was rewarded with a contract from the Ministry of Pensions.

Bader got on very well with the Dessoutter brothers; but, then, Bader could get on with anyone he chose. He could be angry. He could be irritable; but, whenever he wished, he could turn on a supply of charm that never failed to captivate.

When the legs were ready, he began as he intended to continue. He rejected any notion of using a stick and he had no time for parallel bars and the like. He simply strode forth, wobbling sometimes, falling over occasionally, but striding forth nevertheless. In any assessment of his life, his work in encouraging the limbless to carry on regardless of their handicaps must rank as high (one almost dares to say higher) as his career as a fighter pilot. In this, as in everything else, his attitude was positive: to ignore the seemingly impossible on the understanding that, with guts and perseverance, anything could be achieved.

Now, fully shod so to speak, he felt that he could further his budding romance with the fair Thelma Edwards at The Pantiles. Through her cousins, she knew much more about him than he suspected. She was not, however, entirely sanguine about how her parents might react to the idea of her marriage to a legless pilot with little money and whose prospects might be regarded as somewhat limited. To overcome this problem, they were twice wedded. On the first occasion, they went through a secret and very simple ceremony at Hampstead Registry Office in North London. On the second, when Bader's future seemed to be more secure, they did the job properly at St Mary Abbott's Church in Kensington. Both times they went to Cornwall for their honeymoon.

Bader was convinced that he could fly an aeroplane as well as anyone more sufficiently equipped. Among his acquaintances was Sir Philip Sassoon, the Under Secretary of State for Air, who owned a magnificent estate near Lympne in Kent. One day, he invited Bader and a fellow pilot for the weekend. Not far away, there was an aerodrome at which 601 Auxiliary Squadron was based with its Hawker Demon biplanes (related to the Hawker

Hart and a creation of Sydney Camm, who went on to design the
Hurricane). As Sir Philip had half-expected, Bader begged to be
allowed to have a go, and so it was arranged. In a flight that took
him over the RAF station at Kenley and back, he gave ample
evidence that his infirmity had done nothing to impair his ability
as a pilot. His landing was faultless; the instructor who accompanied him was effusive in his praise – and, indeed, in his
amazement. But, by now, all sorts of things were possible. He
could dance, play golf and tennis, and even managed to acquit
himself tolerably well at squash. Rugger, of course, was impossible and cricket proved to be disappointing. When St Edward's
School invited him to play in the Old Boys' Match, he scored
eighteen with somebody doing the running for him. As a fielder,
however, he was a disaster.

He was determined to stay on in the RAF, but on the strict
understanding that he should serve as a pilot. The doctors found
nothing wrong with his health, but it would require a test at the
Central Flying School to determine his fitness to fly aeroplanes.
He passed it with no difficulty whatsoever, but there was a snag.
There was nothing in King's Regulations that applied to cases
such as his. Without it, he could not be permitted to fly solo. He
found out afterwards that the authorities had expected him to fail:
that the whole business had been little more than a sop to his
pride. Bader was furious – and then very depressed. He couldn't
tolerate the idea of remaining on the ground and watching others
fly the fighters he loved so much. In a far from good humour, he
resigned his commission on the grounds of ill-health: was
granted £100 a year as a total disability pension and a further
£99.10s.0d (£99.50) as retirement pay. It was little enough, but
the service may have considered that it had been generous in its
handling of the Court of Enquiry investigating his accident (he
was never called to give evidence) and that was enough. Whatever
the reason, he now had to look for a job.

He was getting on well with his artifical legs. The only problem
was that he would not be able to spend any length of time in the
tropics, where the sweat would chaff his stumps. His first
application was to Unilevers, where he was told that his inability
to work in tropical climes was not disastrous, though it would
impede his promotion (they had tentatively put him down for a
course of instruction about the business of soap – to be followed
by an appointment in West Africa.) The Asiatic Petroleum

Company (part of Shell) was more promising. It seemed that the company was setting up an aviation section to sell petroleum products to governments and airlines. They would be pleased to employ him in their Bishopsgate (London) office at a salary of £200 a year. It was not the kind of work that he relished, but it was work nonetheless. He accepted. He and Thelma were now, both of them, twenty-three.

The years rolled by. Hitler came to power, and the war clouds rolled into position as well. When hostilities broke out on 3 September 1939, Thelma went off to join her parents at a bungalow adjoining The Pantiles. Douglas had obviously put up a satisfactory performance for Shell: the company wanted to list him as 'indispensible'. This was not to be tolerated. Now, surely – King's Regulations or no King's Regulations – good pilots would be needed, with or without legs. He declined the oil company's suggestion and sat down to write a few letters. The upshot was that he was invited to attend a selection board at the Air Ministry.

As it happened, the chairman of the board was an Air Vice Marshal named Halahan who had been commandant at Cranwell when Bader was there. This seemed to augur well for the future until Halahan explained that they were only dealing with ground duties. When Bader explained that he wanted a flying job, Halahan relented somewhat. He scribbled a note and told him to take it to the medical unit. After a series of tests had shown that apart from his missing limbs he was extremely fit, he was shown the letter. It read: 'I have known this officer since he was a cadet at Cranwell under my command. He's the type we want. If he is fit, apart from his legs, I suggest you give him A.1.B. category and leave it to the Central Flying School to assess his flying abilities.' The medics agreed.

On 14 October he received a letter from CFS at Upavon (Wiltshire). It suggested that he should report for a test in four days' time. He felt awkward at first, conspicuous in his civilian clothes when everyone else was in uniform. But he soon came across one or two old friends – among them Rupert Leigh, who had been a junior cadet when Bader was at Cranwell. He was now a squadron-leader. Leigh explained that he would be conducting the test: it would be carried out in a Harvard advanced trainer – a monoplane that was different in this and many other respects from the old Bristol Bulldog. Afterwards, Leigh remarked that to question Bader's ability to fly was 'damn silly'. He would recommend him to be posted to Upavon for a full refresher course.

Bader was back in the fold. He was accepted as a regular officer, his old rank (flying officer) was restored to him, and so was his seniority. In all but one respect, it was as if that eight-year gap had never existed. The exception was that, by some administrative quirk, the authorities insisted that he should continue to receive his 100 per cent disability pension!

He duly reported for duty and was issued with all the necessities for aerial combat. They included a pair of flying boots. When he explained that, in his peculiar circumstances, they were unnecessary, he was told that he had to have them (something about it in KR no doubt). He gave them to Thelma – they might help to keep her feet warm during cold winters.

Rupert Leigh knew soon enough when his old chum was flying solo again. Somebody reported having seen an Avro Tutor charging along upside down at 600 feet in the circuit area. This was breaking just about every regulation that had ever been written. He begged Bader to be more circumspect in future, and he agreed. In any case, the escapade had something to do with the case of the Bristol Bulldog and Woodley Aerodrome. He couldn't explain it fully to himself – let alone to anyone else. It was best to be silent about it. When he completed the course in the following January, his ability as a pilot was rated as 'exceptional'.

Bader first became acquainted with a Hurricane before he left Upavon. He was instantly enamoured with it. He felt a part of the aeroplane and he had never flown anything so responsive to his bidding. There was also a Spitfire on the station, but this was unavailable. Somebody had taken it up to 23,000 feet, passed out from lack of oxygen, and come to at 500 feet. He managed to bring it out of the dive just in time to avoid hitting the ground. The suddenness of the manoeuvre had strained the aircraft's wings.

On 7 February 1940 Douglas Bader was posted to 19 Squadron at Duxford in Cambridgeshire. In two weeks' time he would be thirty, and here he was having the cockpit of a Spitfire explained to him by a callow young man of twenty. But one had to get used to such things, just as one steadfastly stuck to orange squash when all around him others were burying their noses in bottles of beer. ('If I can't be cheerful without a drink, I'm not much good'.)

Nineteen Squadron was part of 12 Group, which was responsible for guarding the Midlands against enemy intruders. Its neighbour, 11 Group, was charged with protecting London. Bader's first operational flight was a convoy patrol, and was totally lacking in incident. Nor were the following outings more exciting, but he was clearly giving satisfaction. In March he was posted to 222 Squadron (also at Duxford), given command of a flight, and promoted to Flight Lieutenant. On 1 June he scored his first victory when he shot down an Me–110 over Dunkirk.

Thelma's reaction to the enemy's awakening and the end of the Phoney War was like that of many other pilots' wives. 'I suppose,' she said, 'you'll all be very happy now.' The implication that she would be less than exuberant cannot have been lost on her husband, but she had spoken nothing but the truth. He was indeed happy, and a succession of moves from one aerodrome to another, and a succession of risings at dawn did nothing to spoil his elation. Eventually, they ended up at Hornchurch (then in Essex, now scooped up into Greater London). Strangely enough, nobody seems to have informed them of what, exactly, was happening on the French beaches at Dunkirk.

Columns of smoke from burning oil supplies gave the first clue. When the clouds permitted, innumerable men on the seashore and the sight of an armada of small boats and larger boats supplied a more detailed explanation. The British Expeditionary Force was pulling out. To encounter the enemy in the sky depended upon both sides being present at the same time. Two-two-two Squadron was not particularly fortunate in this respect. On his darkest day, Bader had to return early: his engine had begun to misfire. Back at the aerodrome, he found a letter waiting for him. It instructed him to answer a charge of exceeding the speed limit in his MG. On other occasions, he fared better. A 109 fell victim to his guns and so did another 110. They were better than nothing, but a small reward for days that began at dawn – long summer days in which patrol followed patrol, and a pilot seldom got out of his cockpit. The operation ended by order of the Prime Minister on 4 June. On that final sortie, he saw a yacht, its white sail billowing, heading away from Dunkirk. It must have been the last vessel to come home. On landing, he retired to bed. He slept for the next twenty hours.

Not long afterwards, he was given command of 242 Squadron. He was bidden to group headquarters at Hucknall in Nottinghamshire, where the AOC, Air Vice Marshal Leigh-Mallory, told him about it. On the day before he was promoted to flight-lieutenant, he had damaged a Spitfire by, uncharacteristically, setting the propeller to the wrong pitch – and thereby discouraging its efforts to take off. By coincidence, on the day before his visit to Hucknall, he had misjudged a landing, and written off another. He admitted as much to Leigh-Mallory, but the AOC didn't seem to mind. The unit, he told him, was the only Canadian squadron in the RAF. It was equipped with Hurricanes. The pilots were a tough bunch and currently very bloody minded. They had been employed in France. The evacuation had been a shambles in which they had lost several aircraft and their morale was very low. They needed firm handling, Leigh-Mallory insisted. Bader, he judged, was the man to provide it. His visitor may have reflected that in eight weeks he had risen from flying officer to squadron leader, which wasn't bad going.

The Squadron was stationed at Coltishall, near Norwich. It was late at night when he arrived in the area. He had trouble in finding the aerodrome, and more trouble getting into it. In the first instance, the locals were reluctant to direct him lest he be an enemy spy. In the second, the sentry not unreasonably became suspicious when he confessed to not knowing the password. It took a 'phone call and twenty minutes to put matters right. As he waited impatiently, he pondered on an ill-disciplined body of men's reactions to the prospect of being led by a legless officer who still wore the two rings of a flight-lieutenant on his sleeve. At least the latter could be put right. He drove into Norwich next morning and got somebody to sew on the extra braid.

He was fortunate in his adjutant, Flight-Lieutenant Peter Macdonald – a member of Parliament of 14 years' standing, who was wise to the ways of human nature and who had contacts that might be useful. The Hurricanes were all new, but there was a snag. Nobody had seen fit to provide tools and spare parts for them. The pilots, when he first met them, might have discouraged the greatest optimist. But Bader was neither optimist nor pessimist. If he was determined that something should happen, it did happen – without the need for fate to give it a helpful push. Nobody seemed to be in charge of A Flight. A man named Turner thought that he might be in charge of B Flight, though he didn't seem certain. Nobody appeared to be impressed by his arrival: the word 'sir' was squeezed out with reluctance and some of the pilots did not even bother to stand up.

Bader decided that the first thing should be to demolish any ideas that might prejudice the idea of a commander who stood on tin legs. He ordered a Hurricane to be readied, put on a magnificent display of aerobatics, and then climbed unaided from the cockpit. Next day, he summoned them all to his office. He castigated them on their appearance, pointing out that a good squadron looks smart. In the mess, for example, they would kindly wear shirts and ties and shoes. Roll-neck sweaters and flying boots would not be tolerated. That was all very well, but, as Turner pointed out, they did not have anything else. All their belongings had been lost in France. Over there, each pilot had had to service his own aircraft, and get himself back to England independently of the others. Seven pilots had been killed, two had been wounded, and one had succumbed to a nervous breakdown. It was a dismal picture, and Bader apologized for his brusqueness.

Many of their needs were obvious, but was there anything else? The engineer officer, a veteran named Bernard West, ventured that there was. Not to put too fine a point on it, they would be the better for two new flight commanders. Bader had anticipated this. He had already arranged it. One of them suffered from a mild stutter, but this was redeemed by the fact that he had been to Cranwell. Anyone who had been to Cranwell was, to Bader's mind, OK. He also placed importance on having been to the Right School – though this did not apply to men from overseas (possibly because they didn't have Right Schools overseas).

He sent them all into Norwich to be kitted out, on the promise that if there were any problems about payment he would personally foot the bills. Morale was already beginning to perk up; the eighteen Hurricanes were a pleasure to behold, but the problem of tools and equipment remained. West was told to make out a list of what he needed. To make out lists and to have their contents fulfilled were two quite different matters. The farther you got from the fighting, or so it seemed, the more lethargic became the attitude, the more prolific the excuses, and the more abudant the red tape. But the bureaucrats of the service clearly did not know their Bader. He fought the matter at ever increasing altitudes until, at last, he found himself in front of Dowding,

Commander-in-Chief of Fighter Command, at his headquarters in Bentley Priory (at Stanmore, Middlesex).

Dowding and Bader were not, by their respective natures, allies. Nevertheless, on this occasion the Air Chief Marshal and the Squadron Leader got on famously. An Air Vice Marshal who attended to all the equipment of Fighter Command was called into the office and told to listen to Bader's story. There was no messing about. The AVM noted every detail and, before long, a fleet of lorries arrived at Coltishall. When they had been unloaded, West reported that he now had sufficient to keep ten squadrons in the air. Bader announced 242 was going to be the best squadron in Fighter Command – even if it killed him. He sent off a signal to the effect that it was now fully operational. It was just as well: the Battle of Britain was soon to begin.

Bader's style was not that of leading from a desk: better by far to be up there in the midst of the fray. Indeed, on one occasion when his clerk had reason to rebuke him for the pile up of paperwork, he solved the problem by tipping the lot into a wastepaper basket. It was clearly better to be airborne, training, training, and then training again for an event that would clearly test the squadron's skills to their limits. His love for 242 Squadron was a possessive love and woe betide anyone who spoke ill of it.

Eleven Group, led by Air Vice Marshal Keith Park, bore the brunt of the Battle of Britain, with 12 Group in what might be described as a supporting role. Two-four-two's first victim in this instance (and Bader's, come to that) was a Dornier that was shot into the sea near Cromer. It filled him with such confidence that even Thelma conceived the idea that he was indestructible.

To make such an assumption with not yet very much evidence to support it may seem to have been foolhardy – a tempting, perhaps, of providence. But Bader had a wardrobe of personae, and he could put on whichever seemed to be suitable. He could charm, he could rebuke, he could argue (seldom budging from his convictions). His enthusiasm was tremendous, and he was determined that he should deserve only one adjective: best.

Nevertheless, this sortie had been no more than a blooding of the Squadron before the big fight. There would be many more and the victories would not only be substantial; they would be achieved at a reasonable price in pilots and aircraft. Despite this prospect of success, Bader (to mention only one of several people) was not happy about the conduct of the battle. For one thing, those at the top seemed to be under the impression that modern fighters, with their very much greater speeds, could not be used in the way that the machines used in the First World War had been employed. Dogfights, or so they argued, were things of the past – and so were the old adages such as 'Beware of the Hun in the sun.' The new idea was that they should fight in close formation, flying in a line – queuing, so to speak, for a share of the action. Bader argued that this was rubbish; that the old aces such as Bishop, McCudden and Ball had known what they were doing. Their methods were not outdated and, for want of anything better, no harm would come of following their examples.

Then there was the problem of getting into the battle before it was too late. Bader insisted that they should have earlier warning; Leigh-Mallory's reply was that they were, after all, supposed to be a reserve. It would not do to overlook this responsibility. To join in the combat that concerned 11 Group was almost as if to trespass. There was, however, one matter on which Leigh-Mallory and his argumentative subordinate did agree. Park was in the habit of committing his aircraft to battle squadron by squadron. Bader's idea was that much greater damage could be inflicted by the formation of 'big wings' comprising two or even three squadrons. The trouble, as his critics were quick to point out, was that, sound though this theory might be, such units took time in which to assemble. Twelve Group had that time; 11 Group did not. But, then again, those who were for the motion insisted that it was better to wipe out a German raid after it had done its work, rather than merely to pick at it beforehand. Eventually, the matter was settled by Churchill, who came down in favour of 'big wings' – much to the dismay and misfortune of Dowding, who was a Park man and had strongly contested the idea.

While the debate was going on, 242 Squadron was inflicting punishment on the intruders. In the last six months of 1940, it accounted for sixty-seven enemy aircraft in return for the comparatively modest loss of six pilots. Bader had been awarded the DSO; nine other pilots, the DFC.

Early in his career with 242, Bader had laid down certain precepts. Basically, the idea was to dive towards an enemy formation and thus, with a bit of luck, to break it up. After that, it was a free for all, with each pilot seizing whatever opportunity fate (or enemy unawareness) offered him. To have the sun behind you was good: to follow a damaged opponent down – hoping to see what happened to him and, perhaps, to gain credit for a kill – was bad. Straggling was disastrous. The lone duck was an easy prey for hostile guns. A pilot's aim should be steady with sufficient allowance made for deflection.

The concept worked and Leigh-Mallory began to call 242 'the disintegration squadron'. Before long, he placed two other squadrons under Bader's command, and thus the 'big wing' came into being.

As Göring turned his attacks towards London, 242's share of the action increased. There was the day when Bader and his pilots were told to patrol North Weald in Essex. In an ideal world, which means to say one in which there was plenty of warning, they would have been in position well above the enemy, waiting for their arrival and then swooping upon them. But the world was not ideal and it was often a matter of desperately trying to gain altitude, of attempting to push the aircraft beyond their capabilities. There were times, too, when the wing wasn't 'big' at all – simply because one or another of the component squadrons had not been able to reach the scene in time.

On this occasion, Bader managed to climb to 15,000 feet. Anti-aircraft fire over Britain was helpful – not least because it served as a guide to where the intruders were. In this instance, it helped to direct the pilots' attention to a formation crossing the Thames to the east of London and heading north. The trouble was that the enemy still had the advantage of 5,000 feet of additional height. As the two sides moved towards each other, Bader could make out about seventy Dornier bombers with Me–110s intermingled with them. Higher still were Me–109s riding shotgun. The Spitfires, whilst faster than the Hurricanes, had a slower rate of climb. Before many minutes had elapsed, Bader and one other pilot found that they were out on their own – with the rest of the pack straining to catch up.

There was no time for the tactics he would have liked to use. The Dorniers were streaking by, their rear gunners pouring out streams of tracer. He treated a 110 to a quick burst of fire, then noticed an Me–109 in his mirror. Another squirt at the 110, and he was pleased to see smoke coming from it. But his pleasure was short lived. The Hurricane began to jolt as cannon shells from the 109 smashed into it. Suddenly the cockpit was full of smoke, and

Bader was afraid. The time had come, he believed, to get out. He hauled back the cockpit hood and undid his straps. There were no flames; the smoke dispersed. It had been caused by cordite from the guns – that, or so it seemed, was the most likely explanation. The fear had gone and so, thankfully, had the Me–109.

He was now diving. Another 110 came into view. When he judged it to be in range, he treated it to three sharp bursts. It plunged into a field near a railway line and exploded on impact.

The Hurricane was now playing up, dropping its left wing and protesting at his attempts to bring it back into level flight. A glance showed him that the port aileron had been almost shot off and that there were holes in the starboard side of the cockpit. Indeed, there was even a gash in his flying suit – another centimetre or so, and his right hip would have been shattered.

He turned towards Coltishall and safety. On landing, he told West that he wanted the aircraft ready for use again in thirty minutes' time. West shook his head sadly; told him that the work would take at least a week, and proceeded to enumerate the damaged items. The tally was far, far greater than Bader had feared. The fuel tank had received four bullets, several of the instruments had been smashed beyond repair, and this was only a beginning. The score for the patrol was eleven enemy aircraft destroyed, one of 242 Squadron's pilots killed, and six Hurricanes severely modified. It should have been a prime example of a big wing in action, but there you were: the other two squadrons never arrived in time to share the action.

That October, Hitler announced that Operation Sea Lion (the invasion of Britain) would be postponed for a year. The *Luftwaffe* turned its attention to the cities. But, before the Battle of Britain was over, Bader was commanding no fewer than five squadrons. He had also conceived a motif for his beloved 242. It showed Hitler being kicked in the backside by a flying boot labelled 242. It was painted on all the squadron's aeroplanes.

When Bader was awarded his first DSO, Leigh-Mallory 'phoned to break the good news. Bader was at home with Thelma at the time, having dinner. He thanked the AVM for telling him and returned to the table without saying anything. Later that evening, a young pilot called round, and Bader happened to mention it to him. Thelma's reaction was, predictably, 'You might have told me first.' In all honesty, however, it seems doubtful whether her husband took much pride in the ribbons on his chest. Two-four-two was what mattered; that and making life as uncomfortable for the enemy as he could.

With the turn of the year, the action under Leigh-Mallory took a different direction. Group headquarters were now at Uxbridge; 242 was still at Hornchurch. Any prospect of an invasion of Europe was obviously some way off. Meanwhile, however, there seemed to be no reason why the *Luftwaffe* should enjoy life in France without any cause for anxiety. As Leigh-Mallory envisaged it, the sorties could take three forms. One was a 'Rhubarb' in which a couple of fighters nipped across the Channel and shot up anything that was German – whether it was in the sky or on the ground. 'Sweeps' were somewhat grander. In their original form, they were very much larger formations of fighters, whilst a 'circus' was comprised of bombers with accompanying fighters. Later on the word 'circus' was abolished and fighter swoops, with or without bombers, were known as 'sweeps'. Later still, a formation of a number of Stirlings (for instance) with, say, 200 fighters in attendance became known as a 'beehive'. The word was Bader's.

By March, the harassing tactics were becoming established. Bader was promoted to Wing-Commander, and moved to Tangmere in Sussex, where he took command of three squadrons. He continued to fly with his men (further evidence, perhaps, that, to some people, aerial combat was addictive) and their names included the great and the good. There was 'Johnny' Johnson, who, by the end of the war, had accumulated two DSOs, a DFC, and who, on his retirement in 1966, had reached the rank of Air Vice-Marshal. 'Cocky' Dundas also earned himself the DSO and Bar and the DFC. By the summer of 1945, he was a Wing Commander. It was during a party in the mess one night that Dundas propounded a theory that was to change Bader's tactical concept. Dundas's idea was that they should fly with four aircraft in line abreast. When they encountered the opposition, two would peel off to the left and two to the right. Having circled the formation, they would join up again on the enemy's tails. Not the least of the advantages was that it produced a situation in which everyone could cover everyone else – at the same time unleashing a burst or two of ammunition.

Bader liked the idea in principle. After trying it out several times against another squadron in the wing, he adopted it. Known as the 'finger four' formation, it was eventually used by other wings. (In all honesty, one has to admit that Werner Mölders had already conceived the gambit and used it to good effect. But Mölders was not in the habit of passing on such useful tips to his enemies. Thus, in an RAF context, Dundas/Bader can be given credit for its conception.)

Nowhere on the Continent close to the Pas de Calais and, indeed, beyond, could consider itself safe from these sweeps, and they had the effect that Leigh-Mallory had intended. Plagued by these intrusions of the RAF, Göring began to withdraw fighters from the Russian front to strengthen his air defences in the west. Much of the burden of using them to good effect fell on the *Geschwader* (group) commanded by Adolf Galland. Just as Galland was seldom without a cigar in his mouth, Bader was not often seen without a pipe in his. One day, returning from a sweep, one of the pilots noticed that Bader (code-named 'Dogsbody' from the initials DB that decorated his aircraft) had the lid of his cockpit open and was happily puffing away at his briar. It was against all the regulations; but, if you were Bader, you could get away with such foibles.

These outings, which took place whenever the daytime weather was suitable, put a considerable strain on Bader. Peter Macdonald noticed the signs of fatigue, and urged him to take some leave – or, at the very least, to spend more time at his desk and less in the air. Thelma became increasingly anxious, too, but her husband was adamant. The war must go on and, for so long as it did, he must be up there wreaking whatever havoc he could. In the end, Macdonald decided to make a pre-emptive strike by arranging the golfing holiday at St Andrews. Bader agreed with not particularly good grace. He insisted, however, on making one more sweep before they departed. It was a sweep too many. The target was Bethune, but Bader never reached it. That night, he was in the hospital at St Omer.

Galland was a generous enemy; a man who believed that there could still be chivalry in wartime. On one occasion, Göring remarked to him that whilst the aircraft they shot down could be replaced without too much difficulty pilots were another matter. How, then, would Galland react to an order that he and the others should shoot down pilots who bailed out? Galland was nothing if not candid. 'I should regard it as murder, Herr Reichsmarschall,' he replied, 'and I should do everything in my power to disobey such an order.' The matter was never raised again*.

Bader had landed in this foreign field with one leg more or less in good order, but the other was badly damaged. Galland's engineers repaired it to the best of their ability, but its long-term prospects were not good. At their meeting, Bader asked whether a message could be sent to England, requesting a spare leg – and, now that he thought about it, a pipe and a supply of tobacco. Galland said that he would try to oblige, and fulfilled part of it immediately. He just happened, it seemed, to have some English tobacco with him. Göring, to his credit, agreed about the idea of a leg drop and a radio message was transmitted on international May Day. It offered free conduct to a British aircraft, which would be allowed to land near the French coast and to offload Bader's requirements. Considered more cynically, of course, it was a nice way of telling the world that this very important aviator was now in German hands.

The RAF did not avail itself of the invitation to land. Intead, the replacement leg was put on board a Blenheim, and encased in a box with a parachute attached to it. Escorted by fighters from the Tangmere wing, it was dropped from a height of 15,000 feet at a point just to the south of St Omer. Stokoe, Bader's devoted batman, had asked to be allowed to accompany it – feeling, no doubt, that his master might be grateful for his services in captivity. Permission was refused.

One account has it that when Winston Churchill heard about it he accused Sholto Douglas (Dowding's successor as head of Fighter Command) of fraternizing with the enemy. Douglas replied that the pilots had accomplished more than a mission of mercy. They had shot down eleven enemy aircraft in return for the loss of only six or seven of their own. The Prime Ministerial grumblings ceased abruptly.

By this time, Bader had already attempted to escape. Returning from his meeting with Galland, he was told that he was to be moved to Frankfurt on the following day. Obviously, the nearer the coast he was, the better would be his chances of getting home. That night, he knotted fifteen sheets together, climbed out of the

---

*By no means everybody, whichever side they were on, shared this view. After a Spitfire pilot had been shot while bailing out over Malta, Beurling was asked what his attitude would be. He said that in such a situation he would have done what the enemy did. 'After all,' he said, 'he might return to duty and shoot *me* down.'

window, and – unnoticed by the Germans and with assistance from the French underground – made his way to a house on the edge of the town. Next day, he was accommodated in an outhouse, but he did not remain at large for long. Somehow, the Germans had got wind of his intentions – even of his hiding place. Among the squad that arrested him was a pleasant Stabsfeld-webel (staff sergeant) who had lived in Streatham for eleven years. He and Bader exchanged reminiscences of dancing at the Locarno Ball Room in the London suburb. However, such pleasantries did not prevent their removing his legs once he was back in St Omer.

The state of leglessness did not last long, and nor did his sojurn in St Omer. When the new artificial limb was delivered to him, he found that Thelma had thoughtfully filled the inside with a pair of socks for his stumps, a supply of talcum powder, chocolate, and tobacco.

Douglas Bader's life in and out of captivity is another story, and one that deserves a book of its own. However, it is worth mentioning that he again tried to escape. This attempt, too, was a failure: he ended up in a cell at Stalag VIIIB in Silesia. Among those present in the camp was a medical orderly of the Seaforth Highlanders, Alec Ross, who had been captured during the 1940 retreat to Dunkirk. He was currently employed in digging ditches – a task that was by no means congenial.

Bader needed somebody to look after him, and Mr Ross was given the task. About four days later, the Wing Commander was informed that he was to be moved to Colditz – that grim example of early fortified architecture that had been adapted to house restless souls whose attentions were directed to escaping to the exclusion of almost everything else. Ross, who preferred his new role to that of ditch digging, asked whether he might accompany him. Bader asked, 'Do you really want to go? It's the camp for the bad boys.' Ross assured him that he did.

At first, the Germans turned down the request, but then they relented. On 16 August 1942, the two of them arrived at Schloss Colditz where they were to spend the rest of the war.

What did Ross think of Bader? 'I liked him,' he said. 'He was very, very regimental. He was the boss. Wherever he was, he liked to be the head one. When he shouted, you ran to do whatever he wanted. Even the Germans respected him, although he pushed them to their limits.'

After the war, Douglas Bader rejoined Shell as head of its aviation fleet. He also did a great deal of work encouraging the disabled to overcome their handicaps – work which earned him a CBE in 1956 and created him a KBE in 1979. He died on 5 September 1982 on his way home from a dinner in honour of Marshal of the RAF Sir Arthur Harris, former head of Bomber Command.

10

Pierre Clostermann
THE FLYING FRENCHMAN

On 22 June 1940, France bowed ruefully to the power of German military might and concluded an armistice. But there were some Frenchmen who would never surrender. One of them was General de Gaulle; another, in a somewhat less exalted position, was a young flier named Pierre Clostermann. At the time of the surrender, the latter was living with his parents at Brazzaville in the Congo. His father was a captain attached to French military headquarters. Doubtless, young M. Clostermann could have ridden out the storm of war beneath the calmer skies of Africa – in tolerable comfort and not very much danger. That, however, was not how he saw things. His place was in the line of battle – which is to say in England with the RAF. Not without difficulty, he made the journey and, in the spring of 1942, we find him serving as sergeant with an Operational Training Unit in Wales. He was coming to terms with that most willing of combat accomplices, the Spitfire.

Pierre Clostermann wanted to keep a record of his activities as what he describes as one of 'General de Gaulle's mercenaries'. Wherever he went, he took with him a notebook in which he jotted down his thoughts and experiences. He attached to it a copy of his will, which was rather pathetic. In his present circumstances, Pierre Clostermann had very little to bequeath. A note attached to the flyleaf of the book instructed that in the event of his being killed or reported as missing it should be sent to his father in Brazzaville.

All told, he flew on 420 sorties (another source puts the figure at 293, but Clostermann surely must be correct. It was, after all, his life). He shot down nineteen enemy aircraft (confirmed)*, was awarded the DFC and Bar, and attained the rank of Squadron Leader. Notebook after notebook became filled with his impressions, and for this we must be grateful. They provided the material for *The Big Show* (*Le Grand Cirque* in France), a book that became a bestseller on both sides of the Channel, and rightly so. It provides a vivid, thoughtful record of one man's war in the air: a record that is not without humour and which moves at the pace of the Spitfires that feature so prominently in it.

Clostermann had a splendid way with words and he must have been a most endearing companion. He was a consummate extrovert – a young man who thought few things better than a good party. He liked to play his mandolin; he also enjoyed a game of chess. He was something of a showman who never gave up. Throughout his time in the service there were occasions when prudence must have suggested bailing out as the wisest course. But Clostermann refused to make the jump that led only to a prison camp. He soldiered on and executed landings that may have been fatal to his aircraft but which, against all the laws of physics, he survived.

From the OTU, he was posted to Turnhouse (not far from Edinburgh) where the 341 Free French Fighter Squadron (otherwise known as the 'Alsace' Squadron – thus giving us a clue to Clostermann's apparently Germanic name) was being formed. The strength, in terms of pilots, was himself and three others. In terms of aircraft, it was nil. But the Spitfires and the rest of the personnel presently arrived, and the unit was posted to Biggin Hill.

As he recalls in his book, there were a number of axioms that a pilot forgot at his peril. 'The Hun is always in the sun.' 'Wait to shoot till you see the whites of his eyes.' 'Never go after the Jerry you have hit. Another will get you for certain.' 'It is better to come back with a probable than to be shot down with the one you've confirmed.' 'Look out! It's the one you don't see that gets you.' 'Silence on the radio. Don't jam your RT channel.' 'If you are shot down over enemy territory, escape. If you are caught, keep your trap shut.' And 'Don't dream about your popsie. If you don't see the Hun who is going to get your mate, you are a criminal.'

*His own estimate is thirty-three – fourteen of them achieved in a Tempest displaying the double cross of Lorraine. See Chapter 1.

Such sayings were fresh in his mind when he set off on his first operation. His enthusiasm was considerable; but, just the same, he was nervous. The mind is an often uncomfortable instrument that sometimes projects a thought or a memory when it is least wanted. On this occasion, his recalled a football match at school in which, as goalkeeper, he let the ball through for fear of being hurt by the studs on an opponent's boots. It was by no means one of his most glorious moments and the recollection brought with it fear. He had no appetite for the soup, sausages and mash that were being served for lunch.

As the moments passed, however, he found himself being curious as well an anxious. He wanted to know how he would react in the face of a danger more real than that posed by the studs on football boots. He wanted to know what absolute fear felt like – and he wanted to know why a Canadian in 611 Squadron, whose baptismal combat flight this was also to be, could actually order a second helping of potatoes, whilst he could not manage a first.

The operation was to be a 'circus' in which the fighters were to escort 72 Flying Fortresses intent on bombing the airfield at Glissy near Amiens. The weather was superb. By 1.15 pm, he was sitting in the cockpit of his Spitfire with an empty feeling in his stomach and rather regretting the lunch he had never eaten. A white Verey light fired from the control tower gave the signal to depart. Once in the sky, he began to feel very cold and, as he gained altitude, it became harder to breathe. He turned his oxygen supply full on. He also felt a curious sense of isolation. Despite all the other aircraft round and about, a pilot in a single-seater aeroplane, he reflected, is so very much alone.

At some point during his climb to 15,000 feet, the engine cut out. Through inexperience, he had used up the fuel in the auxilliary tank in his scramble to keep up with the rest of the flight. He switched on to the main tank and there he was – not yet over the target and with no reserves. Radio silence was essential; any pilot who had to turn back had to waggle his wings which would be more than sufficiently eloquent. But Clostermann had no intention of turning back. He continued climbing to 27,000 feet and resolved to be more careful in future about conserving petrol.

The action over Glissy was a kind of controlled confusion – if that is the right expression. The opposition was fielding a team of FW–190s. Now and again, one or another of them flashed through Clostermann's sights; but, on none of these occasions, did he see the whites of anyone's eyes. And then, quite suddenly, the sky was empty. That was how it always was: a complex pattern of writhing aircraft, climbing, diving, rolling, looping, doing any manoeuvre that seemed to be propitious – with the din of engines and cannon fire as an accompaniment. Then silence and solitude and an urgent desire to get away from it all ('it's the one you don't see that gets you.') With his engine sucking out the last dregs of petrol from the tank, Clostermann made his way back to Biggin Hill. When he landed, he found that one school of opinion was pretty sure that he had 'bought it'. He had done nothing of the kind. What was more, he had gone through the wall of fear. It seldom troubled him again.

Not long afterwards, he made his first kills. It was over Le Havre, where the opposition was known to be the 'Yellow-Nose' Richthofen wing led by Major von Graff. They had the latest FW190s and the pilots were hand picked. As he put it, 'there was probably going to be the hell of a scrap.'

At first it seemed that he was to play no part in it. His name had not been put down as one of the participants. Clostermann, however, was a very determined young man who meant to have his own way. It may have been that, when considering the odds, whoever had been responsible had judged this comparative novice to be too easy a prey for von Graff's experienced aviators. Whatever the reason, Clostermann reacted in what seemed to him a reasonable manner. He raised hell. It worked, and there he was, a puppy in a pack of battlewise hounds. As things turned out, it was as well that he had made his protest at exclusion. When the sky was empty again and silent, too, Pierre Clostermann had accounted for two of the enemy. To accomplish this in what was only his second sortie was not bad going. But, then, he seldom lacked self-confidence. The only snag on this occasion was that – despite his resolution – he really did run short of petrol and had to come down at Shoreham to refuel. He very nearly muffed the landing, which may contain some sort of moral – isn't there something called hubris, the price one had to pay for excessive pride?

He always obeyed his instincts, and he had little faith in that abstraction called luck. He knew very well that one unguarded moment could create disaster. As time went by, he formed an assessment of the enemy pilots. Something like 15 or, say 20 per cent of them were as good as – possibly better than – anyone the

Allies could put into the sky. But, once you had said that, you had said everything. The rest of them were (his words) 'not up to much. Very brave but incapable of getting the best out of their aircraft.' He also, in one of his excursions into self-analysis, came across a rather surprising discovery about his reactions after a kill. Far from feeling elated, he experienced 'a sudden panic that grips your throat . . . All your pent-up energy is suddenly relaxed and the only feeling left is one of lassitude. Your confidence in yourself vanishes. The whole exhausting process of building up your energy again, of sharpening your concentration, of bracing your battered muscles, has to be started all over again.'

This, however, did not diminish his jubilation on returning from a successful sortie. He relished victory rolls – despite the fact that aerobatics of any kind over airfields were frowned upon (Bader would not have approved. He never went in for victory rolls). He was, of course, doing very well and, in September 1943, he received a commission. Later, after the Allied invasion of France, Archibald Sinclair, the Secretary of State for War, presented him with the DFC during a visit to the British foothold on the Continent.

Clostermann's experiences began at a transitional phase of the air war – when the Allies were moving from the defensive to the offensive. The fighters were protecting bombers rather than towns (during a brief posting to the Orkneys Clostermann was protecting warships). They were also being equipped with bombs (the Mk V Spitfire could carry a 500-lb bomb. In the Typhoon, which he flew later, two 500 pounders could replace eight rockets if need be; and the Tempest, his final mount, could be used to convey a bomb load of anything up to 2,000-lbs). Thus they could be used for ground strafing, and we find among Clostermann's list of victims 72 railway trains, 225 vehicles, and even a couple of boats).

The Allied fighter, it seemed, was carrying out the role the Junkers 87 was intended to perform, but accomplished only under favourable conditions.

During the late spring of 1944, Clostermann was flying with 125 Wing which, on 4 May, was transferred from the airfield at Detling in Kent to Ford (near Brighton). Among the inhabitants of Ford were several Thunderbolt squadrons recently arrived from America. The United States pilots seemed to be surprised that an aircraft such as the Spitfire could fly in the kind of weather that is apt to mar what ought to be a season of sunny skies and burgeoning blossom (his comment: 'What did they expect? – England isn't California'). They were also impressed by an aircraft that could take to the sky in fifty yards, whilst a laden Thunderbolt required 600 yards.

The idea was clearly to prepare for D-Day by cutting lines of communication to the Normandy beaches. They were now flying the Mk IX Spitfire, which was reckoned to be a match for the redoubtable FW–190, and which could be used as a dive bomber. The programme was strenuous. Two missions a day were commonplace, and some were damnably dangerous. After attacking the viaduct at Mirville, even the RAF communiqué described the aircraft has having dived through 'a wall of flak', and such press releases were not given to overstatement. The viaduct was hit in the middle and at the northern end, though it was hard to tell who had scored the vital blows. Clostermann knew that he had not: his bomb had exploded at least 200 yards from the target. As this may suggest, for all his bounce, he was not devoid of self-criticism. After another foray, he admitted that 'As for me, my shooting was beneath contempt.'

It was a punishing business. 'At this tempo,' he confessed, 'we were quickly reduced to wrecks.' And, 'As for me, I was completely creased.' However, respite of a sort was in the offing when his commanding officer, Group Captain Rankin, was called to the Allied Expeditionary Air Forces GHQ at Uxbridge. He decided to take Clostermann with him on the grounds, as he put it, that the latter's French uniform 'provided a bit of local colour.'

The object was to plan the role of the Allied air forces during the coming invasion. The proceedings took place in the station's underground vaults; the array of brass, top and less than top, was staggering. Air Marshals seemed to be ten a penny, and so did Generals in the US Army Air Force. Possibly out of argument comes truth, and out of truth a sensible plan of action. Certainly, according to Clostermann, there was a lot of friction between members of the RAF and those who belonged to the American 9th Air Force. Not the least of the matters in dispute was the strength of the opposing fighter cover. The British regarded their American allies' estimate of the destruction they had wrought as ridiculous – statistics that might be good for propaganda purposes, but which were too unrealistic to be of any strategic value. For example, in a formation of 72 Flying Fortresses, you had something like 300 or 400 machine-gunners. Suppose they were attacked by twenty FWs, and five of the German aircraft were shot down. That was reasonable; but the score might be considerably increased by reports of gunners who, in all sincerity, *believed* that they had erased a Focke-Wulf from the sky. The statistics then slid into fiction, and it was no use pretending that such things did not happen. One thing about human nature is that people are apt to see what they want to see. Nothing can change it.

Again, after a raid on Augsburg, 900 British and American fighter pilots claimed that they had demolished 118 German aircraft, whilst the gunners in the 500 Flying Fortresses reported 350 victims. All this, according to Clostermann's reckoning, suggested that a third of the German fighter strength had been destroyed in one operation. The idea was laughable. Who was kidding whom?

Despite the arguments, a plan was forged and, two weeks after he had arrived, Clostermann was able to leave these not very comfortable corridors of power. He was not sorry to be back at Ford – even if his release from the realm of higher thought had been conditional. Because he was now privy to all the secrets of D-Day's aeronautical plans, an embargo was placed on his activities. He had, indeed, to sign an undertaking that he would divulge nothing to anyone, and that he would not fly over enemy-occupied territory until D-Day plus ten hours. The reason was obvious. As the cliché has it, the German interrogators had ways of making their victims talk. If he were shot down, they would employ them ruthlessly – so ruthlessly that even a man of Clostermann's calibre might crack. He was (to continue our excursion into clichéland) a man who knew too much.

When he did get back into the sky, he was surprised at the lack of German fighter response. The main hazards seemed to be the possibility of running out of fuel, or colliding with another aircraft. This state of affairs could not continue: the war was far from over and the pressure on pilots was considerable. The *Luftwaffe*, too, seemed to have regained its strength – whatever other shortages the Third Reich might be experiencing, there seemed to be no lack of those pesky FW–109s. On one day, he accounted for two of them (confirmed) and another (probable) and damaged two others – all in the space of forty minutes. To celebrate, he indulged himself by executing five victory rolls over the town of Longues – much to the delight of the folk down below.

You can push yourself so far. Assisted by drugs, you can push yourself a little bit farther. But there comes a time when you must discipline yourself to the idea of resting. His diet during these days in France consisted mostly of corned beef and carrots, which was doubtless nourishing. To it, however, was added double the normal dose of benzedrine tablets. The medical officer was becoming concerned and reported his disquiet. He may also have reported the fact that Clostermann had lost seventeen pounds of weight in a fortnight and had developed a nervous tic which, according to one of his friends, caused him to resemble 'a decrepit drug-addict'.

As a result, he was removed from combat, placed on board a tank landing craft at Arromanches, and sent back to England and a staff job. During the Channel crossing, the ship's second officer gave him his cabin. The date was 7 July. Some miles from the coast, the battle for Caen was blazing away. Pierre Clostermann was left on his own to ponder that the war was going well: that it would not be long before Paris was liberated and (dismally) the liberation would most likely take place without his assistance.

Nature's staff officers have no ambitions to take part in aerial combat, and those engaged in said combat seldom wish to become staff officers. Clostermann did not settle happily into his new duties. As he put it, 'I didn't really breathe freely in that HQ atmosphere, and the three months I spent there, in spite of the many charming people I met, were painful.' Paris fell to the Allies, just as he thought it would, and France returned to business as an ally. That was all very fine, but two forces were now engaged in a tussle about who owned Pierre Clostermann. The RAF wanted him back on operations. The Ministère de l'Air, now established in Paris, claimed that this lively and very much more than competent pilot belonged to them and that they had every intention of keeping him. To strengthen its case, the Ministry pointed out that General de Gaulle had compiled a list of pilots he wished to preserve for some other purpose, and who were not to be sent back into battle. Clostermann's name was on it.

Clostermann never admitted defeat. What was more, he knew people – people who might very well foster his cause. One of them was Colonel Coustey, the Officer Commanding French Air Forces in Great Britain. Coustey saw his point and took it upon himself to authorize his return to the RAF. 'At the same time,'

Clostermann recalled, 'he begged me not to get myself killed, else he would get into trouble.'

That afternoon, he set off for Aston Down in Wiltshire to do a quick conversion course on Typhoons and Tempests. When the station commander had studied his log-book, he said that he could skip the theoretical part and get straight to the business of flying. If the weather held good, he promised, he could be in Holland (now in Allied hands) within a week.

Pierre Clostermann kept his promise to Colonel Coustey: he survived. There were occasions when he very nearly did not. To take one example, after carrying out forty sorties in twenty days, he was asked to lead a patrol of four aircraft with the object of keeping watch on the *Luftwaffe* airfield at Rheine. A number of Me–262 jet fighters were based there, and it seemed probable that the Germans might try to use the last minutes of twilight to evacuate them to the interior of Germany. He was dog tired and he tried to find a replacement. Nobody was available.

The enemy airfield had been badly bombed. Most of the aircraft had been removed to the cover of neighbouring woodland, and it was difficult to get even a reasonably clear picture. To confuse matters yet more, a Junkers 88 night fighter wandered on to the scene. Clostermann fired at it and scored some hits. But the *coup de grace* was accidentally administered by his number two, who, following him, collided with the German aircraft. There was a fearful fire and then the darkness returned. Clostermann was wretchedly disturbed, but being disturbed was a luxury he could not afford. With his mind on the tragedy, he blundered into a barrage of flak. He climbed desperately, but the gunners were on form. Two bits of shrapnel sliced through his aircraft. His radio was put out of action, his instruments were in a state of chaos, and a lot of blood was coming out of his right leg. It was probably painful as well, but he was too preoccupied to notice. His first reaction was to believe that this was how life ended – the mystery of death was soon to be unravelled.

But whatever secrets death may have were not to be revealed. His mind calmed down – helped by cold air that was now seething through the cockpit. To judge by the aircraft's behaviour, his tail plane had been badly damaged; but, and one had to look on the bright side, he was still in the sky. Eventually – with assistance from rivers, a canal, and a railway line – he and his stricken aeroplane groped, limped, and sometimes staggered, back to base near the Dutch town of Volkel. All feeling had gone out of his feet and he couldn't sense the rudder bar any more. To make matters worse, the people at Volkel seemed to be taking an uncommonly long time to switch on the landing-strip lights.

At last, the lights came on. He could not communicate by radio, and so he waggled his wings to show that he was in distress. The message was received. He could see an ambulance and the crash wagon hurrying to meet him.

There was no question of being able to lower the undercarriage. This would have to be a belly landing, which was not the kind of thing anyone would enjoy doing in a Tempest weighing seven tons. The aeroplane bounced and hurled him against the side of the cockpit. The hood flew off; the wings disintegrated; the plates of the fuselage were torn apart. At some point, his face was smashed against the gunsight and he tasted a great deal of blood. A fire started; a shell exploded in the flames. But, somehow, they managed to extract him and inject him with a large dose of morphine. When he woke up, he was in Eindhoven hospital. A pleasant Scottish doctor was sitting beside his bed. The M.O. suggested that, next time, his patient should try to make a better landing – and, yes, he should stop collecting scrap iron in his legs. Clostermann was both hungry and sleepy, but he did not have long in which to debate which need to satisfy first. Sleep won.

Six days later he was back in business – flying in the duty Ansor to Warmwell in Dorset, where he was to select a brand new Tempest for himself.

The shoot out in the sky above Germany continued remorselessly – almost until the bitter end. On 3 May 1945, less than a week before the Nazi surrender – we find Clostermann (now in temporary command of a wing) in action over Grossenbrode, a lonely fragment of land, added as a careless afterthought to German soil and situated near the western entrance to the Baltic. The target was a naval air base, where more than 100 large transports were preparing to evacuate troops. Strong fighter cover was expected from the opposition.

In all conscience, it was strong enough, and so was the flak. About 100 enemy aircraft were swarming about the sky and to reasonably good effect. Clostermann ended the life of a Blohm und Voss 138 flying boat which was riding at anchor in the roads. He went on to destroy a Dornier Do 24 flying boat and, later still, another. He was also partly responsible for the demise of an

FW–190: indeed, he probably would have got it, but his ammunition ran out. The kill was accomplished by one of his pilots. When it was all over, eleven aircraft out of the wing's twenty-four failed to return.

Nor had fate finished with him. Ironically, it saved up a master stroke for a day when the war was over – for an occasion that should have been a celebration. The purpose was a victory fly-past over Copenhagen. The performance was immaculate until almost the end. As he prepared to land, only fifty per cent of his undercarriage came down. The engine failed to respond when he tried to manoeuvre himself out of trouble. At 200 mph, the Tempest smashed itself to pieces on the ground. Amazingly, Clostermann was stunned, bewildered, and then able to realize that he was unharmed.

On 27 August he applied for demobilization. There was a last show of aerobatics, many emotional farewells, and finally the journey to Paris, sitting in the co-pilot's seat of a Mitchell bomber. Pierre Clostermann had lived to fly again – and, indeed, did fly again during the French trouble in Algeria. But that is another story. The days of *Le Grand Cirque* were over. He was as pleased as anyone else at the return of peace; but, within his pleasure, there was sadness. He mourned for the friends who had been killed, and for the companionship of those who had not. He mourned, too, for the separation from aircraft he had come to love. They had helped him to come through a lot of danger with minimal damage to himself. They had also caused the Nazi regime a good deal of trouble and that, after all, had been their object.